DISABLING BARRIERS

DISABILITY CULTURE AND POLITICS

**Series Editors: Christine Kelly (University of Manitoba)
and Michael Orsini (University of Ottawa)**

This series highlights the works of emerging and established authors who are challenging us to think anew about the politics and cultures of disability. Reconceiving disability politics means dismantling the strict divides among culture, art, and politics. It also means appreciating how disability art and culture inform and transform disability politics in Canada and, conversely, how politics shape what counts as art in the name of disability. Drawing from diverse scholarship in feminist and gender studies, political science, social work, sociology, and law, among others, works in this series bring to the fore the implicitly and explicitly political dimensions of disability.

DISABILITY
CULTURE AND
POLITICS

DISABLING BARRIERS
Social Movements, Disability History, and the Law

Edited by Ravi Malhotra and Benjamin Isitt

UBCPress · Vancouver · Toronto

25 24 23 22 21 20 19 18 17 16   5 4 3 2 1

Printed in Canada on FSC-certified ancient-forest-free paper (100% post-consumer recycled) that is processed chlorine- and acid-free.

Library and Archives Canada Cataloguing in Publication

Disabling barriers : social movements, disability history, and the law / edited by Ravi Malhotra and Benjamin Isitt.

(Disability culture and politics)
Includes bibliographical references and index.
Issued in print and electronic formats.
ISBN 978-0-7748-3523-7 (hardcover). – ISBN 978-0-7748-3525-1 (PDF). – ISBN 978-0-7748-3526-8 (EPUB). – ISBN 978-0-7748-3527-5 (MOBI).

1. People with disabilities – Canada – Social conditions.   2. People with disabilities – United States – Social conditions.   3. People with disabilities – Government policy – Canada – History.   4. People with disabilities – Government policy – United States – History.   5. People with disabilities – Legal status, laws, etc. – Canada – History.   6. People with disabilities – Legal status, laws, etc. – United States – History.   I. Malhotra, Ravi, editor   II. Isitt, Benjamin, editor   III. Series: Disability culture and politics

HV1559.C3D63 2017   362.40971   C2017-902923-1
                                                              C2017-902924-X

Canadä

UBC Press gratefully acknowledges the financial support for our publishing program of the Government of Canada (through the Canada Book Fund), the Canada Council for the Arts, and the British Columbia Arts Council.

This book has been published with the help of a grant from the Canadian Federation for the Humanities and Social Sciences, through the Awards to Scholarly Publications Program, using funds provided by the Social Sciences and Humanities Research Council of Canada.

Printed and bound in Canada by Friesens
Set in Warnock Pro and Futura by Apex CoVantage, LLC.
Copy editor: Barbara Tessman
Indexer: Megan A. Rusciano
Cover designer: Gabi Proctor

UBC Press
The University of British Columbia
2029 West Mall
Vancouver, BC V6T 1Z2
www.ubcpress.ca

Contents

Part 2: Debates in Disability Studies

Part 3: Legal Debates

Foreword

BRYAN D. PALMER

Capitalism disables.[1] This was understood by those early figures, such as William Dodd, who experienced directly the physical toll the Industrial Revolution exacted on the first factory labourers, some of whom were children. Dodd, author of *A Narrative of the Experience and Sufferings of William Dodd, a Factory Cripple* (1841), was born in 1804 and was working eighteen-hour days in England's textile mills before he reached his teenage years. He earned his first meagre wage as a five-year-old. Thirty years later, his body wracked by the consequences of textile toil, he had to have an arm amputated, and in the 1830s he became associated with Lord Ashley's investigations into the conditions of child labour.

In *The Factory System: Illustrated* (1842), Dodd outlined how proletarians bore the marks of capital on their bodies, a point that, as Mark Leier notes in his contribution to this volume, would also later be made by the Wobbly agitator "Big Bill" Haywood, who by the age of nine had lost an eye and entered the mining workforce. Dodd wrote that factory labourers could be distinguished by their physical appearance: "Either the knees are in, the ankles swelled, one shoulder lower than the other, or ... [they are] round-shouldered, pigeon-breasted, or in some other way deformed."[2]

Marx's more poignant passages in *Capital*, addressing the disabling consequences of a working day that too often extended well into the night, detailed the disfiguring of working-class bodies. He drew on a plethora of sources, including medical assessments of workers in the pottery districts.

"Each successive generation of potters is more dwarfed and less robust than the preceding one," testified one physician. Another doctor, in charge of an infirmary, regarded the potters as "a degenerated population" that, as a rule, was "stunted in growth, ill-shaped, and frequently ill-formed in the chest; they become prematurely old, and are certainly short-lived."[3] Engels' *The Condition of the Working-Class in England in 1844* (1845) quoted copiously from similar reports, detailing malformations of the spine, knees that were bent inwards, and enfeebled ligaments.[4]

This was but the half of it. Industrial accidents took lives and limbs at random. In Canada, where the factory system came later than it did in England, a Royal Commission on the Relations of Labor and Capital resulted in extensive published commentary in 1889. Its six volumes of testimony were riddled with accounts of disabling, often lethal, industrial accidents.[5] Eric Tucker, author of the final chapter in the present volume, has provided a pioneering and comprehensive account of the origins of the law and politics of occupational health and safety regulation in Ontario in the years 1850–1914.[6] But this history and subsequent developments, however much they suggest an augmented sensitivity to disability and an enhanced apparatus of workplace protection and regulation in the modern era, have never really adequately addressed the disabling nature of capitalism, as many of the essays in this volume suggest. Death, disfigurement, and diseases spawned of industrial toxins stalk employment in Canada and throughout the world, to this day.[7]

This is not to suggest that our approach to disability narrow discussion, dialogue, and debate to the class dimensions of disability alone, telescoping all consideration into capitalism's causation of problems and prejudice. As Anne Finger's account of Franklin Delano Roosevelt's disability suggests, and as critical disability studies have established, the ways in which physical impairment can limit human possibility reach past a simplified origin in the injuries of class, hidden or otherwise. That said, Roosevelt's "management" of his disability was certainly facilitated by his class privilege, just as the inabilities of others to negotiate their way through and around specific disabling realities were not unrelated to their subordinate place in a class hierarchy.

The historical figure who first drew Ravi Malhotra and Benjamin Isitt to this project of exploring the historical conjucture of social movements, disability history, and the law, E.T. Kingsley, certainly understood the class nature of capitalist oppression and exploitation. He did not dwell on his specific disability, which arose from an industrial accident that resulted in the amputation of both of his legs. Recovering from this traumatic event, Kingsley read Marx, became a revolutionary and an advocate of Daniel De-Leon's Socialist Labor Party, gaining a reputation as an ardent propagandist in California during the 1890s. As the Socialist Party of British Columbia seemed poised to veer from its resolute conviction to wage "uncompromising political warfare against the capitalist class," Nanaimo's vigilantly class-conscious miners, in an attempt to shore up the theoretical acumen and political resolve of provincial socialists, brought Kingsley to Vancouver Island on what was supposed to be a short-lived propaganda tour in 1902. So great was Kingsley's influence and the respect he commanded that his advocates decided to retain him permanently, setting him up as a Nanaimo fish-seller and, subsequently, a printer. As Malhotra and Isitt recount in their introduction to this volume, Kingsley's influence in the British Columbia revolutionary left was, for the next decades, unrivalled.[8] They point out, rightly so, that Kingsley's appearance in published works of political and labour history has often been cameolike, and he has never in such writing "occupied centre stage."[9] That may be the case, but to the revolutionary socialists of pre–First World War Canada, Kingsley was himself something of the stage. A 1910 article in the *Western Clarion* assessing the history of the Socialist Party of Canada declared decisively that, "the movement today in Canada is the result of one man's interpretation of Marx."[10] That man, of course, was Kingsley.

I understand exactly what Anne Finger is suggesting in the concluding sentence to her chapter in this volume when she refers to what might be lost by simply assimilating Kingsley as "one of us." By this statement she is rightly accenting that his disability should not be discounted, as he perhaps himself understated its significance, in routinely stressing the disabling universalism of capitalism as a class system. In the particularity of Kingsley's special oppression as a double amputee – as someone who paid a very large price and whose life was irrevocably altered by the dangers of exploitative work under capitalism – lay an important social commentary that can never be simply and one-dimensionally distilled to a particular anticapitalist politics. After all, disability pre-dated capitalism and the making of class society, and it will continue to exist under socialism, even into the reaches of imagined utopias that may finally transcend the exploitative essence of class society.

What is evident in Kingsley's example, however, is the extent to which he himself sought out answers in the body of critical socio-political theory of his time, the ideas and orientations developed in revolutionary Marxism as a critique of consolidating capitalism. That animating conceptualization of capitalism demanded that exploitation be recognized as the foundation of a market-oriented system elevating "individual freedom" to the commanding ideological heights of society; that this regime of accumulation for profit be appreciated as one in which various oppressions were intrinsic to the routines of material life; that an economic order of this nature must be overthrown so that production could be for social use, not individual acquisition; and that humankind must struggle to organize society so that each might be provided according to their needs, and that each would be called on to contribute according to their abilities.

Kingsley believed in this Marxist critique and understanding of the possibilities of human development with all of his being, a being that was truncated by capital's insatiable appetite for profit. He was marked by capital in ways that many of us who are able-bodied find unfathomable. But he will always, given his legacy of intractable resistance to capitalism, be counted as "one of us" among socialists who strive to see capitalism itself disabled, so that its disabling imperatives can finally be brought to a halt.

This project of social transformation is a grandiose undertaking. Too often, its large vision obscures particular needs, and the difficult struggle to realize its ultimate goals can, at times, seem to obscure specific components of a complex and multifaceted effort to achieve far-reaching change. Within this anticapitalist endeavour, addressing disability usefully and humanely will be central. It will not be the end of efforts to achieve what needs to be accomplished, but it will be a fundamental leap in the right direction. Small steps are currently being taken, by labour historians and by others, to recognize the importance of disability in a variety of intellectual fields and research initiatives.[11] This important collection of essays on social movements, disability history, and the law, inspired by E.T. Kingsley, similarly prods us to where we need to be going, engaging with and contributing to critical disability studies the better to understand the social relations of our times and how they contain within them the potential seeds of human liberation and transformation.

NOTES

1 See the discussion in Marta Russell & Ravi Malhotra, "Capitalism and Disability" in Colin Leys & Leo Panitch, eds, *Socialist Register* (London: Merlin, 2002) 211.
2 William Dodd, *The Factory System: Illustrated* (1842) 112–13, quoted in E.P. Thompson, *The Making of the English Working Class* (Harmondsworth, UK: Penguin, 1968) at 363.

3 Karl Marx, *Capital: A Critical Analysis of Capitalist Production*, vol 1 (Moscow: Foreign Languages Publishing House, 1961) at 245.

4 Frederick Engels, *The Condition of the Working-Class in England in 1844* (London: George Allen and Unwin, 1968) esp. at 153.

5 See, for an abridgement, Gregory S Kealey, ed, *Canada Investigates Industrialism: The Royal Commission on the Relations of Labor and Capital, 1889* (Toronto: University of Toronto Press, 1973).

6 Eric Tucker, *Administering Danger in the Workplace: The Law and Politics of Occupational Health and Safety Regulation in Ontario, 1850–1914* (Toronto: University of Toronto Press, 1990).

7 See, for instance, among many possible texts: Charles E Reasons, Lois L Ross & Craig Paterson, *Assault on the Worker: Occupational Health and Safety in Canada* (Toronto: Butterworth's, 1981); Doug Smith, *Consulted to Death: How Canada's Workplace Health and Safety System Fails Workers* (Winnipeg: Arbeiter Ring, 2000); Robert Storey, "Social Assistance or a Worker's Right: Workmen's Compensation and the Struggle of Injured Workers in Ontario, 1970–1985" (2006) 78 Studies in Political Economy 67; Robert Storey, "'Their Only Power Was Moral': The Injured Workers' Movement in Toronto, 1970–1985" (2008) 41 Histoire sociale/Social History 99. On one particular industry in Atlantic Canada, see Elliott Leyton, *Dying Hard: The Ravages of Industrial Carnage* (Toronto: McClelland and Stewart, 1975); Richard Rennie, "The Historical Origins of an Industrial Disaster: Occupational Health and Labour Relations at the Fourspar Mines, St. Lawrence, Newfoundland, 1933–1945" (2005) Labour/Le Travail 107; Harry Glasbeek, *Wealth by Stealth: Corporate Crime, Corporate Law, and the Perversion of Democracy* (Toronto: Between the Lines, 2002) at 61–66.

8 Malhotra's and Isitt's forthcoming biography of Kingsley will no doubt provide much new detail and perspective on Kingsley's life. I rely on the undoubtedly partial and somewhat skewed account in A Ross McCormack, *Reformers, Rebels, and Revolutionaries: The Western Canadian Radical Movement, 1899–1919* (Toronto: University of Toronto Press, 1977), and the unpublished Ross A Johnson, *No Compromise – No Political Trading: The Marxian Socialist Tradition in British Columbia* (PhD Dissertation, University of British Columbia, 1975), as well as a selected reading of Kingsley's political journalism and pamphlets, which often hit hard at the lack of class consciousness among wage earners.

9 See p. 5 of this volume. Curiously, Ian McKay's representation of Kingsley in *Reasoning Otherwise: Leftists and the People's Enlightenment in Canada, 1890–1920* (Toronto: Between the Lines, 2008) is rather jaundiced. It presents Kingsley's critique of the "wage slaves" who embrace the project of capitalist acquisitive individualism as "dumber than wild animals," raises eyebrows at Kingsley's "arrogance" and "indifference" with respect to women's suffrage demands, and suggests that Kingsley was insensitive to Aboriginal peoples, denigrating their homelands in remote northern regions. This may all be true enough, if judged from present-day sensibilities, but it builds on selective use of quite restricted quotation and takes Kingsley very much out of his historical context. In McKay's strained effort to amalgamate quite different strands of left-wing experience into what he designates the common politics of "first formation leftists," he assimilates the experience of Kingsley and the discernibly

more moderately social democratic James Simpson. McKay also characterizes Kingsley as a member of the "petite bourgeoisie," citing his occupations as "fish merchant, print shop proprietor, and publisher," albeit acknowledging that "he was also a man who had lost both of his legs in an industrial accident – perhaps formally irrelevant to a strictly Marxist definition of his class location, but not likely to have been personally irrelevant to either him or to his own sense of class identity." It is a bit much to mechanically label Kingsley a "merchant." And while Marxist understandings of what McKay calls "class location" may tend towards an "objective" structuralism, they can hardly be weighted down with this kind of wooden reductionism. Kingsley was a professional revolutionary, an occupation that fits uncomfortably with the notion "petite bourgeoisie." His British Columbia "occupations" were all funded by the cooperative impulses and material support of the working-class socialist movement he dedicated his life to advancing. It is difficult not to see Kingsley's early labouring life as working class, his disabling injury as pushing his life in certain directions that were anything but a denial of proletarian status. All of this reveals the ahistorical social construction of the Canadian revolutionary left that animates McKay's "reconnaissance," in which awkward complexities are congealed in simplified categories. (Quotes and other comments from pp. 156–58, 162–63, 185, 196, 301, 393, 506, 518.)

10 Quoted in McCormack, *supra* note 8 at 61.
11 See, for instance, Audra Jennings, "'The Greatest Numbers ... Will Be Wage Earners': Organized Labor and Disability Activism, 1945–1953" (2007) 4 Labor: Studies in Working-Class History of the Americas 55.

Acknowledgments

We are grateful to a number of scholars, most notably the authors who have contributed towards this volume, as well as colleagues affiliated with the Canadian Law and Society Association (CLSA), for their ongoing support for the production of critical legal scholarship. Members of the CLSA Board, and Eric Reiter in particular, provided assistance at key stages in the production of this volume and at a symposium in Winnipeg that provided inspiration for several chapters. In addition to our respective families, Christine Malone, Frank Smith, Richard Jochelson, and Lynda Collins provided hours of support and encouragement. Superb copy-editing was provided by Robin Whitehead. Megan Rusciano, author of one of the chapters in this volume, prepared the index. We also wish to thank the anonymous peer reviewers. Randy Schmidt at UBC Press was endlessly patient as we progressed on the manuscript. Deans Bruce Feldthusen and Nathalie Des Rosiers at the Faculty of Law, Common Law Section, University of Ottawa, have been exemplary advocates of critical scholarship and superb mentors. We gratefully acknowledge the financial support of the Social Sciences and Humanities Research Council (SSHRC) and Ilia Starr for his erudite assistance on all things related to SSHRC. All remaining errors are our own responsibility.

DISABLING BARRIERS

Introduction
Bringing History and Law to Disability Studies

RAVI MALHOTRA AND BENJAMIN ISITT

This volume of essays had both a long gestation period and a complicated history in its own right. The editors hail from different cultural backgrounds, scholarly traditions, and geographical spaces. Malhotra, a legal scholar and disability rights advocate in Ottawa, and Isitt, a historian and city councillor in Victoria, met fortuitously as a result of a long – and long-distance – collaboration on another distinct but related project. The duo came together in 2010 to research the life of double amputee and political radical Eugene T. Kingsley (1856–1929).[1] This was a vast project, involving dozens of meetings, intricate financial planning, and an army of research assistants who, under our direction, scoured archives across North America in search of any trace of the American-born Kingsley.

Almost completely forgotten today, Eugene Kingsley became a prominent member of the San Francisco branch of the Socialist Labor Party of America (SLP) in the closing decade of the nineteenth century, after experiencing a serious railway accident in 1890, when he was in his early thirties and working as a brakeman on a railway car in Montana. Despite losing his legs and requiring artificial limbs to ambulate, Kingsley went on to become a political radical and rabble-rouser, running in California as an SLP candidate for the US House of Representatives in 1896 and 1898. Hounded by the state in a forgotten "free speech fight" in San Francisco, and battered by inner-party strife, Kingsley moved to Nanaimo, British Columbia, in 1902 and ultimately to Vancouver, where he became a founder and leader of the

Socialist Party of Canada (SPC). Serving for many years as editor of the SPC organ, the *Western Clarion*, Kingsley soon became a household name in Vancouver and working-class communities around the province, running several times for election to both the BC Legislature as well as the Canadian House of Commons. Although he was never elected to public office, Kingsley remained a political radical and leading theoretician of the Canadian left throughout his life, and his impossibilist vision of socialism leaves a rich legacy that is all the more pertinent in these times of deep austerity and political contestation in Canada and globally.[2]

Our interest in Kingsley's story and his legacy led us to convene a workshop of scholars in Winnipeg in 2014. This symposium, convened in partnership with the Canadian Law and Society Association and financially supported by SSHRC, brought together Canadian and American scholars from a variety of disciplines to discuss and debate issues relating to disability rights and the place of people with disabilities in the world. The workshop provided the genesis for this anthology, which traces the thematic and theoretical contours of the worlds of disability studies, law, and the history of social movements.

Disability as both a topic of inquiry and basis for theoretical discussions has long been marginalized in both law and history. Too often, legal scholars have disregarded the fact that people with disabilities are one of the largest – and most marginalized – minority populations. Yet, people with disabilities are actors in their own right and make their own history. Since the publication of Michael Oliver's now classic text, *The Politics of Disablement*, there has been a sea change away from the medical model of disablement, which focused primarily on medical rehabilitation as the strategy to improve the quality of life of people with disabilities, to an embrace of the social model of disablement.[3] The social model identifies barriers as the main problem facing people with disabilities. It marks a shift from a focus on correcting physiological impairment to one on removing those barriers that create disabilities – imposing a positive obligation on a host of institutions to provide resources and take action in pursuit of substantive equality. Whether one considers staggering poverty rates or dismal labour market participation rates, it is apparent that people with disabilities have been largely excluded from a society that has been filled with systemic physical and attitudinal barriers that have impeded their progress. Be it an inaccessible university campus or a workplace staffed by managers hostile to the presence of workers with disabilities and eager to speed up production to meet growing neoliberal demands for efficiency and just-in-time production, people with disabilities face a litany of barriers to participation in everyday life. Yet relatively few established legal scholars, particularly in Canada, have devoted their full attention to analyzing disability rights issues.[4] Even fewer have approached disability rights through an overt lens of social justice and critical scholarship. More often, disability is mentioned as an afterthought after a long list of identity categories, without any real engagement about the richness or diversity of the disability community. Or discussion of disability rights is glaringly absent, notwithstanding the fact that legal issues permeate every aspect of the lives of people with disabilities.

Similarly, despite some exciting new scholarship in the past few years and with the partial exception of biography, disability history as a discipline is largely in its infancy.[5] People with disabilities have rarely been regarded as historical actors, despite significant evidence that they have participated in the political process, lobbied for change, and even mobilized against the state at times. Groundbreaking work in the area of social history since the 1970s – illuminating the stories, experiences, and struggles of working people, women, Indigenous people, immigrants, people of colour, and, more recently, members of the queer community – has failed to inquire into the lives of people with disabilities. This historiographical lacuna is apparent is the story of E.T. Kingsley. Widely recognized as the leading theoretician of the western Canadian left in the first two decades of the twentieth century, Kingsley has often made a cameo appearance in works on political and labour history, but he has never occupied centre stage. Historians in Canada and other lands have been more inclined to interrogate the past through the lenses of class, race, gender, and sexuality than through the prism of ability and disability. We hope that the chapters that follow are able to push the discussion forward, ask new questions about the past, present, and future, and encourage scholars from law, history, and disability studies to rethink their assumptions about people with disabilities and their place in the world. We hope this questioning will inform policy debates and play a role in transforming social, legal, economic, and political relations, with a view towards removing barriers and achieving substantive equality.

Our volume is divided into three parts, with a degree of overlap and fluidity between them. The first, entitled Historical Debates on Work and Disability, features chapters by historians and other historically minded scholars on a range of topics affecting people with disabilities. In the first chapter, Mark Leier provides an overview of working-class political struggles in British Columbia in the first two decades of the twentieth century. Leier demonstrates the contradictions of a labour movement that sought to redress the injustices imposed by an exploitative system and yet too often excluded those whom it regarded as inferior, whether on the basis of race or gender, to the white men who dominated the movement. This critique of the exclusionary impulse within the labour movement helps to illuminate some of the prejudices and barriers that confront workers with disabilities, both then and now.

In Chapter 2, Dustin Galer tackles disability rights in the workplace in a different setting and time period, post–Second World War Canada. Galer capably shows how returning veterans and civilian polio survivors played a pivotal role in leading campaigns to encourage the employment of people with disabilities. Yet, as Galer notes, returning veterans were typically entitled to services and benefits superior to those available to other disabled workers, creating tensions and frictions with the disability community. It would be some years before hiring campaigns seeking to alter ignorant and discriminatory attitudes of employers began to have a discernable impact, gradually culminating in the declaration by the United Nations of the International Year of Disabled Persons in 1981.

In Chapter 3, historian Geoffrey Reaume uses the prisms of gender and work to examine several distinct areas of disability history, considering people with physical, sensory, and intellectual disabilities; the elderly; workers; and mad people. Interestingly, Reaume discusses how gender is most effectively addressed in "mad history," showing how women confined to mental institutions were expected to perform work and how this work was defined and constrained on a gendered basis. Reaume's insightful and engaging overview demonstrates a nuanced appreciation of the intersections between disability, gender, and class, pointing towards new approaches for historians of disability.

The second part of this volume, entitled Debates in Disability Studies, opens with a powerful contribution from the past president of the Society for Disability Studies, scholar Anne Finger (Chapter 4). She documents how American president Franklin Roosevelt undertook significant efforts to disguise the effects of his impairments, which were a result of what contemporaries and historians have generally assumed to be polio. At the same time, to the extent that his disability was public knowledge, Roosevelt sought to rearticulate the narrative of disability as one of overcoming adversity. In an era before television, the president's iconic fireside chats effectively emphasized his voice and intellectual gifts. Finger documents the lengths to which Roosevelt and his aides went to minimize any negative press attention about his impairments, even while Roosevelt privately enjoyed the company of others with disabilities.

In Chapter 5, Mark Walters closely examines the history of the physiology of the ear to demonstrate how the construction of deaf people as having disabilities was critical to scientific understanding of the inner ear's role in regulating balance. Moving effortlessly between the traditionally discrete disciplines of sound studies, disability studies, and the history of the senses, Walters' imaginative contribution critically assesses three models of understanding balance and embodiment. He constructs an original intervention that shows how "disabled bodies defy translation, overflow with excessive meanings, and threaten commonly held beliefs about the proper relationship not only between sensory modalities but also of the sensory body to its world."

Finally, we close this part with a contribution from Jen Rinaldi and Jay Dolmage (Chapter 6). Combining disability studies, the field of rhetoric, and legal studies, they trace early twentieth-century Canadian immigration policy, using legislative histories, archival documents, and popular texts. Rinaldi and Dolmage effectively show how immigrant bodies were rigorously inspected for fear they were sites of contamination. Racial bigotry merged with eugenic conceptions of disability to create a highly invasive immigration policy. This confluence was manifested in the notorious anti-Asian head tax and a statutory framework enacted in British Columbia and elsewhere in the country to limit Chinese immigration, the response to which demonstrated deep divisions within the working class in Canada. The authors conclude by indicating how this racist and ableist legacy has relevance for current policy debates around immigration. Rinaldi and Dolmage's exploration of the relationship between race and ability complements the method advanced in the preceding chapter by Reaume.

Part 3 is devoted to debates in legal theory and laws, regulations, and legal decisions affecting people with disabilities. In Chapter 7, Odelia Bay examines the barriers experienced by people with chronic illness in the workplace in a Canadian context. She argues that antidiscrimination case law has to date largely failed people with chronic illnesses, according greater recognition and protection to people with visible rather than invisible disabilities. In order to make real progress, Bay argues that we should look to the experience of case law that concerns caregiving and addresses gender and family status discrimination. By emphasizing flexibility, work-life balance, and the importance of workplace benefits, Bay points to an effective and transformative strategy that can improve the lives of people with chronic illnesses.

In Chapter 8, Megan Rusciano examines the issue of poverty among people with disabilities through an analysis of a single case: the Ontario Human Rights Tribunal 2014 decision in *Garrie v Janus Joan Inc.* That case concerned a woman with intellectual disabilities who was paid a training honorarium of one dollar per hour for her labour, far below the prevailing statutory minimum wage. Rusciano illustrates how the relevant domestic jurisprudence, the United Nations *Convention on the Rights of Persons with Disabilities,* and the *Accessibility for Ontarians with Disabilities Act* all provide limited remedies for people with disabilities facing discrimination in wages. One of the more challenging issues raised in this chapter is the possibility that the legal capacity of workers with intellectual disabilities to litigate may be called into question. This issue raises profound philosophical questions about inclusion in society: it seems deeply ironic that one may be qualified to perform wage labour for an employer yet have one's capacity to litigate to ensure that one is treated fairly on the job subject to legal challenge. Rusciano's discussion thus links to many of the reflections made in previous chapters on the exploitation of workers with disabilities.

Finally, in Chapter 9, Eric Tucker eloquently traces the history of debates surrounding workers' compensation, with particular reference to Ontario, and how the law has been employed in the context of the market's desire to commodify labour and the concomitant tendency of injured workers to fight for decommodification under certain circumstances. Tucker demonstrates how the rise of the negligence model of liability came about as a result of deep dissatisfaction with the contractual principles that dominated the nineteenth century and largely exonerated employers from responsibility for workplace accidents. Yet the negligence model soon faltered, as employers were concerned about potentially significant liability claims, while employees were often reluctant to sue because they risked having to pay the legal costs of their employer should they lose. Furthermore, there was always a risk that an initial victory for an employee in tort might be overturned on appeal. Tucker's timely chapter traces this complex history and situates the circumstances of injured workers within the changing political times and the ebbs and flows of class struggle.

Collectively, the chapters in this volume provide a rich array of approaches, case studies, paradigms, and perspectives. They propel several fields of scholarly inquiry in exciting and challenging new directions, honouring the experiences and struggles of people with disabilities, who have hitherto operated on the margins of academic research and many societal institutions. Rather than slavishly following a single ideological or methodological path, each chapter contributes in a small way to paint one facet of a larger picture: the deep and persistent inequalities that pervade the lives of people with disabilities today – and potential strategies for attacking inequality, removing barriers, and pursuing substantive equality. All the authors aim to interrogate critical questions in history, disability theory, and law to make a better world for people with disabilities. We hope that this volume raises new questions in history and law, challenges misconceptions about people with disabilities, creates pathways for new research, and offers hope for the future.

NOTES

1 Their resulting biography of Kingsley is in development with UBC Press.
2 For one account of impossiblism, see Frank Girard & Ben Perry, *The Socialist Labor Party 1876–1991: A Short History* (Philadelphia: Livra Books, 1991).
3 Michael Oliver, *The Politics of Disablement* (London: Macmillan, 1990).
4 Some major exceptions include the landmark anthology by Dianne Pothier and Richard Devlin, Michael Lynk's work on the duty to accommodate people with disabilities in the workplace, and a recent volume on disability and narratives by Ravi Malhotra and Morgan Rowe. See Dianne Pothier & Richard Devlin, eds, *Critical Disability Theory: Essays in Philosophy, Politics, Policy, and Law* (Vancouver: UBC Press, 2006); Michael Lynk, "Disability and the Duty to Accommodate: An Arbitrator's Perspective" in *Labour Arbitration Yearbook, 2001–2002* (Toronto: Lancaster House, 2002) 51; Ravi Malhotra & Morgan Rowe, *Exploring Disability Identity and Disability Rights through Narratives: Finding a Voice of Their Own* (London: Routledge, 2013).
5 See, e.g., Kim E Nielsen, *A Disability History of the United States* (Boston: Beacon Press, 2012); Susan Burch & Michael Rembis, eds, *Disability Histories* (Urbana-Champaign: University of Illinois Press, 2014); Paul K Longmore & Lauri Umansky, *The New Disability History: American Perspective* (New York: New York University Press, 2001). Canadian disability history remains more tenuous. For a full discussion in the context of gender, see Chapter 3 by Geoffrey Reaume in this volume. There has also been growing interest in the life story of Deaf-blind radical activist Helen Keller, yet many people remain unaware of Keller's radical politics. See, e.g., Keith Rosenthal, "The Politics of Helen Keller: Socialism and Disability" (2015) 96 Intl Socialist Rev, online: <http://isreview.org/issue/96/politics-helen-keller>.

PART 1

Historical Debates on Work and Disability

1

Bearing the Marks of Capital
Solidarities and Fractures
in E.T. Kingsley's British Columbia

MARK LEIER

"I've never read Marx's *Capital*, ... but I have the marks of capital all over me."[1] So "Big Bill" Haywood, the best-known organizer for the Industrial Workers of the World (IWW), declared at rallies, strikes, and demonstrations across North America. From the founding of the revolutionary union in 1905 until 1921, Haywood put his body on the line, rhetorically and literally. Injured in a mining accident, attacked by police, his health broken by prison and hard living, Haywood and his testimony were appreciated by his working-class audiences, who bore their own marks of capital.

The connections between work, death, and disability were expressed in popular working-class culture as well as in speeches and manifestos. In 1908, another member of the IWW, using the pen name "An Unknown Proletarian," kept the structure and some of the imagery of Rudyard Kipling's poem, "The Song of the Dead," changed the title to "The Cry of Toil," and replaced the British admiralty with employers as the cause of death and injury. The poem was later set to music by another member of the IWW and became better known as "We Have Fed You All for a Thousand Years":

We have fed you all, for a thousand years
And you hail us still unfed,
Though there's never a dollar of all your wealth
But marks the worker's dead.
We have yielded our best to give you rest

And you lie on crimson wool.
Then if blood be the price of all your wealth,
Good God! We have paid it in full.
There is never a mine blown skyward now
But we're buried alive for you.
There's never a wreck drifts shoreward now
But we are its ghastly crew.
Go reckon our dead by the forges red
And the factories where we spin.
If blood be the price of your cursed wealth
Good God! We have paid it in.
We have fed you all for a thousand years –
For that was our doom, you know,
From the days when you chained us in your fields
To the strike of a week ago.
You have taken our lives, and our babies and wives,
And we're told it's your legal share;
But if blood be the price of your lawful wealth
Good God! We have bought it fair.[2]

In British Columbia, where Haywood spoke on several occasions, the socialist writer, editor, and organizer E.T. Kingsley was a more vivid example of the marks of capital. As Ravi Malhotra and Ben Isitt's introduction to this volume indicates, both of Kingsley's legs were amputated in 1890, the result of an accident while working as a railway brakeman. Unlike Haywood, Kingsley seems to have made little public reference to his disability; indeed, his political opponents and the children of his colleagues more often referred to and recollected his bald pate than his missing limbs.[3] Nonetheless, his loss was so well known it served as a plot device for the novelist A.M. Stephen in his 1929 *roman à clef* of the BC labour and left movements, *The Gleaming Archway*. In the novel, the protagonist is won over to the cause of socialism by Bob Tacey, a powerful orator who had lost his left arm in a railway accident and "took to readin' books and pretty soon went in for Socialist work altogether."[4]

While injury and dismemberment at the hands of the employer may have led workers such as Haywood and Kingsley to the IWW, the Socialist Party of America, the Socialist Labor Party, and the Socialist Party of Canada, most workers did not turn to revolutionary unions and radical parties. Nor, on the other hand, was injury necessary for people to become radicals: class exploitation, in which surplus value was created by workers and expropriated by the employers, was reason enough for many to "rally 'round the standard when the red flag is unfurled," as Joe Hill put it in a song for a 1912 IWW strike in British Columbia.[5] BC workers, like workers elsewhere, responded to capitalism in many ways, from supporting those candidates and policies of the traditional Liberal and Conservative parties that were labour friendly, to creating labour and socialist parties, and to eschewing political action altogether in favour of strikes, walkouts, and even sabotage. New organizations sprang up, collapsed, and were replaced, as workers struggled to create new solidarities. Nor did the common experience of injury and death unite workers across lines of race, gender, and occupation. Yet we may nonetheless trace a red thread through the early BC labour and left movements, a thread of violence, injury, and death that shaped work and resistance.

That thread began with the early years of industrial capitalism in the province. On Vancouver Island, coal miners began to create informal local organizations as early as 1848. By the early 1890s, several strikes had been launched, though with little success. Strikes in 1877, 1883, and 1891 were aimed at Robert Dunsmuir, whose company was labelled by Samuel Gompers, the long-serving head of the American Federation of Labor, as "one of the most villainous corporations who ever lived."[6] A former miner himself, Dunsmuir had little concern for the safety of the workers: in the nine years between 1879 and 1888, more than 260 died in mining accidents on Vancouver Island. Dunsmuir used his political connections to deploy the violence of the state, calling upon the militia and police to evict and arrest strikers and ensure that scabs could work with impunity. With the failure of the 1883 strike, miners explored new forms of organization beyond the local association. Led by Samuel Myers, an Irish labourer and miner, they turned to the Knights of Labor. The Knights, created in the United States in 1869, promised to unionize all workers, regardless of trade, craft, or skill. That approach was very different from most of the union movement, in which trade, craft, and skill were too often code for white, male, and anglophone privilege. In contrast to those unions that made exclusion the basis of their organization, the Knights set out to create an inclusive working-class organization and culture that would bring in all who worked, regardless of race, gender, ethnicity, or skill. Thus, the Great Seal of the Knights incorporated a sketch of North and South America and a triangle linking economics (production, distribution, and consumption) with human existence (birth, life, and death), all encircled with the motto "That is the most perfect government in which an injury to one is the concern of all." In the United States, the Knights were among the first unions to organize white and African American workers in the same union and local.

On the west coast of the United States and Canada, however, the Knights' ideology of inclusion did not extend to Chinese workers, as events in Vancouver make clear. Just three years after the city was chartered in 1886, workers created the Vancouver Trades and Labour Council (VTLC), giving several independent unions mutual support and a single voice. The council was made up largely of craft unions, such as carpenters and printers, but it also included the Knights, who signed on to the first principles of the VTLC: the fight for the nine-hour day and Asian exclusion. The anti-Asian movement in the city culminated in an attack on Chinese workers by a mob that included members of the Knights of Labor.[7]

In the Vancouver Island coalfields, white miners often subcontracted Chinese labourers to do semi-skilled ancillary tasks in the mines, freeing the white miners to concentrate on the actual mining. During the 1883 strike, Robert Dunsmuir was quick to hire these Chinese workers, whom the white miners had not organized, to dig coal and keep the mines producing. The reaction of the white miners was not to expand the union to include Chinese; rather, it was to add to the list of strike grievances the demand that Dunsmuir stop using Chinese workers at the coal face. That demand, like their others, went unheeded. In the end, the failure of white miners to organize Chinese workers was one reason for the failure of the strike. Dunsmuir had learned an important lesson: that race could be an effective tool to divide workers. White miners too learned from the strike but drew two contradictory conclusions. They had learned the need for political action, and so they drafted Samuel Myers to run in the provincial election of 1886, no doubt hoping that a friendly presence in the legislature would help constrain state violence against strikers. They had not, however, learned that, because racism was a useful tool for the employer, it was a problem that had to be overcome by workers. Indeed, one of Myers' political demands was the exclusion of Asians from the province. This plank did not give Myers much traction in the election, for he finished last among seven candidates, and was outpolled 10–1 by the winner, Robert Dunsmuir. The consequence of failing to make "an injury to one the concern of all" was soon brought home in grisly fashion. Less than nine months after the election, a mine explosion killed 150 workers, white and Chinese alike. Among the dead was Samuel Myers.[8]

The 1883 strike revealed some of the differences in occupation, political integration, gender, and ethnicity that were difficult to overcome as workers searched for tactics and strategies to meet the exigencies of everyday life. Too often it was easier for more privileged workers, paraphrasing the IWW singer and storyteller Utah Phillips, to shift the blame pattern downward, easier to attack the weak within their own class than to attack the power of the capitalist class, easier to find accommodations with capital than to mobilize broadly against it.

Thus, even as the VTLC newspaper, *The Independent,* called in 1900 for working men to come together and form unions and raise money for a labour hall, it warned that in BC, "one in four is a Mongol." The article then argued that such a high proportion of Chinese and Japanese would have the effect of stopping desirable immigrants from coming to the province and would have the tendency to "stop capital more than the eight-hour law, for it is impossible to have confidence in a British colony peopled by Japanese and Chinese."[9] When Joseph Watson, a stalwart member of the VTLC, the boilermakers union, and the Liberal Party, set out to organize fishers on the Fraser River in 1900, he refused to sign up Asian and First Nation workers, insisting that it was "better to starve the Mongol out than to starve our white worker out of an occupation."[10]

Yet the same labour council, with many of the same members who had pushed for Asian exclusion in 1889, soon repudiated Watson's racism. When his organizing drive failed, he was replaced by Frank Rogers, who brought Asian, First Nation, and European fishers along the Fraser River into the union and led a strike in 1900. Fishers won some modest gains and were better prepared for another strike the following year. But as with the Vancouver Island miners, the fishers were met by state violence used on behalf of the employers, this time in the form of the Duke of Connaught's Own Rifles. The newly formed unit's first deployment was to escort strike-breakers across picket lines, giving ironic meaning to its regimental motto, "Clear the Way."[11]

While it was clear that capital could rely upon the power of the state in the struggle with labour, it was also prepared to use violence on its own and with no pretense of acting to preserve the public good. When in 1903, a new union, the United Brotherhood of Railway Employees (UBRE), organized the so-called unskilled workers of the Canadian Pacific Railway (CPR), including navvies, baggage clerks, and freight handlers, the company swore to "spend a million dollars to kill the UBRE." The fierce reaction of the CPR was, on the surface, surprising, for many of its workers – the firemen, brakemen, conductors, and engineers who made up the running trades of the railway – had long been unionized. But their high wages were subsidized by the low wages of the unskilled, and the CPR was determined to stop the organizing drive of the UBRE. The railway hired private detectives to infiltrate the union and provoked a strike by firing a worker. When the American president of the UBRE, George Estes, came to Victoria to support the strikers, the CPR used its influence to have him arrested and jailed for three weeks.[12]

The company was also able to take advantage of splits in the labour movement. Joseph Watson, still a member of the VTLC and still a force for division, herded scabs to break the UBRE picket lines. Watson then organized a new union to compete with and siphon off support for the UBRE and attacked members of his own union who wanted to strike in sympathy. Other Vancouver workers, however, notably longshoremen, teamsters, and seamen, refused to handle CPR goods and went out in sympathy strikes to defend the UBRE. Frank Rogers, then active in the longshore union, was instrumental in building solidarity for the strike. In response, the CPR literally put him in its gunsights. When Rogers went to a UBRE picket line at the Vancouver railway terminal, he was shot and killed by someone among the group of police agents and strike-breakers hired by the CPR. One man was charged with murder, but his lawyer, retained by the railway, had the case dismissed.[13] Not even Rogers' death could heal the rifts in the labour movement: hundreds of workers turned out for his funeral march, but none of the railway running trades sent representatives. And when the question of who would pay for the funeral arose, the VTLC refused to accept the bill, worried that it would set a precedent that would leave it liable for other claims and debts incurred by the UBRE. The result was that Rogers was buried in a grave that remained unmarked until the 1980s, when labour activists and historians raised funds for a modest stone.[14]

The same year saw ferocious strikes in the Crowsnest Pass and Vancouver Island led by the radical Western Federation of Miners, and the relations between labour and capital increasingly resembled the overt class conflict predicted by Karl Marx and other revolutionaries. So intense were class relations that the federal government intervened in the way that it does whenever an issue threatens to rend the country: it created a royal commission. Future prime minister William Lyon Mackenzie King, not yet thirty years old, was dispatched to serve as the secretary of the commission, which was charged with investigating industrial disputes in British Columbia.[15]

The increased readiness of the labour movement to strike was supported with political action. Recovering from Myers' disappointing showing in the 1886 provincial election, labour elected two candidates in 1890. In the following election, that of 1894, three labour candidates ran. None were elected, but, in one riding, the working-class candidate received nearly 49 percent of the vote; in another, over 45 percent. The third candidate, Ralph Smith, garnered fewer votes, but in the 1898 election, Smith trounced his opponent, winning over 78 percent of the popular vote; that year, Vancouver workers elected Robert Macpherson as a labour-affiliated candidate. Smith was re-elected in 1900, and five other avowed labour candidates, including Joseph Dixon, the first president of the Vancouver Trades and Labour Council, also ran in that election. Such political involvement was an important step for the craft unions, which made up the bulk of the council, for it indicated their disavowal of the conservative American Federation of Labor leader Samuel Gompers and his policy that the trade union movement should not engage directly in political action by running their own candidates under the banner of labour. Even more notable perhaps, 1900 saw the first socialist candidate: William MacClain, a comrade of Frank Rogers, polled about 5 percent of the vote in the riding of Vancouver City. If MacClain's showing was not invigorating, by February 1901, the left had reason to add optimism of the intellect to optimism of the will: James Hawthornthwaite, running as an Independent Labour Party candidate, won by acclamation the seat left vacant when Smith resigned to run as a Liberal in the federal election of 1900. In the next provincial election, just six months after the murder of Rogers, Hawthornthwaite ran and won as a member of the Socialist Party of British Columbia. He was joined in the legislature by fellow socialist Parker Williams and by William Davidson, a Labour candidate in Slocan. The Socialist Party of BC ran ten candidates, and while there was no provincial labour party, five people ran as labour-supported candidates. Thus, over one-third of the forty-two seats in the provincial legislature were contested by labour or left candidates; in the finest tradition of left sectarianism, Socialist Party, Vancouver (Independent) Labour Party, and Socialist Labor Party candidates fought each other in the riding of Vancouver City.[16]

The move to the left continued, as BC workers created the Socialist Party of Canada (SPC) in 1904 and brought E.T. Kingsley to the province as an organizer and newspaper editor. Kingsley was known as an "impossiblist," rejecting both trade union activity and political reformism for political action and socialism. His political impossiblism was adopted and adapted from the US Socialist Labor Party, led by Daniel DeLeon. DeLeon defined socialism as "that social system under which the necessaries of production are owned, controlled, and administered by the people, for the people and under which, accordingly, the cause of political and economic despotism having been abolished, class rule is at an end. That is socialism, nothing short of that."[17] Kingsley's philosophy of no compromise and no political trading, which was promulgated in his newspaper, the *Western Clarion*, found significant support in British Columbia.[18]

Some have seen British Columbia as an example of "western exceptionalism," a province propelled by terrible conditions to greater radicalism, but such analysis is too simplistic. Radical movements flourished across North America, and there is little evidence that the conditions of work and political repression in BC were exceptional. At the same time, the BC labour movement, for all its initiatives and gains, for all its new solidarities and radicalism, remained riven. The SPC, for example, combined its official impossiblism with a strong element of reformism, notably around questions of workers' safety. When the party held the balance of power in the provincial legislature for a few years before 1912, it pressed for an eight-hour day in the mining industry and for a workers' compensation board to inspect workplaces and insure workers against injury on the job. Parker Williams, part of the surge of socialists elected in 1903, retained his seat until 1917, when he left politics to become the head of the newly established Workmen's Compensation Board. As further evidence of a divided movement, both conservative trade unionists and revolutionary socialists committed to political action could denounce the IWW for its insistence on direct action, up to and including the strategies of the general strike and sabotage. In the United States, Bill Haywood was removed from the national executive committee of the Socialist Party of America for refusing to renounce sabotage, while in British Columbia, labourists and electoral socialists were quick to disassociate themselves from Wobblies, who hinted at the need to take the fight directly to employers and political figures.[19]

Questions of gender could also both unite and fracture labour and the left. The VTLC, composed entirely of men until the tailors' union sent Helena Gutteridge as its delegate in 1912, had gone on record as early as 1900 in support of equal pay for equal work and had supported women telephone operators in a strike in 1902. Yet it still argued that women should not do "men's work" and held to the ideal of the family wage to support the male breadwinner as the head of the household. Often men in the labour movement believed that the chief contribution women could make was in "ladies' auxiliaries" rather than as members of unions. Members of the socialist movement too would take contradictory positions. Bertha Merrill Burns was elected to the executive of the Socialist Party of BC, the short-lived precursor to the SPC, receiving just three fewer votes than E.T. Kingsley. Burns wrote a column, "We Women," for the party newspaper, but she and other women had to face the opposition of many men in the movement. The SPC did not even come out unequivocally in favour of women's suffrage: as one writer put it, "the suffragette movement has no connection with the working class movement for the overthrow of capitalism."[20]

Tensions arising from solidarities and divisions continued in the province. In 1910, workers created the BC Federation of Labour, an umbrella organization that called for industrial unionism and socialism, and by 1913 Helena Gutteridge was editing the "women's page" in its newspaper, the *BC Federationist*. The violence in the workplace and on the picket line also continued, most graphically during the 1912–14 coal mining strike on Vancouver Island. Workers' safety was the precipitating issue for the strike. Since the death of Samuel Myers and 149 others in 1887, over 170 more miners had been killed in explosions and cave-ins in the island's mines. When a member of the miners' safety committee was fired in September 1912, outraged miners, who were by then organized in the United Mine Workers of America (UMWA), first took a "holiday" in protest and were then locked out. The call for a broader strike went out, and soon most of the coal pits were behind picket lines.

A cartoon published in the *BC Federationist* during the strike made it clear that the action was directly tied to the threat of death and disability that workers faced on the job. In the cartoon, Death, represented by a skeletal figure, holds in one hand a torch labelled "EXPLOSION." With the other hand, he extends a full bag marked "Extra Profits" to a collier proprietor while a government safety inspector and a miners' delegate watch helplessly from a distance. "So long as you allow me the run of your pits," says Death to the proprietor, "So long as you drop in for these extras, d'you see? You turn your back on me and listen to those fellows behind, and your extras stop. It is for you to choose."[21] At one of its rallies, the BC Miners' Liberation League drew explicitly on the IWW song "We Have Fed You All for a Thousand Years," with a large banner reading "There is never a mine blown skyward now but we're buried alive for you." Beside the lyric was printed a death toll: "27 Men Killed on Vancouver Island Every Year for 25 Years."[22] Miners, their wives, and children again faced the violence of the militia, this time the 72nd Seaforth Highlanders in its first action. The regiment was transported to the area via the Esquimalt and Nanaimo Railway, first owned by Robert Dunsmuir and two US railway barons, Leland Stanford and Collis P. Huntington, and sold to the CPR in 1905. The regiment, which proudly displayed its

Maxim gun, a machine gun capable of firing six hundred rounds a minute, remained stationed in the coalfields for nearly two years.

As they had done previously, BC workers split over questions of militancy and radicalism. When members of the IWW joined with others to call for a general strike to free imprisoned miners and break the deadlock of the strike, some respectable and pragmatic union leaders insisted such a thing was impossible. Four times miners and their allies called for a general strike, and each time the call was ignored, tabled, or opposed by conservatives and labour bureaucrats. By the summer of 1914, miners were leaving the region or quietly returning to work; by summer's end, they voted to accept the offer they had soundly rejected just a few months earlier. The conservative trade unionists preferred to blame the loss of the strike on economic conditions and Asian labour rather than on their own failure to develop a more inclusive and militant solidarity.[23]

The international violence of the First World War put even more pressure on labour and the left, and the movements in BC and elsewhere nearly collapsed under the strain. Government repression banned some organizations and censored much of the left-wing press. Patriotism claimed some members, who abandoned ideals of international solidarity in favour of national chauvinism. Some trade unions were quick to support the war because military production resulted in good jobs for their members; many workers chose to sign up in the armed forces because the prospect of regular meals and pay was better than the unemployment they had faced in the prewar depression. Gradually, the horrors of the war became evident, while war profiteering exposed in particularly stark ways the class nature of Canada. The imposition of conscription in 1917 provided the impetus for the labour and left movements in BC to remobilize and begin to organize again.[24] When the popular union organizer, BC Federation executive, and SPC member Ginger Goodwin was killed by a police agent on Vancouver Island in 1918, Vancouver workers were angry and confident enough to launch a one-day general strike in protest, something they had been unable or unwilling to do during the two years of the Vancouver Island coal strike.

That general strike was a harbinger of the strike wave that would crash across Canada from 1919 to 1920. While the six-week-long Winnipeg General Strike is the best known, workers from Amherst, Nova Scotia, to Victoria turned to the general strike, making 1919 the year in which more worker-days were lost to strikes than any other in Canadian history. Workers took up the lessons that had long been taught by socialist and IWW agitators, and they increasingly insisted that production for profit had to give way to production for need, that something more like Kingsley's vision of socialism was necessary and worth fighting for. Led by socialists and unionists from British Columbia, a new organization, the One Big Union (OBU), was created in 1919 and set out to organize the unorganized (especially in the logging industry) and the "misorganized" – that is, workers such as miners who were represented by conservative and undemocratic unions.[25]

The upsurge of radicalism and militancy was met with a backlash from the government, business, and conservative labour. The VTLC was again the site of a struggle over tactics and directions. When OBU militants came to dominate the council, conservative unionists, led by Percy Bengough of the machinists union, set up an alternate council and fought against the OBU, even siding with employers and the state to dislodge the radical union. Such division weakened both sides of the labour-left movements, and, in the face of government repression that included massive deportations, employer intransigence that made wide use of the yellow dog contract and the black list, and an economy that shrank rapidly after the wartime boom, many of the gains of these movements were lost. These losses ranged from the theft of VTLC records to the forfeiture to the provincial government of the Labour Temple to the revival of racism and Asian exclusion as dominant currents in the labour movement. The socialist movement too foundered, as the SPC broke apart on the question of support for the Bolsheviks and the Russian Revolution. Attempts to create new organizations, notably the Federated Labour Party and the Canadian Labour Party, had some small successes, but these two organizations fought with each other and were wracked as well by internal conflict, often in response to the newly formed Communist Party. By 1928, the labour and left movements in British Columbia were exhausted.[26]

So too were the old militants and leaders. Bill Haywood, convicted under the US *Espionage Act* of conspiring to interfere with the draft, fled the United States for the Soviet Union in 1921. Dispirited and ill, worn out from his work as an activist, Haywood died in Moscow in 1928. Kingsley, largely ignored in the last years of his life, ran unsuccessfully in the Canadian federal election of 1926 and died in his Vancouver room, possibly of suicide, in 1929, aged seventy. Their careers, like the trajectories of the movements of labour and the left in British Columbia and North America, remind us that solidarity – the only weapon workers have – is never formed as a simple response to terrible conditions, even those of workplace injury and death. Workers interpret their class experience, and they do so through different lenses at different times. These range from their personal circumstances to larger cultural, economic, and political trends and movements. The activism in Kingsley's time was no less contentious and fractious than in our own. That history may serve as both a caution and an inspiration as we confront a capitalism no less predatory and exploitative and as we strive to develop new solidarities and strategies.

NOTES

1 J Anthony Lukas, *Big Trouble: A Murder in a Small Western Town Sets Off a Struggle for the Soul of America* (New York: Simon and Schuster, 1997) at 233.

2 See Archie Green, David Roediger, Franklin Rosemont & Salvatore Salerno, eds, *The Big Red Songbook* (Chicago: Charles H. Kerr Publishing Co, 2007) for the words and history of "We Have Fed You All for a Thousand Years." The editors note that "the poem has been erroneously attributed to Rudyard Kipling," and they are correct to point out he did not write this version. However, comparing it with Kipling's "The Song of the Dead, Part II," first published in 1893, makes it clear the Wobbly poet was inspired by Kipling.

3 See William Pritchard, interview with David Millar, 1970, online: <www.abletolead. ca>, accessed 13 January 2015. Una Larsen was the daughter of Parmeter Pettipiece, a friend and comrade of Kingsley for many years. Reflecting on Kingsley, she commented on his baldness, though not his disability. Una Larsen, interview with Mark Leier, February 1989.

4 AM Stephen, *The Gleaming Archway* (London and Toronto: J.M. Dent and Sons, 1929) at 33–34.

5 For Hill's song and a brief description of the strike, see Philip J Thomas, "Where the Fraser River Flows," in *Songs of the Pacific Northwest* (Saanichton, BC: Hancock House Publishers, 1979) at 95–98. See also Mark Leier, *Where the Fraser River Flows: The Industrial Workers of the World in British Columbia* (Vancouver: New Star Books, 1990) at 47–56.

6 *Nanaimo Free Press* (21 March 1891), cited in Allen Seager & Adele Perry, "Mining the Connections: Class, Ethnicity, and Gender in Nanaimo, British Columbia, 1891" (1997) 30:59 Histoire sociale / Social History 55 at 58.

7 See Mark Leier, *Red Flags and Red Tape: The Making of a Labour Bureaucracy* (Toronto: University of Toronto Press, 1995) at 43–70 for the founding of the Vancouver Trades and Labour Council. See also Robert AJ McDonald, *Making Vancouver: Class, Status, and Social Boundaries, 1863–1913* (Vancouver: UBC Press, 1996). For the Knights of Labor more generally, see Gregory S Kealey & Bryan D Palmer, *Dreaming of What Might Be: The Knights of Labor in Ontario, 1880–1900* (New York: Cambridge University Press, 1984).

8 For Myers and the Knights, see H Keith Ralston & Gregory S Kealey, "Myers, Samuel H." in *The Dictionary of Canadian Biography*, vol 11, *1881–1890* (Toronto/Quebec: University of Toronto/Université Laval, 2003), online: <http://www.biographi.ca/ en/bio/myers_samuel_h_11E.html>.

9   *The [Vancouver] Independent* (31 March 1900).

10   *Ibid.* See also Leier, *supra* note 7 at 125–42.

11   Jeremy Mouat, "Rogers, Frank" in *Dictionary of Canadian Biography*, vol 13, *1901–10* (Toronto/Quebec: University of Toronto/Université Laval, 2003), online: <http:// www.biographi.ca/en/bio/rogers_frank_13E.html>; HK Ralston, *The 1900 Strike of Fraser River Sockeye Salmon Fishermen* (MA Thesis, University of British Columbia, 1965) [unpublished].

12   *Province* (6 March 1903) cited in McDonald, *supra* note 7 at 113.

13   J Hugh Tuck, "The United Brotherhood of Railway Employees in Western Canada, 1898–1905," (1983) 11 Labour/Le Travail 63; A Ross McCormack, *Reformers, Rebels, and Revolutionaries: The Western Canadian Radical Movement, 1899–1919* (Toronto: University of Toronto Press, 1977) at 44–47; Mouat, *supra* note 11.

14   Tuck, *supra* note 13; McCormack, *supra* note 13 at 44–47; Mouat, *supra* note 11; Leier, *supra* note 7 at 111–12.

15   Allan D Orr, *The Western Federation of Miners and the Royal Commission on Industrial Disputes with Special Reference to the Vancouver Island Coal Miners' Strike* (MA Thesis, University of British Columbia, 1968) [unpublished]; Paul Craven, *"An Impartial Umpire": Industrial Relations and the Canadian State, 1900–1911* (Toronto: University of Toronto Press, 1980) at 240–70; McCormack, *supra* note 13 at 44–52.

16   British Columbia, Elections British Columbia, *An Electoral History of British Columbia, 1871–1986* (Victoria: Queen's Printer for British Columbia, 1988), online: <http://elections.bc.ca/docs/rpt/1871-1986_ElectoralHistoryofBC.pdf>.

17   Daniel De Leon, "Industrialism," *The Daily People* (23 January 1906), online: <https:// www.marxists.org/archive/deleon/works/1906/060123.htm>.

18   Kingsley's life and politics are examined more closely in the introduction to this volume, by Ravi Malhotra and Ben Isitt. See also McCormack, *supra* note 13, c 4, "The Ascendancy of the Socialist Party of Canada"; RA Johnson, *No Compromise – No Political Trading: The Marxian Socialist Tradition in British Columbia* (PhD Thesis, University of British Columbia, 1975) [unpublished]; Peter Campbell, *Canadian Marxists and the Search for a Third Way* (Montreal & Kingston: McGill-Queen's University Press, 1999); Peter E Newell, *The Impossibilists: A Brief Profile of the Socialist Party of Canada* (London: Athena Press, 2008).

19   John Thomas Keelor, *The Price of Lives and Limbs Lost at Work: The Development of No-Fault Workers' Compensation in British Columbia, 1910–1916* (MA Thesis, University of Victoria, 1996) [unpublished]; Mark Leier, *Rebel Life: The Life and Times of Robert Raglan Gosden, Revolutionary, Mystic, Labour Spy*, 2d rev ed (Vancouver: New Star Books, 2013).

20   Linda Kealey, *Enlisting Women for the Cause: Women, Labour, and the Left in Canada, 1890–1920* (Toronto: University of Toronto Press, 1998) at 100–7; the quote on socialism and suffrage is cited at 119–20. See also Janice Newton, *The Feminist Challenge to the Canadian Left, 1900–1918* (Montreal & Kingston: McGill-Queen's University Press, 1995).

21   *BC Federationist* (November 1913), in Charles Hou & Cynthia Hou, *Great Canadian Cartoons, 1820–1914* (Vancouver: Moody's Lookout Press, 1997) at 211.

22 Photograph, Vancouver, City of Vancouver Archives (CVA 259–1, dated 20 December 1913).
23 Much has been written on the Vancouver Island coal strike. For the strike and particularly Ginger Goodwin's life and death, see Roger Stonebanks, *Fighting for Dignity: The Ginger Goodwin Story* (St. John's, NL: Canadian Committee for Labour History, 2004).
24 Dale M McCartney, *A Crisis of Commitment: Socialist Internationalism in British Columbia During the Great War* (MA Thesis, Simon Fraser University, 2010) [unpublished].
25 Gregory S Kealey, "1919: The Canadian Labour Revolt" (1984) 13 Labour/Le Travail 11; David Bercuson, *Fools and Wise Men: The Rise and Fall of the One Big Union* (Toronto: McGraw-Hill, 1978); Todd McCallum, "*A Modern Weapon for Modern Man": Marxist Masculinity and the Social Practices of the One Big Union* (MA Thesis, Simon Fraser University, 1995) [unpublished].
26 Paul Phillips, *No Power Greater: A Century of Labour in BC* (Vancouver: BC Federation of Labour, Boag Foundation, 1967) at 82–93; Ben Isitt, "Elusive Unity: The Canadian Labour Party in British Columbia, 1924–28" (2009) 163 BC Studies 33.

2

Employers, Disabled Workers, and the War on Attitudes in Late Twentieth-Century Canada

DUSTIN GALER

In the aftermath of the Second World War, a new war was fought in and around the Canadian workplace by people with disabilities and their allies. Wounded soldiers returning from abroad faced new obstacles in the labour market, as a growing rehabilitation industry and postwar welfare state stepped up to meet their needs. Hiring campaigns conducted across North America were devised by veterans groups and their allies in response to employer attitudes and practices that blocked disabled people from obtaining paid employment. Initially conceived as an extension of wartime efforts to "support the troops," disability hiring campaigns eventually made their way into the postwar political and legal discourse of disability as they were recycled to address the chronic unemployment and poverty in the broader disability community. Rehabilitation organizations, including the Canadian Rehabilitation Council for the Disabled and the Canadian Council of Rehabilitation Workshops, initiated massive awareness campaigns, becoming disability advocates that promoted their own unique vision of disability to a wider audience. These organizations advocated a proto–social model of disability that underscored the limitations and restrictions of impairment while noting the significant barriers caused by social attitudes and conventional responses to disability. While this approach helped to dismantle barriers to integration, it also served to promote the interests of the rehabilitation industry, given that awareness campaigns also constituted advertisements for the expansion of rehabilitation services.

Hiring campaigns used rhetoric that reflected a hybridized social and medical model of disability. "Hire the Handicapped" campaigns originated in the United States and made their way into Canada due in large part to the cooperation of rehabilitation service agencies and political authorities. These campaigns presented attitudes towards people with disabilities as the "biggest," as opposed to the only, source of people's handicaps, in order to rebrand disabled people as capable workers to promote their full participation in the labour market. Campaign terminology challenged the focus on individual medical pathology by highlighting the role of socially constructed barriers. Despite growing awareness of disability issues in Canada, as a result of awareness and hiring campaigns, there was no political framework that enabled Canadian policymakers to effectively address the exclusion of people with disabilities from the labour market. Problems posed by a lack of consensus on how to address barriers to labour market participation raised in these campaigns were exacerbated by few enforceable political commitments.

This chapter examines the role of hiring campaigns in Canada as part of broader efforts to promote the economic integration of people with disabilities during the late twentieth century. Examination of the origins of hiring campaigns in the United States and their extension into Canadian discourse is followed by analysis of employer attitudes and responses to initial efforts to promote employability. The final section discusses the limitations of awareness campaigns within the context of employment practices, as disability activists and their allies attempted to challenge employers' prejudicial attitudes towards disability.

Veterans and the Origins of Hiring Campaigns

Canadian hiring campaigns built on longstanding "Hire the Handicapped" campaigns in the United States, which developed in response to thousands of Second World War veterans with amputations, visual impairments, and other physical and mental disabilities who returned to inaccessible homes, workplaces, and public spaces. Many injured veterans could not find employment, despite undergoing intensive physical and vocational rehabilitation, and faced a life of poverty and unemployment common among other disabled people. Although many Canadians with disabilities were excluded from workforce participation, most politicians and the wider Canadian public considered the economic dislocation of injured veterans particularly unacceptable. As a result, a variety of initiatives specifically targeting injured veterans were introduced in the postwar period to promote their reintegration into the paid workforce. The 1951 National Conference on the Rehabilitation of the Physically Disabled, for example, occurred in response to the growing needs of decommissioned injured veterans. The conference provided a watershed moment that led to the creation of a federal coordinator for vocational rehabilitation programming and new cost-sharing agreements with the provinces in an effort to rapidly expand the rehabilitation system to meet the needs of a growing disabled population.[1] Federal-provincial cost-sharing in the area of vocational rehabilitation for veterans set the stage for the rapid development of the rehabilitation industry.

Canadians belonged to a society that placed a heavy emphasis on the importance of work. This ethic distanced workers from the "burden" narrative, to which disabled people belonged, by virtue of individual effort and self-achievement. Eager to re-establish themselves as independent wage-earners, veterans formed associations and service organizations that encouraged employers to hire them. Canadian-born Harold Russell, whose hands were amputated and replaced with prosthetic hooks following a war-related injury, wrote in his 1981 memoir about the development of well-known hiring campaigns. Russell achieved celebrity status as a result of his role in the acclaimed Hollywood film *The Best Years of Our Lives*, about the troubled postwar lives of veterans, and subsequently served as the long-time chair of the President's Committee on the Employment of the Handicapped (PCEH). As the flagship campaign of the PCEH, National Employ the Handicapped Week worked to raise awareness about disability, with the aim of encouraging employers to change their attitudes towards the employment of disabled people.[2] By 1949, organizers began to promote the tagline "Hire the Handicapped – It's Good Business," which quickly caught on as a popular slogan in this broader awareness campaign.

Hiring campaigns were firmly rooted in the promotion of the contemporary rehabilitation system, which originated largely in the development of supports and services to reintegrate injured veterans into the social and economic fabric of society. The aftermath of both world wars and outbreaks such as the mid-century polio epidemic enhanced the public's trust in medical authorities while boosting the role and importance of the rehabilitation industry.[3] As Jerome Bickenbach observes, "The social problems brought about by returning veterans and the underclass of unemployed people with disabilities were seen as problems arising from the impact of impairments."[4]

Faced with the dismal alternative of social marginalization, unemployment, and poverty, which they observed among civilians with disabilities, injured veterans organized themselves into lobby groups and service agencies to actively improve the rehabilitation system. Veteran activists and associations lobbied relentlessly for the expansion of the rehabilitation system to help other veterans live within inaccessible communities and acquire work-related skills that would ensure their independence.[5] Organizations such as War Amps, established in 1920 by Great War veterans on the principles of a fraternal association, assisted fellow injured veterans to acquire prosthetics, vocational training, and other rehabilitation services at a time when few other options existed.[6] Sir Arthur Pearson's Association of the War-Blinded and the National Council of Veterans' Associations were also influential national lobbyists that pushed for improvements to pensions, legislation, and therapeutic services.[7] In the interwar and postwar periods, veterans' organizations such as these pressured federal and provincial governments to increase their direct involvement in rehabilitation programs for both disabled veterans and civilians.

Civilians with disabilities increasingly complained that the rehabilitation system favoured veterans over civilians despite the fact that all people with disabilities living in the community needed similar access to work supports and rehabilitation services. Indeed, veterans were among the first to gain access to new accessible technologies and rehabilitation facilities, which often enabled them to access job opportunities and generally achieve social and economic reintegration more expeditiously than civilians without such benefits.[8] Civilian disabled people argued that all people with disabilities needed equal access to work supports and rehabilitation services, regardless of the origins of their impairments.[9] Yet, war-wounded veterans existed within a moral economy separate from other people with disabilities. It was widely held in Canada that war-related injuries and permanent disabilities were the result of a patriotic sacrifice, which qualified veterans as particularly "righteous" and "worthy beneficiaries" of specialized supports and services.[10] A landmark study conducted in the mid-1970s by Cyril Greenland, for example, included approximately two thousand participants across the country and found that "[t]he more basic services the CNIB [Canadian National Institute for the Blind] provided them compared poorly to the generous government pensions and other funding for the war-blinded veterans."[11]

As wartime coordination agreements between federal and provincial governments expired in the aftermath of the Second World War, nonveteran people with disabilities also enjoyed greater access to rehabilitation services that were critical to their economic success. The volume and social dynamics of war veterans returning to Canadian communities stimulated the development of treatment and rehabilitation facilities for civilians.[12]

Veterans with physical disabilities pushed for the rapid expansion of such community-based physical and occupational therapies as well as other disability-related programs, services, and supports, which stimulated the rehabilitation industry. The spotlight on large cohorts of injured veterans who made their way through the rehabilitation system convinced policy-makers to initiate programs to increase access to rehabilitation services. While veterans received funding through the Department of Veterans' Affairs (DVA) and injured workers accessed the workers' compensation system, Mary Tremblay and her colleagues found that civilians largely continued to deal with congenital and acquired disabilities on their own or through private insurance.[13]

Nevertheless, the prioritization of vocational rehabilitation in Canadian public policy in the postwar period flowed directly from the experiences of veterans and reflected the general belief that a speedy return to financial independence and paid employment effectively paved the way for full participation in the community. Wartime Orders-in-Council designed to provide vocational rehabilitation to disabled veterans were replaced in 1961 with the *Vocational Rehabilitation of Disabled Persons Act* (VRDPA), which enabled the rapid expansion of rehabilitation and job training for disabled civilians.[14] Attentive to the economic reintegration of disabled people, vocational rehabilitation "stressed the importance of serving people with disabilities within their communities (as opposed to residential institutions) creatively helping people with disabilities overcome the challenges of daily life to attain self-sufficiency and personal fulfillment."[15]

Rebirth of Hiring Campaigns in Canada

By the 1970s, the Canadian rehabilitation industry was seen by policymakers and the broader Canadian public to speak on behalf of the disability community. The Canadian Rehabilitation Council for the Disabled was the leading advocacy organization and undertook an ambitious hiring campaign with the slogan "Your Attitude Could Be Their Biggest Handicap." Television and print advertisements rolled out across the country, featuring people in wheelchairs, wearing leg braces, and with other physical disabilities, with the provocative caption encouraging people to discard the association of disability with medical pathology to consider the impact of social attitudes. Such campaigns encouraged people to discard seemingly ancient wisdom that rooted disability in an individual's medical pathology and embrace the concept that overcoming impairment required a combination of personal strength and professional intervention.

Despite the introduction of revised terminology in hiring campaigns, the traditional slogan "Hire the Handicapped" continued to have wide influence in the conceptualization of awareness programs and activities in Canada. A popular Canadian television program called *The Littlest Hobo*, for example, in 1984 featured a short vignette set in Toronto, where construction foreman Victor Corrano (played by local television legend Al Waxman) received a phone call regarding promotional materials sent to him. The pamphlet read: "Hire the handicapped. It's good business." Victor responded, "I got your brochure and the book. Well look, Mr. White, I appreciate what you're trying to do, really I do, but this is ... well, I got enough problems with normal guys. I don't need crutches and wheelchairs here. This is construction work here, Mr. White. I don't make handbags here. That's all right. Goodbye."[16] The fictionalized exchange revealed what ostensibly would have been understood at the time as a common response by an employer who believed that disabled people were unproductive and "hard to employ."[17] Only when Victor acquires paraplegia after falling from faulty scaffolding and subsequently experiences a readjusted self-image does he realize that his preconceptions about disabled people's abilities were inaccurate.

The architects of awareness campaigns believed that disability issues were misunderstood and underappreciated in the public sphere, and that such misunderstanding fuelled social barriers to the employment of disabled people. In particular, the campaigns reflected a developing consensus in the rehabilitation industry that an ill-informed public was partly responsible for contributing to the cultural acceptance of the marginalization of disabled people. Rehabilitation professionals repeatedly observed disabled clients (such as the fictionalized Victor Corrano) make their way through the rehabilitation system only to find their integration blocked by physical barriers and unspoken prejudices.[18] Accordingly, these professionals saw lack of awareness about disability as creating and reinforcing "disabling" attitudes that undermined the ultimate objective of meaningful social and economic integration.

The Problem of Attitudes

Through television and other means, the ubiquitous slogan "Hire the Handicapped" was firmly entrenched in the Canadian discourse on disability and work from the 1950s through the 1970s. In 1976, the Toronto Mayor's Task Force on the Disabled and Elderly noted, "All of those Hire the Handicapped campaigns, however well-intentioned they may have been, have done little to alleviate the situation, possibly because they were saying, in effect: 'Do the crippled a favour.'"[19] Goodwill Industries similarly noted that the slogan had become a "tired old line."[20] Human rights officials asserted that, despite longstanding campaigns to promote the hiring of disabled people, people with disabilities were "constantly being denied the opportunity even to try for jobs that are within their competence."[21] Canadian governments were forced to differentiate diversity employment programs such as affirmative action as "not a program to 'hire the handicapped'" since "increased employment opportunities for the handicapped is the overall goal but this involves much more than a hiring program."[22] Still, organizers of local campaigns continued to use the slogan in order to highlight efforts to improve the employment of people with disabilities in their community, confident that the popular tagline would resonate with employers and the wider public.[23]

There was often deep-seated resistance, however, to the notion that limitations experienced by disabled people were caused by the attitudes of others. Many people found it counterintuitive to prioritize social change when the traditional understanding of disability was that it resulted from an individual's physical or mental disability. The reconceptualization of disability as the effect of attitudinal barriers constituted an entirely new paradigm that would take time to be fully accepted by the public. In his landmark 1978 text, *Handicapping America*, once considered a manual for disability rights activism in North America, Frank Bowe asserted that attitudes can be remarkably inflexible, even when people are presented with ample evidence regarding the prevalence of "disabling" attitudes and the results of socially and economically sidelining disabled people. Bowe discovered that attitudinal barriers were in many ways much more resilient than architectural barriers, in that they could not be erased simply with legislation. Bowe also concluded that more than thirty years of Hire the Handicapped Weeks and similar awareness campaigns had resulted in little appreciable change in employer attitudes or workforce participation rates.[24]

A variant of the "Hire the Handicapped" campaigns promoted the abilities of the "able disabled," suggesting the prefix "dis-" in the word "disability" wrongly characterized people as incapable when medical status did not necessarily reflect capacity to undertake productive work. In 1973, corporate chemical giant DuPont conducted a landmark study of its disabled employees, evaluating their effect on insurance rates, absenteeism, job performance, taxes, and motivation.[25] The report, titled "The Able Disabled" but widely known as the "DuPont study" echoed earlier hiring campaigns, arguing that fears around hiring disabled people were unfounded and that many disabled workers were just as "able" as nondisabled workers despite widespread prejudice against them. The DuPont study had wide international influence on the business community in Canada, and the term "able disabled" quickly succeeded "hire the handicapped." The Toronto Dominion Bank, for example, embarked on a nationwide hiring campaign, and Canadian human resource professionals organized events featuring the DuPont study as a model for Canadian employers.[26]

Deprived of a diverse set of experiences with people with disabilities, many people in mainstream society relied upon culturally mediated stereotypes that reinforced the ideological and actual separation of disabled people from normative settings. In response to this status quo, Ontario Minister of Labour Bette Stephenson noted in her 1976 address to the Seminar on the Employability of the Handicapped in Toronto, "We may ramp the steps and widen the doors and redesign the washrooms, but until attitudes change, progress will be illusory."[27] As a reflection of the developing consensus among rehabilitation professionals and consumer activists regarding the attitudinal barriers to rehabilitation, Stephenson observed that attitudinal and psychological barriers could not be undone as readily as physical accessibility and rehabilitation could be provided. Despite a collective desire to "help the handicapped," Stephenson found there was often a tendency to seek out simplistic solutions.[28]

In preparation for the International Year of Disabled Persons in 1981, Canadian authorities promoted the underlying message in the DuPont study in various educational seminars, television commercials, posters, and print advertising, and in a touring exhibit, with new slogans, "Label Us Able"[29] and "We Are All Able."[29] The *Globe and Mail* raised the profile of the campaign by promoting workplaces and employers that reflected the ideals of the campaign.[30] One television commercial connected to the campaign began with a camera panning over a production studio where an advertisement was to be shot. The scene bustled with the activities of various workers, including "carpenters, technicians and musicians." At the end of the commercial, it was revealed that all the workers were disabled. A screenshot showed the group of workers exuberantly throwing up their hands in front of giant letters that read "Label Us Able."[31] While the producers of the commercial encountered difficulty finding qualified disabled workers and had to instead hire disabled actors, the wider campaign built upon earlier hiring campaigns with concrete examples of people with disabilities who had found work.[32]

Given the limited results of earlier hiring campaigns, much skepticism surrounded these updated campaigns. University of Toronto's *Varsity* newsletter warned that the undisputed success of the 1981 International Year of Disabled Persons in achieving greater awareness of disability issues might backfire due to a "distressing tendency of people to jump on a popular bandwagon, subsequently jumping off when it has run its course."[33] A growing movement of disability identity politics reflected an unresolved tension surrounding popular attitudes towards disability and systematic practices promoted by the rehabilitation industry to integrate people with disabilities.[34] Rehabilitation thus became an increasingly politicized experience, particularly for disabled people who continued to face barriers to full participation despite witnessing the progressive expansion of the rehabilitation system.

Disabled Need Not Apply

The relative success of people with disabilities who sought "full participation" in the labour market during the latter part of the twentieth century in Canada ultimately rested primarily upon the hiring preferences and employment practices of employers. As Brian Doyle observes in his study of the relationship between disability and employment discrimination, "It is the employer's perception which matters, not the employee's actual medical status."[35] Employer responses to disability were conveyed through workplace policies regarding recruitment, compensation, accommodation, promotion, termination, and other key aspects of the employment relationship. Yet recruitment preferences and the treatment of disabled employees ultimately reflected a discursive relationship between broader social attitudes around disability and decisions by employers in the work environment. Disabled people were generally expected to present themselves to employers as fully self-aware of the limitations of their impairments yet positive, optimistic, and energetic in an effort to anticipate and challenge stereotypical and likely negative perceptions of disability. One pamphlet on job-hunting advice produced by the Ontario Ministry of Labour's Handicapped Employment Program, for example, emphasized that people with disabilities were partly responsible for challenging employer attitudes. The pamphlet argued, "Your own attitudes are also important. Handle your disability in a positive way and employers will be more receptive to hiring you. You have to believe that you will be an asset to an employer and that productive work is fulfilling."[36]

Despite ongoing campaigns across the country that raised awareness of disability issues in the workplace and specifically targeted employers, repeated studies from the 1970s to the 1990s demonstrated few substantive changes in the attitudes and practices of employers. The Canadian Chamber of Commerce (CCC), for example, conducted a study that provided a comprehensive assessment of small-, medium-, and large-scale employers across Canada and concluded that employers' attitudes were among the most important factors that shaped the exclusion of people with disabilities from mainstream employment. Thirty percent of survey respondents acknowledged they had never hired or considered hiring a disabled person and were unaware that the public sector might be a source for new employees. Nearly 75 percent stated there was no job that disabled workers could handle or that the nature of their business was inappropriate for disabled people, and a further 61 percent stated that a disabled person had never applied for available jobs. Many employers believed that disabled workers were inherently at greater risk of accidents or that they might contravene fire regulations or generally result in increased insurance premiums. Other employers believed that their workplace was inaccessible to many disabled people and could not be adapted to become accessible. Finally, many employers believed that disabled workers would be chronically absent, result in greater turnover, have emotional problems, require too much supervision, and ultimately would negatively affect production rates.[37]

The CCC study and many subsequent reports found that these concerns about how disabled workers would upset the typical employment relationship gave rise to a general attitude of resistance to hiring disabled people. Employers were perplexed by the needs of people with disabilities and how disabled workers intended to negotiate an inaccessible workplace and broader environment, which fuelled general uncertainty about disabled workers and the potential dangers they presented to their organization. Importantly, these studies concluded that, while there was a serious lack of awareness of disability issues among employers, there was also a general willingness to learn more about disability should the opportunity arise.

The CCC report was highly influential within the public sector and business community, promoting awareness and self-reflection about prejudices held against disabled people. The Chamber of Commerce and the Department of National Health and Welfare (DNHW) built on positive feedback from the report by subsequently organizing a Seminar on Employability of the Handicapped in 1979 in Toronto, wherein key stakeholders met to discuss the report's findings. The event brought together an unprecedented array of key multisectoral stakeholders, including representatives from the DNHW, the Canadian Council of Rehabilitation Workshops, the

Ontario Ministry of Labour, municipal and provincial disability activist organizations, and others in an attempt to brainstorm strategies for increasing the employment of disabled people.[38] Many members of the local Toronto Chamber of Commerce sat alongside senior federal and provincial government officials, representatives from rehabilitation agencies, and consumer activists to discuss strategies for improving disabled people's job opportunities.[39] In advance of the seminar, disability activists lobbied political officials to use the conference as an opportunity to make firm commitments to reforming policies that would effectively promote the inclusion of disabled people in the labour market.[40] In her keynote speech at the seminar, Ontario Minister of Labour Bette Stephenson highlighted the general atmosphere of optimism at the seminar, noting the attendance of many business leaders gathered to work with government officials and voluntary agencies in order to create realistic job opportunities for disabled people seeking work.[41]

By the mid-1980s, provincial and federal government officials learned that awareness-boosting activities and training seminars undertaken since the 1970s were not having their intended effect, which led to the development of innovative measures to address the problem of employer attitudes. The 1983 report of the Ontario Task Force on Employers and Disabled Persons, entitled *Linking for Employment*, envisioned the creation of community councils linking businesses with local agencies and government departments in an innovative network that promised to connect qualified disabled people with job vacancies.[42] The task force, led by Jean Pigott, believed that the concept of community councils situated employers as active participants with an integral role in cultivating employment opportunities for people with disabilities.[43] Pigott also envisioned a vocational rehabilitation system that fully included employers in the process of finding job opportunities for people with disabilities.[44]

Justice Rosalie Abella, the sole commissioner of the federal Royal Commission on Equality in Employment, built on Pigott's findings shortly thereafter by encouraging employers to redesign their recruitment and workplace practices to promote the employment of people with disabilities, as well as other designated groups.[45] After a series of consultations with people with disabilities across Canada, Abella issued a number of recommendations to promote the improvement of employment opportunity structures for people with disabilities across Canada by challenging barriers to employment created in part by employer attitudes.[46] Abella introduced the term "employment equity" to refer to a system of special measures taken to accommodate differences that would surmount barriers to participation in the labour market.[47] Employment equity was distinct from the "duty to accommodate," which reflected employers' legal responsibility to accommodate workers with disabilities in the workplace up to the point of undue hardship.[48] Abella's term, which was based on the American conceptualization of affirmative action, laid the foundations for the federal *Employment Equity Act* in 1986 and confirmed that employers' discriminatory recruitment, hiring, and promotion practices had no place in an equitable labour market.[49] Reminiscent of the conclusions reached by earlier studies, the Abella commission found that disabled people as well as women, Aboriginal people, and visible minorities were denied job opportunities as a result of systemic discriminatory attitudes and practices by employers and the wider public, which presented obstacles to equitable employment.[50]

Hiring campaigns failed to produce a substantive impact on employment practices with respect to disabled people in both Canada and the United States. While the premise of awareness projects was generally accepted, there was often deep-seated resistance in the public sphere to the notion that an attitudinal overhaul was needed to lower barriers faced by people with disabilities. Borrowing slogans developed in the United States to "hire the handicapped," campaigns in Canada continually evolved to present slightly reworked taglines and scenarios helped along by a developing disability rights movement and discourse of work and disability. Hiring campaigns relied upon a negative ontology of disability, gesturing towards employers' charitable impulses and connecting disabled people's economic dislocation with broader systems of welfare.

These campaigns concluded that employers figured prominently in the disability community's pursuit of economic integration during the late twentieth century in Canada. Employer attitudes towards disability in general and disabled workers in particular shaped recruitment preferences and employment practices that rendered many people with disabilities unemployable in the mainstream labour market. Discrimination in recruitment and employment was often unconsciously projected upon people with disabilities, undermining their attempts to achieve full participation in the community. These prejudices, and the awareness campaigns that arose to combat them, reflected a pervasive and deep-seated undervaluation of disabled people's potential as productive members of society. The chronic unemployment and poverty of disabled people in Canada, which persisted throughout the postwar period and late twentieth century, led many critics to point to the limitations of awareness campaigns and question the value of sensitivity training for employers. In spite of these challenges, many people with disabilities and their allies remained committed to the work of awareness building, hopeful that attitudes would change and barriers to labour market participation would recede.

NOTES

1   Paul Wright, *The Status of Disabled Persons in Canada: A Historical Analysis of the Evolution of Social Policy to Develop Effective Change Strategies Directed Toward Achieving Equality* (MA Thesis, Carleton University, 1990) at 78 [unpublished].

2   Harold Russell, *The Best Years of My Life* (Middlebury, VT: P.S. Eriksson, 1981) at 155.

3   Anne Finger, *Elegy for a Disease: A Personal and Cultural History of Polio* (New York: St Martin's Press, 2006).

4   Jerome Bickenbach, *Physical Disability and Social Policy* (Toronto: University of Toronto Press, 1993) at 105; David Cameron & Fraser Valentine, "Comparing Policy-Making in Federal Systems: The Case of Disability Policy and Programs" in David Cameron & Fraser Valentine, eds, *Disability and Federalism: Comparing Different Approaches to Full Participation* (Montreal: Institute of Intergovernmental Relations, 2001) at 95.

5   Fred Pelka, *What We Have Done: An Oral History of the Disability Rights Movement* (Amherst: University of Massachusetts Press, 2013) at 131.

6   Aldred Neufeldt, "Growth and Evolution of Disability Advocacy in Canada" in Deborah Stienstra, Colleen Watters & Aileen Wight-Felske, eds, *Making Equality: History of Advocacy and Persons with Disabilities in Canada* (Concord, ON: Captus Press, 2003) at 19; The War Amps of Canada, "The War Amps History," online: <http://www.waramps.ca/history.html>. For more information on the history of how fraternal associations worked to improve the lives of people with disabilities, see Dustin Galer, "A Friend in Need or a Business Indeed? Disabled Bodies and Fraternalism in Victorian Ontario" (2010) 66:1 Labour/Le Travail 9.

7   Serge Marc Durflinger, *Veterans with a Vision: Canada's War Blinded in Peace and War* (Vancouver: UBC Press, 2010) at 250.

8   Mary Tremblay, Audrey Campbell & Geoffrey Hudson, "When Elevators Were for Pianos: An Oral History Account of the Civilian Experience of Using Wheelchairs in Canadian Society: The First Twenty-Five Years, 1945–1970" (2005) 20:2 Disability & Society 103.

9   *Ibid.*

10 Peter Blanck, "The Right to Live in the World': Disability Yesterday, Today, and Tomorrow" (2008) 13:2 Texas J on Civil Liberties & Civil Rights 367 at 375–76; for more information on the relationship between the Great War and disability, see Nic Clarke, "'You Will Not Be Going to This War': The Rejected Volunteers of the First Contingent of the Canadian Expeditionary Force" (2010) 1:2 First World War Studies 161.

11 Durflinger, *supra* note 7 at 316; Cyril Greenland, *Vision Canada: The Unmet Needs of Blind Canadians* (Toronto: Canadian National Institute for the Blind, 1976) at 3.

12 Tremblay et al, *supra* note 8 at 107.

13 *Ibid.*

14 Michael Prince, "Designing Disability Policy in Canada" in Alan Puttee, ed, *Federalism, Democracy and Disability Policy in Canada* (Montreal: Institute of Intergovernmental Relations, 2002) 31; Peter Graefe & Mario Levesque, "Accountability and Funding as Impediments to Social Policy Innovation: Lessons from the Labour Market Agreements for Persons with Disabilities" (2010) 36:1 Canadian Public Policy 50; Michele Campolieti & John Lavis, "Disability Expenditures in Canada, 1970–1996: Trends, Reform Efforts and a Path for the Future" (2000) 26:2 Can Public Policy 241.

15 Allison Carey, *On the Margins of Citizenship: Intellectual Disability and Civil Rights in Twentieth-Century America* (Philadelphia: Temple University Press, 2009) at 97.

16 "One Door Closes," *The Littlest Hobo*, Canadian Television Network (CTV) (1984).

17 Michael Stein, "The Law and Economics of Disability Accommodations" (2003) 53:79 Duke L J 79.

18 Colin Barnes, *Cabbage Syndrome: The Social Construction of Dependence* (New York: Falmer Press, 1990) at 155; Sara Lock et al, "Work after Stroke: Focusing on Barriers and Enablers" (2005) 20:1 Disability & Society 33.

19 "This City Is for All Its Citizens" (report, June 1976), Toronto, Archives of Ontario [AO] (RG 7-148, box B353847, file Mayor's Task Force).

20 Goodwill Quarterly (newsletter, Spring 1978) AO (RG 7-148, box B100558, file Speeches/TV).

21 Ontario Human Rights Commission, *Life Together: A Report on Human Rights in Ontario* (Toronto: Ontario Human Rights Commission, 1978).

22 Handicapped Employment Program, "A Conference on Education Now – Employment Later: The Hearing Impaired Job Candidate and the Changing Employment Scene" (November 1980), AO (RG 7-148, box 100615, file Speeches/TV), at 10–11.

23 Letter, Vocational Rehab Advisory Committee to Handicapped Employment Program (26 March 1980), AO (RG 7-149, box B363026, file Public Relations).

24 Frank Bowe, *Handicapping America: Barriers to Disabled People* (New York: Harper & Row, 1978) at 181.

25 James Sears, "The Able Disabled" (March/April 1975) 41:2 J Rehabilitation 19.

26 "Hiring The Handicapped: Why More Companies Are Beginning to Look into It," *Management* (30 March 1981); Personnel Association of Toronto, "Hiring the Handicapped" (December 1981), AO (RG 7-148, box B100660, file News Clippings), at 3–4.

27 Speaking notes (26 November 1976), AO (RG 7-149, box B367312, file Dr. Stephenson's Speech).

28 *Ibid.*

29 Handicapped Employment Program, "A Conference on Education Now – Employment Later: The Hearing Impaired Job Candidate and the Changing Employment Scene" (10–11 November 1980), AO (RG 7-148, box B100558, file Speeches).

30 "Jeweller Honored for Hiring Disabled," *Globe and Mail* (2 July 1982).

31 Kirk Makin, "Label Us Able – but Legibly," *Globe and Mail* (1 July 1981) 1.

32 University of Toronto, "Queen's Park Says 'They're Able!'" *The Varsity: Supplement on Disabled Persons* (9 November 1981).

33 University of Toronto, "Label Them Able," *The Varsity: Supplement on Disabled Persons* (9 November 1981).

34 *Ibid.*

35 Brian Doyle, *Disability, Discrimination and Equal Opportunities: A Comparative Study of the Employment Rights of Disabled Persons* (New York: Mansell, 1995) at 174.

36 Pamphlet, Program for Employment of the Disadvantaged, "It's Up to You: Disabled People Can Work! Job Hunting Hints for the Handicapped" (1981), Manitoba Archives (box P5364, file 21).

37 Canadian Chamber of Commerce, Ottawa Liaison Committee, "Role and Initiatives of the Federal Government Regarding Rehab and Employment of the Handicapped" (31 May 1979), Ottawa, Library and Archives Canada (box 238, file 4314-3-1-9(1)).

38 *Ibid.*

39 *Ibid.*

40 "A Letter to the Premier," *The Third Eye* (newsletter), vol 10 (10 December 1976), AO (RG 7–148, box B100558, file Publications).

41 Speaking notes, *supra* note 27.

42 Ontario, Task Force on Employers and Disabled Persons, *Linking for Employment: Report of the Task Force on Employers and Disabled Persons* (Toronto: Task Force on Employers and Disabled Persons, 1983).

43 *Ibid.*

44 *Ibid.*

45 Canada, Royal Commission on Equality in Employment, *Report of the Royal Commission on Equality in Employment* (Ottawa: Royal Commission on Equality in Employment, 1984) [Royal Commission].

46 *Ibid.*

47 Rosalie Silberman Abella, "A Generation of Human Rights: Looking Back to the Future" (1998) 36:3 Osgoode Hall LJ 597.

48 Ravi Malhotra, "The Legal Genealogy of the Duty to Accommodate American and Canadian Workers with Disabilities: A Comparative Perspective" (2007) Washington UJL & Policy 1.

49 *Ibid.*

50 Royal Commission, *supra* note 45.

Gender and the Value of Work in Canadian Disability History

GEOFFREY REAUME

This chapter provides a historiographical discussion of how gender and the value of work intersect in the history of Canadians with disabilities. It examines the value, or lack of value, placed on the work of Canadians with disabilities in institutional settings like asylums and in the wider community, considering, for example, people who acquired disabilities on the job and who afterwards sought compensation and/or re-entry into the job market. The gendered dimension of the historical exploitation and devaluing of disabled people's labour is a central part of this chapter: I analyze how mainstream society viewed the worth of disabled women's labour compared to that of disabled men in regard to both unpaid and paid work. When considering this topic, it is essential to note that most of the authors whose work is cited in this chapter were not writing from a critical disability studies perspective, let alone suggesting future directions for such work. The works are chosen to provide examples of how a gendered analysis of work in Canadian disability history can be gleaned from existing studies, in an attempt to see what has been done and where to go from here.

People with Physical and Sensory Disabilities
In her work on people with spinal cord injuries, which began in 1993, Mary Tremblay was among the first historical scholars in Canada to use an analysis derived from the new field of disability studies.[1] While her studies do not explicitly employ gender as a basis for analysis, there are clear dimensions of

her work that bring this topic to light, most notably in the masculine assumptions inherent in expectations surrounding work for disabled male veterans of the Second World War. One person she interviewed, Dr. Albin Jousse, noted the irony of these expectations in the context of the different roles men were expected to play, first as able-bodied unemployed men and then, after war service, as disabled employed men to whom the state felt an obligation: "They couldn't get a job during the thirties when they were able-bodied ... [But h]aving been in the army, having become a paraplegic, they were expected to go to work. Nobody wanted them before. Now they were encouraged to do what they were never able to do of their own volition."[2] In her work, Tremblay notes the way in which people with paraplegia undergoing rehabilitation in Toronto "could be most happy only when living at home and when usefully and gainfully occupied."[3] While it is unremarked upon in this context, it is important to note that Tremblay's point initially referred to males with paraplegia, specifically veterans of the Second World War. In this sense, according to Tremblay, the value of work was primarily focused on males' paid work outside the home in the early years of rehabilitation of disabled veterans.

Women with spinal cord injuries became eligible for rehabilitation programs in late 1946 and early 1947 at Lyndhurst Lodge in Toronto. Afterwards, they were expected to do certain kinds of gendered work. For example, after returning from Lyndhurst to her hometown of Chatham, Ontario, in the late 1940s, Ruth Clark ran a business from her house.[4] Given the bias towards work that was considered appropriate for men, along with masculine attitudes and practices in rehabilitation programs for people with spinal cord injuries that originated with disabled veterans, it is not surprising that gendered forms of work were ingrained early on and tied to an individualistic "pull yourself up by your own bootstraps" mentality. This perspective is hardly unique to this historical period or country. In the aftermath of the American Civil War, disabled Confederate veteran James E. Hanger, reflecting on his own work experiences, stated, "I have been no idler ... even though I am a cripple."[5] Similar attitudes are evident in the following quote from Ken Langford, when commenting on fellow veteran John Counsell, one of the founders of the Canadian Paraplegic Association and Lyndhurst Lodge: "Through sheer determination he rehabilitated himself. Solved most of his own problems ... He was a very strong personality."[6] Keywords like "determination," "solved," and "strong" were as gendered as they were value-laden, yet they reflected key beliefs. In addition, when considering Counsell, who came from a wealthy, very well-connected family, one needs to note the great importance of his elite social status and personal resources. These allowed him more leeway to approach rehabilitation in a way that stressed "willpower," given that he had a private safety net to fall back on – something that less well-connected disabled people did not have.[7] Thus, when considering the topic of gender and the value of work, it is important to underline how work, and rehabilitation, could also be subsidized in ways that privileged some over others. The experience of a wealthy male war veteran with family connections in a centrally located city was in many ways different from that of an isolated disabled woman civilian who lived in one room by herself in a distant, much smaller city and who had, by chance, read about and made a successful application to a place where rehabilitation was being offered.

Gender, class, and race were of central importance in views about disability and labour. In *A Disability History of the United States* (2012), Kim Nielsen writes that, in the United States between 1865 and 1890,

> white women of middle- or upper-class status, were considered *incapable* of performing labor. Class- and race-based definitions of femininity presumed them unfit for labor. Race and gender paradoxically impaired and privileged such women. Working-class women, however, regardless of race or ethnicity, frequently engaged in rigorous manual labor ... The increasing bureaucratic and social tendency to define disability as the incapacity to perform manual labor had radically different implications for different groups of people.[8]

Natalie Dykstra's 2001 article on Alice James reflects this point, using the experiences of a wealthy disabled American woman in the late nineteenth century to show how class, race, and gender influence notions of "work." James's chronic illness and subsequent inability to walk left her immobile during her final years, an experience Dykstra describes as "a specific form of women's work. Such immobility was positioned as an ideal feminine vocation, for it was in keeping with not only dictates of gender but also a longstanding requirement for women's work: its invisibility."[9] This invisibility was true for wealthy disabled women as well as poor disabled women, yet the obvious economic differences resulted in gradations of invisibility. When considering Ruth Clark's experiences in mid-twentieth-century Ontario, it is evident, even from the much more limited information available, that she needed to find a source of income to survive. To what extent Clark was visible or invisible is not revealed by the sources, but, compared with a much more privileged disabled woman such as Alice James, it is likely that, given her need to run a business from home to make a living, Clark did have some visibility in a small community like Chatham, even if she was not as physically visible on a daily basis as were contemporary able-bodied labourers. That the histories recorded here do not discuss racialized disabled people indicates how "hidden" they were during their own lifetimes from mainstream disability services available to the white majority disabled population, while also underlining their absence from critical disability historiography. What can be stated for certain is that the invisibility of women's work had different meanings for women with mobility impairments based on class, race, and social location.

Of all the disabled people whose labour is considered here, disabled male veterans were the most visible – disabled women war veterans were far less so. The active involvement of the state in rehabilitating disabled veterans is the focus of Peter Neary's 2011 study about the way in which Canadian veterans were rehabilitated during and after the Second World War. However, the study contains only a brief reference to disabled women veterans; the focus is the needs of disabled men veterans, without a gendered analysis either of disability or labour issues.[10] When the work of women veterans in general is discussed, it is clear from the absence of disabled women that, unlike for men, the state devoted little concern to establishing employment programs for disabled women who returned to civilian life. In 1942–43, the following question was asked in the federal Subcommittee on the Special Problems of Discharged Women: "How would women fare in vocational training, professional education, and establishment in individual enterprises and agriculture?" The answer was succinct and simple: "The subcommittee assumed throughout that many women in the armed forces would not need any retraining or employment assistance because they would get married and become homemakers."[11] Moreover, those women who would find work outside the home would be in traditional gendered occupations, including nursing, teaching, clerical work, and cleaning. Within this discussion, Neary briefly notes the "exceptional care" expected by policymakers for women who became disabled during war service – such as someone who had a limb amputated or who became blind or deaf – but the references to employment that follow do not mention employment prospects for disabled women. Thus, although the state paid serious attention to the employment prospects of disabled male veterans, it failed to extend the same consideration to disabled women veterans. Neary's brief mention of disabled women vets is more a recounting than an analysis, and thus the biases inherent in the assumptions by wartime officials do not come under serious scrutiny in his historical study.

Similarly, Serge Marc Durflinger's 2010 study of Canada's veterans who were blinded during war service in the twentieth century, while showing more awareness of the new disability history than does Neary, nevertheless does not engage in a critical analysis around gender, disability, and labour. Throughout his discussion of efforts to find employment for war-blinded veterans, Durflinger refers only to "men," which raises the question of why there is no reference to women veterans who experienced blindness or to their employment prospects.[12] Although Neary included a brief reference to the supports blind women veterans would need, neither his book nor Durflinger's makes any reference to their consideration for employment programs after becoming disabled. Whether this was because their prospects were not taken seriously or because the sources are lacking is not indicated in either study. Either way, the historiographical silence on this issue speaks volumes about how disabled women's work – and specifically disabled women veterans' work – was significantly undervalued and not even considered worthy of mention.

Euclid Herie's 2005 historical study of the Canadian National Institute for the Blind (CNIB), to its credit for an in-house history, does examine some of the less savoury parts of the CNIB's history. These include its neglect of employment opportunities for blind women, beyond a few sparse sheltered workshops where they were poorly paid (as were male workers). By 1925, the CNIB was taking the employment of blind men more seriously than it had previously, but it was still neglecting blind women. Herie blames wider social prejudices for this neglect, thus somewhat obscuring the CNIB's sexist attitudes: "As for women, society had few expectations of them or opportunities for them beyond home, church, and perhaps a little genteel charity work, and how well they did in life was tied to marriage, not education and employment. Blind women in those days were marginalized and would remain so for generations."[13] Nevertheless, Herie does note one type of job for which blind women were hired more than men: dictatyping – that is, typing up audio documents, a job that appeared in the early 1930s.[14] Similar to the uniform employment discrimination that Herie describes for blind Canadian women was the overall employment marginalization of deaf people, especially women, during this period. Although Canadian historians have yet to examine this area, the point is made by Susan Burch in her 2002 study on deaf history in the United States during the first half of the twentieth century.[15]

In contrast to Herie's book, Joanna Pearce, in her 2011 study of the Halifax Asylum for the Blind, incorporates analysis from the new disability history and provides a brief gendered analysis of male and female graduates of this institution. In particular, Pearce notes how blind women were initially excluded from loans to purchase tools with which to earn a living after graduation, though several years after the fund was established, female music teachers were able to obtain access to it.[16] As the next section illustrates, more extensive gendered interpretations of work in Canadian disability history were produced in studies that focused on labour history.

Old Age and Labour Histories

In her 2003 book on the history of old age homes in British Columbia, Megan Davies analyzes how gender, ethnicity, and class influenced when and where a person ended up in an old age home. She shows how, during the late nineteenth and first half of the twentieth century, white males of European descent ended up in old age homes significantly more frequently than did females, a fact that Davies notes was not too surprising, given that men vastly outnumbered women in the province around 1900. Davies analyzes how these men, many of whom worked in resource industries, became completely marginalized economically due to their perceived lack of usefulness as workers in an economic system that valued physical strength, which diminished with age. The impact of their changed status – from strong, macho workers to men who were shunted aside once it was presumed that their bodies could no longer do the heavy lifting that had defined their occupational lives – is a common theme in Davies' analysis. As older women were fewer in number in the earlier period of this study, their experiences are consequently less visible.[17] While Davies' work does not focus solely on people categorized as disabled and old, and she does not draw on the then developing field of disability history, the topic of her book lends itself to inclusion in this category, given that many of the people who are discussed acquired disabilities as they aged. She also clearly shows how perceived or actual diminished physical ability with age led to a consequent devaluing of the worth of previously valued male workers. Whether this trend was similar for female workers as they aged awaits further research.

Two articles borrow from the new disability history in their analysis of labour history and provide a clear picture of the impact of recent historiographical developments in the field. In her 2006 study of disabled miners, specifically men suffering from silicosis, Nancy M. Forestell integrates gender and disability as part of an overarching analysis of how both men and their families dealt with this lung disease. Her work includes a discussion of how historians have heretofore ignored the unpaid toil that wives performed caring for their disabled husbands, at a time when women had few options for work outside the home, in this case, in Timmins, Ontario, the focus of much of her article. Forestell critiques historians for neglecting this essential part of working-class histories: "Scholars of labour and working-class history have much to gain from this kind of approach, although with notable exceptions we have proven rather reticent to do so ... And thus important aspects of working-class life remain underdeveloped, including the boundaries of working-class communities, who has counted as a worker, and the meanings of work and dependency."[18] Reflecting on her earlier work on this topic, she further states, "I return to the gold-mining camp, the Porcupine, and the nearby community of Timmins, Ontario (the scene of my historiographical crime as it were) to examine the consequences of and responses to workplace accidents and diseases over the decades from 1920 to 1950."[19]

Forestell writes that men with silicosis were "left physically diminished for the rest of their lives" and that "debilitating accidents and diseases seriously undermined their masculinity."[20] Furthermore, she argues that the solidarity that existed between disabled and nondisabled miners needs to be seen as perpetuating male control of both family life and the workplace, as women were kept in a subservient place no matter how much they helped their families survive the stress of the main male breadwinner's becoming injured on the job in a remote community. Indeed, unpaid work by women in the home included taking care of men disabled as a result of their work in the mines, an area that Forestell emphasizes is in need of more study. She notes that miners challenged the notion that a physical impairment should disqualify a miner from work; on the contrary "a crushed finger, for example, was an inevitable part of working underground for any length of time and thus an indication of experience and skill."[21] Masculine notions of "toughness" obviously played a role in such self-perceptions of ability and impairment. In Forestell's recounting, disability was thus far from universally viewed as a negative experience. The varied impact of impairment on miners and their families needs to be addressed more seriously among labour historians than has previously been the case. Her article is an important advance in this direction.

The way in which working-class men's disabled bodies were valued, or devalued, by fraternal insurance associations in Victorian Ontario is the focus of a 2010 article by Dustin Galer. Like Forestell, Galer uses a gen-dered analysis that incorporates interpretations from labour, feminist, and disability historians. Noting that a male worker's physical state reflected on his monetary worth, Galer points out that very little research has been done on physically disabled workers in Canadian history; he also notes the dearth of primary sources on this topic, which hampers research, es-pecially for the period prior to the twentieth century. What he did find reveals that fraternal insurance promoters used manipulative tactics to attract buyers, including claiming that workers who did not take out in-surance were "lesser men" who would not live up to their responsibili-ties to family members in the event of death or disability.[22] Yet, Galer also shows that men with impairments, or who engaged in work categorized as dangerous (such as mining and railroad work), were more susceptible to being screened out by medical examiners than were able-bodied men. The lack of primary sources leaves an incomplete picture, given that it is not known how many men belonged to fraternal insurance associations after becoming disabled. Even when they did belong, their insurance mon-ey usually ran out within one to three years at best (usually it lasted no more than two years). Thus, a disabled worker's body was "an incomplete body,"[23] and a disabled worker had fewer chances of obtaining or main-taining adequate insurance for himself or his family. The impact that this had on a disabled worker's family was to have the wife and children sent out of the home to find paid work. Galer notes that the fraternal insurers "could have afforded to reach out more enthusiastically to women and the physically impaired," both of whom were discouraged from belonging.[24] Of the sources I reviewed for this chapter, the articles by Forestell and Galer provide the clearest and most recent examples of work that incorporates the new disability history approach within a gendered analysis. Their work also shows how the worth of workers was tied into notions of "normative," able-bodied male labourers, and thus how the value of workers declined significantly with their impairment.

Galer's path-breaking doctoral dissertation, "'Hire the Handicapped!' Disability Rights, Economic Integration and Working Lives in Toronto, Ontario, 1962–2005" (2013), recounts the efforts of disabled activists and their allies to challenge barriers to employment for people with various physical, sensory, and mental disabilities over four decades. Galer inter-viewed eleven male and twenty female disabled workers and includes an analysis of the influence of gender on the types of work that were avail-able to the individuals interviewed. More broadly, Galer acknowledges the importance of gender history at various points in his dissertation, including in his analysis of the loss of economic power experienced by men injured on the job; in his discussion of maternal feminism among parents of children with intellectual disabilities, particularly in the context of activist mothers as discussed by Melanie Panitch (2008);[25] and in regard to the increasing number of women in employment outside the home and the subsequent change in gender dynamics within unions, whereby women became more prominent as activists and leaders.[26] As such, Galer's work is an important addition to this topic from a critical disability studies historical perspective. His point that women activists were the leaders in advocating equity issues within unions from the 1970s onwards, followed by people with disabilities, raises issues about the possible connections between equity-seeking groups at this time.[27] The question arises as to how much mutual support existed between equity-seeking groups in the labour movement, which included people with disabilities. Such support was particularly important at a time when, as one interviewee in Galen's dissertation noted in regard to the early 1980s, "Being a disability activist in the trade union movement was lonely."[28]

A 2009 historical study by Robert Storey provides a gendered history of legal discrimination against women who became impaired on the job. It focuses on how, from the inception of the 1914 *Workmen's Compensation Act* in Ontario, injured women workers had their labour devalued in contrast to that of men. While Storey describes more recent changes to gender-neutral language in legislation, largely due to injured workers' protests from the 1970s on, his study makes it clear that this change has not lessened the fact that women's work continues to be devalued more than that of men, including when it comes to compensation for on-the-job injuries.[29] While Storey, a sociologist, does not incorporate critical disability studies analyses in his study of people who acquired workplace injuries, his research nevertheless provides one of the most systematic attempts at a gendered analysis, and to a lesser extent a racialized analysis, in Canadian disability historiography, even if he himself does not frame it as such. In particular, Storey documents the racialized discrimination towards workers of southern European immigrant backgrounds, specifically male Italian construction workers whose musculoskeletal injuries were derided by Anglo-Saxon doctors and compensation board officials as "Italian back." To resist this ethnic prejudice, the affected community "offered the gendered image of the honest, hard-working man."[30] His findings in this regard reflect a 2005 historiographical article by Sarah Rose on disability and labour in the

United States. Her article includes discussion of occupational injuries leading to disability and how such injuries were particularly common among the most oppressed labourers; she notes that, due to "assumptions about race and gender, some groups of workers have sacrificed more than others," particularly African American labourers and working-class women who acquired disabilities on the job.[31]

Storey reveals further historically based discriminatory practices within the supposedly gender-impartial provincial compensation system in Ontario, whereby injured women workers are paid less than men, as their compensation is based on a wage system that pays men more to begin with. To add insult to injury, "women injured on the job are more likely to have their injuries/illnesses downplayed and/or dismissed by compensation boards and appeals tribunals."[32] With the insights offered in his article on disability, gender, and compensation for injured workers, Storey's research demonstrates the important contributions of scholars who are nominally "outside" the field of disability history but are very much part of the dialogue about a past that has great importance for contemporary labour relations.

One further aspect of labour and Canadian disability history that needs further investigation is the largely unexplored area (in this field) of biography. Ravi Malhotra's 2011 article on the political career of labour activist, Marxist, and later social democrat E.T. Kingsley describes his activities in both the United States and Canada. After losing his legs in an accident when he was working on the railway in Montana, he became a political activist in California before, in 1902, moving to British Columbia, where he stayed until his death in 1929. Kingsley ran for office in both California and British Columbia and, although he was never elected, he ultimately became an influential figure in the Socialist Party of Canada. Interestingly, although he used a cane and had artificial limbs, these details were not mentioned in reports about his activism in California.[33] While disability was not the central focus of his political activism, Kingsley did critique capitalists on an issue he was particularly familiar with when he wrote in 1916: "The most reckless indifference to the welfare of the slaves of industry is manifested throughout the entire employing world, and not the slightest safeguard is afforded the lives and limbs of the workers, if it can in any way be avoided."[34] As Malhotra points out, Kingsley's views on disability itself were less notable than the fact that he, a visibly injured and disabled worker, was publicly engaged in writing, speaking, and running for elected office on a platform of workers' rights at a time when such opportunities largely did not exist for disabled people.

People with Intellectual Disabilities

The labour history of people with intellectual disabilities has been touched on but not extensively examined in any area of Canadian history. A few scholars have referred to the exploitative labour practices intellectually disabled people have endured in institutions in Ontario and how some worked in the community in British Columbia before being confined in sheltered workshops.[35] None of these brief references, however, offer a gendered interpretation of these labour practices. My 2004 article on the exploitative nature of work for people defined as mentally disabled in Ontario from 1964 to 1990 briefly discusses the gendered nature of the province's sheltered workshop system, which segregated work according to "masculine" and "feminine" occupations in a way that reflected similar practices in the broader community; the one area of gender "equality" was that men and women were both paid at the same rate, which was far below the minimum wage.[36] Yet, such brief references only underline how much more work needs to be done on the gendered work of people with intellectual disabilities in Canadian disability history.

An important collection of first-person accounts, *Hear My Voice: Stories Told by Albertans with Developmental Disabilities Who Were Once Institutionalized* (2006), includes accounts by two men and two women who speak of their toil while confined in institutions. Given the brevity of their interviews, it would be difficult to make a gendered analysis from this small sample, in which three of the four people registered negative memories of their institutional labour while one person had good memories.[37] Nevertheless, it is possible to get a sense of how these individuals viewed the value of their work. Harold Barnes, recounting work on a farm at the Michener Centre in Red Deer, Alberta, recalled, "I worked in the greenhouse and I worked in the root cellar, sorting potatoes and stuff like that ... That was slave work, man."[38] Similarly, both Tedda Kaminski and Terry McGee recalled the difficult working conditions on the wards and demeaning treatment by staff, with McGee recalling how inmates were warned that they had to do certain tasks to get food.[39] In contrast, Diane Nabess recalled institutional work as "fun. Getting off and not having to deal with things on the unit [was good]. Because the vocational training was an interesting place to work because when I was working I would enjoy doing my job and enjoy working with other residents I knew. Just getting off the unit for a few hours of the day made me feel good."[40] While Kaminski, McGee, and Barnes had negative experiences of their work life in Alberta's institutions, the tone of their recollections had a similar ring to the positive perspective of Nabess: their assessment of their work, whether the labour was unpleasant or not, was directly related to their sense of dignity and how the work affected them. They each placed value on their toil, whether they viewed it as exploitive or not. If any conclusion can be drawn from this small sample of first-person accounts from formerly institutionalized people with intellectual disabilities, it is that there was a crossgender agreement among interviewees on the connection between work, the value of their toil, and their sense of their own dignity.

Mad People

Of all the areas in Canadian disability history where labour is discussed, it is in mad people's history that a gendered analysis of the value of work is most extensively addressed. This is likely due to the major focus on work therapy in mental institutions, although a strong focus on rehabilitation aimed at the employment of people with physical disabilities has not thus far resulted in similar studies in other areas of disability labour history. Works by Cheryl Krasnick Warsh (1989), James Moran (2000), and myself (2000, 2006), discuss the nature and scope of mad people's labour, including gendered dimensions of this topic, such as where men were expected to toil more outside on grounds maintenance and construction projects than women were allowed to do.[41] Both males and females toiled extensively inside asylums, with women's work concentrated particularly in the laundry, sewing, and tailoring areas; women worked in the kitchens serving their own wards, and men did the same on their wards. These studies analyze institutional supervisors' devaluation of work done by both male and female inmates, finding no gender differentiation in derogatory references to inmates' labour. Moran writes of an asylum in Quebec: "For their part, the proprietors of the Beauport Asylum argued that no real profit could be extracted from the labour of patients in the asylum. 'The labour of lunatics, generally speaking,' they noted, 'does not pay.'"[42] While Moran does not critically analyze this claim, my work does point out the contradictions of asylum superintendents stating one thing – the supposed poor quality of inmates' work – and then complimenting individual mad people on their toil and noting the overall savings to the institution achieved by exploiting inmate labour.[43]

According to these studies, the gendered dimension of inmates' work is reflected in the distinct tasks males and females were required to do, and the fact that their collective efforts were denigrated without distinction between male and female workers. Thus, gender was predominant in assigning the type of work that was done within the institution, while the label of madness was predominant in the devaluing of this same work by the overseers. Yet, the agency of mad labourers comes through clearly in how they valued their work. For example, Mary A., after seventeen years' toil in the Toronto Asylum laundry, wrote letters demanding to be paid a specific amount calculated for her years of work, compensation she would not receive before her death in 1923.[44] Another woman, Audrey B., worked in the sewing room at the same asylum for over thirty years in the first half of the twentieth century, a job for which she was known as a skilled seamstress. This was an unpaid job that she wanted to do, as it enabled her to see her friends, get out of the locked ward, and engage in work that obviously meant a great deal to her self-esteem.[45] The power dynamics of inmate labour within institutions needs to be a central part of our understanding of their toil. Inmates hardly had a choice about where they could work in the asylum; for Audrey, the only way to get out of the confined space of her ward was to go to another confined space where she worked for no pay among people with whom she enjoyed socializing. Beyond the policies and practices of administrators, physicians, and health officials, far greater research is needed to uncover the most important part of this history – the views of the disabled men, women, and, in some cases, children who toiled behind the scenes in institutions, or in the wider community, about their own work. Lykke de la Cour's doctoral dissertation, *From "Moron" to "Maladjusted": Eugenics, Psychiatry, and the Regulation of Women, Ontario, 1930s–1960s* (2013), while focusing on which women were categorized as "feeble-minded" and why, also includes a discussion of how women's labour was directed into domestic work within and outside the asylum.[46] Her study is an example of the value of including both intellectual and psychiatric disabilities in a gendered analysis of the value of work, and it indicates further how much more research needs to be done in this area.

As the studies discussed in this chapter indicate, scholars have only recently begun to examine gender and the value of work in Canadian disability history, just as the field of disability history is itself only starting to emerge in this country, as elsewhere. Given historical views of women's work, it is not surprising that disabled women's work is devalued more than men's. In that sense, this survey of existing literature reveals nothing new. Yet, what can be said is that, as more studies are undertaken on various aspects of disability history, it is essential to provide a more extensive historical analysis of gender and the way in which the work of male and female disabled workers was valued, in order to fully understand and appreciate the contributions that both groups made to the communities in which they lived, willingly or unwillingly. There could be some surprises that will make us revise our interpretations, as where Nic Clarke has uncovered some evidence of pre-confinement labour among people regarded as "mentally deficient" in late nineteenth- and early twentieth-century British Columbia.[47] From what we know, the extent of this labour was vast, but so too is the lack of historical research on this toil and how it affected males and females, both adults and children, in various ways.

It is also essential to stress how the valuing, or devaluing, of disabled people was very much tied into the perceptions of policymakers as well as institutional and medical officials. These people had the power to judge disabled men, women, and children as economically productive or unproductive, and their eugenic perspectives contributed to the idea of a disabled person being a "burden" on society. As Kim Nielsen has pointed out, by lowering the economic value of disabled people, the able-bodied officials who assessed their worth were, at the same time, privileging their own value to themselves and society.[48] In other words, economic value was based on the highly subjective standards of people who were not themselves disabled, and these standards reflected all of the interconnected inequities related to gender, race, class, and ability.

The underlying injustice of this way of thinking has been critiqued in a contemporary context by Sunny Taylor in her article "The Right Not to Work" (2004). As she points out, the notion that disabled people are dependent is misconstrued to make it sound as if able-bodied people do not have dependencies, when in fact all people are interdependent in various ways. Instead, Taylor argues, given the structural barriers disabled people have to finding employment, and the reality of their usually being slotted into low-paying, precarious jobs when paid work is found, it is essential to avoid linking a person's worth to productivity. Instead, a more socially just approach would recognize varied ways of being a member of society, including being wary of using paid employment "as a sign of equality and enfranchisement" in an inequitable capitalist system.[49] This critique needs also to be borne in mind when analyzing gender and the value of work in Canadian disability history. By critiquing the unpaid and underpaid exploitation of disabled people's toil, the purpose is not to imply that disabled people have no value if they have not been engaged in what society views as economically productive tasks. Rather, it is to point out that the historical diminishing of disabled people's labour lends further credence to the devaluing of the abilities and societal status of *all* disabled people, whether or not they are engaged in what is viewed as work. In this context, what is regarded as work needs to be reconsidered and reconceptualized as this historical research proceeds. Feminist scholars and activists have long critiqued the ways in which women's unpaid work in the home has been ignored and uncredited, in the past and present. Such critiques constitute an essential reference point when analyzing disabled people's work. Along similar lines, Taylor writes about attending public demonstrations for disabled people's rights and producing visual art for herself and others as efforts that are seldom recognized for the worth they bring to both the person engaged in such activities and the wider community. Both of these activities are also work, even if they are not considered regularly paid work by most of society (unless one happens to be an employed community organizer or a very fortunate artist). As the work that disabled people have engaged in during the past continues to be uncovered and analyzed, it is essential that the gendered nature of both work and what is perceived of as work is reinterpreted in a way that brings new light to a long-hidden topic.

NOTES

Thanks to Kim Nielsen for her helpful response to an earlier version of this paper on a panel at the Berkshire Conference on the History of Women, University of Toronto, 23 May 2014. Thanks also to Ravi Malhotra and Dustin Galer for their comments on this article.

1 Mary Tremblay, *Living with Disability: The Early Pioneers. A Life History Account of the Experience of Individuals with Spinal Cord Injury before 1967 Who Lived in the Community in Ontario* (PhD Thesis, State University of New York at Buffalo, 1993) [unpublished]; Mary Tremblay, "The Canadian Revolution in the Management of Spinal Cord Injury" (1995) 12:1 Can Bull of Medical History 125 [Tremblay, "Canadian Revolution"]; Mary Tremblay, "Going Back to Main Street: The Development and Impact of Casualty Rehabilitation for Veterans with Disabilities, 1945–1948" in Peter Neary & JL Granatstein, eds, *The Veterans Charter and Post World War II Canada* (Montreal & Kingston: McGill-Queen's University Press, 1998) 160.
2 Tremblay, "Canadian Revolution," *supra* note 1 at 143.
3 *Ibid* at 133.
4 Geoffrey Reaume, *Lyndhurst: Canada's First Rehabilitation Centre for People with Spinal Cord Injuries, 1945–1998* (Montreal & Kingston: McGill-Queen's University Press, 2007) at 62.
5 Jennifer Davis McDaid, "'How a One-Legged Rebel Lives': Confederate Veterans and Artificial Limbs in Virginia" in Katherine Ott, David Serlin, & Stephen Mihm, eds, *Artificial Parts, Practical Lives: Modern Histories of Prosthetics* (New York: New York University Press, 2002) 119 at 134.
6 Langford was interviewed by Mary Tremblay and cited in "Canadian Revolution," *supra* note 1 at 132.

7   Reaume, *supra* note 4 at 20–21.

8   Kim E Nielsen, *A Disability History of the United States* (Boston: Beacon Press, 2012) at 86–87.

9   Natalie Dykstra, "'Trying to Idle': Work and Disability in *The Diary of Alice James*," in Paul Longmore & Lauri Umansky, eds, *The New Disability History: American Perspectives* (New York: New York University Press, 2001) 107 at 122.

10 Peter Neary, *On to Civvy Street: Canada's Rehabilitation Program for Veterans of the Second World War* (Montreal & Kingston: McGill-Queen's University Press, 2011) at 114, 227–41.

11 *Ibid* at 114–15.

12 Serge Marc Durflinger, *Veterans with a Vision: Canada's War Blinded in Peace and War* (Vancouver: UBC Press, 2010) at 185–90.

13 Euclid Herie, *Journey to Independence: Blindness – The Canadian Story* (Toronto: Dundurn Press, 2005) at 107.

14 *Ibid* at 108.

15 Burch writes that in the early 1900s, deaf women "sought to defend deaf education, sign language, the Deaf community, and Deaf men from both oralism and displacement by hearing teachers. In so doing, they fell into even more subordinated roles." Susan Burch, *Signs of Resistance: American Deaf Cultural History, 1900–1942* (New York: New York University Press, 2002) at 20.

16 Joanna Pearce, *"Fighting in the Dark": Charles Frederick Fraser and the Halifax Asylum for the Blind, 1850–1915* (MA Thesis, Dalhousie University, 2011) at 88–89 [unpublished].

17 Megan Davies, *Into the House of Old: A History of Residential Care in British Columbia* (Montreal & Kingston: McGill-Queen's University Press, 2003).

18 Nancy M Forestell, "'And I Feel Like I'm Dying from Mining for Gold': Disability, Gender, and the Mining Community, 1920–1950" (2006) 3:3 Labour: Studies in Working-Class History of the Americas 77 at 78–79.

19 *Ibid* at 80.

20 *Ibid* at 87.

21 *Ibid* at 91.

22 Dustin Galer, "A Friend in Need or a Business Indeed? Disabled Bodies and Fraternalism in Victorian Ontario" (2010) 66 Labour/Le Travail 9 at 18.

23 *Ibid* at 19.

24 *Ibid* at 34.

25 Melanie Panitch, *Disability, Mothers, and Organization: Accidental Activists* (London: Routledge, 2008).

26 Dustin Galer, *"Hire the Handicapped!" Disability Rights, Economic Integration and Working Lives in Toronto, Ontario, 1962–2005* (PhD Thesis, University of Toronto, 2013) [unpublished].

27 *Ibid* at 292.

28 *Ibid* at 309.

29 Robert Storey, "From Invisibility to Equality? Women Workers and the Gendering of Workers' Compensation in Ontario, 1900–2005" (2009) 64 Labour/Le Travail 75.

30 *Ibid* at 88.

31   Sarah F Rose, "'Crippled' Hands: Disability in Labor and Working-Class History"
     (2005) 2:1 Labour: Studies in Working-Class History of the Americas at 38. It
     should be noted that this article focuses on the historical "experiences of people
     with noncongenital disabilities." *Ibid*, at 54. It is equally important to include the
     experiences of people with congenital disabilities in labour histories to ensure
     that their toil and exploitation is addressed, past and present.
32   Storey, *supra* note 29 at 98.
33   Ravi Malhotra, "Electioneering and Activism at the Turn of the Century and the
     Politics of Disablement: The Legacy of E.T. Kingsley (1856–1929)" (2011) 7:3&4
     Rev of Disability Studies 34 at 36.
34   *Ibid*, quoting E.T. Kingsley, at 39.
35   Madeline Burghardt, *Narratives of Separation: Institutions, Families, and the
     Construction of Difference* (PhD Thesis, York University, 2014) at 179 [unpub-
     lished]; Nic Clarke, "Sacred Daemons: Exploring British Columbian Society's
     Perceptions of 'Mentally Deficient' Children, 1870–1930" (2004–05) 144 BC
     Studies 61; Bruce Kappel, "A History of People First in Canada" in Gunnar Dyb-
     wad & Hank Bersani, eds, *New Voices: Self-advocacy by People with Disabilities*
     (Cambridge, MA: Brookline Books, 2008) at 117, quoting Pat Worth.
36   Geoffrey Reaume, "No Profits, Just a Pittance: Work, Compensation and People
     Defined as Mentally Disabled in Ontario, 1964–1990" in Steven Noll & James W
     Trent Jr, eds, *Mental Retardation in America: A Historical Reader* (New York:
     New York University Press, 2004) 466 at 478–79.
37   See Karen Melberg Schwier, ed, *Hear My Voice: Stories Told by Albertans with
     Developmental Disabilities Who Were Once Institutionalized* (Edmonton: Al-
     berta Association for Community Living, 2006): Tedda Kaminski at 23–25;
     Harold Barnes at 77; Terry McGee at 117–19, 121, 123; and Diane Nabess at
     206–7.
38   *Ibid* at 77.
39   *Ibid* at 23–25, 117.
40   *Ibid* at 206.
41   Cheryl Krasnick Warsh, *Moments of Unreason: The Practice of Canadian Psych-
     iatry and the Homewood Retreat, 1883–1923* (Montreal & Kingston: Mc-
     Gill-Queen's University Press, 1989); James Moran, *Committed to the State
     Asylum: Insanity and Society in Nineteenth-Century Quebec and Ontario* (Mont-
     real & Kingston: McGill-Queen's University Press, 2000); Geoffrey Reaume, "Pa-
     tients at Work: Insane Asylum Inmate Labour in Ontario, 1841–1900" in James
     Moran & David Wright, eds, *Mental Health and Canadian Society: Historical
     Perspectives* (Montreal & Kingston: McGill-Queen's University Press, 2006) 69
     [Reaume, "Patients at Work"]; and Geoffrey Reaume, *Remembrance of Patients
     Past: Patient Life at the Toronto Hospital for the Insane, 1870–1940* (Toronto:
     Oxford University Press, 2000) [Reaume, *Remembrance*].
42   Moran, *supra* note 41 at 93.
43   Reaume, "Patients at Work," *supra* note 41 at 76–80.
44   Reaume, *Remembrance, supra* note 41.
45   *Ibid* at 169–71.

46 Lykke de la Cour, *From "Moron" to "Maladjusted": Eugenics, Psychiatry, and the Regulation of Women, Ontario, 1930s–1960s* (PhD Thesis, University of Toronto, 2013).

47 Clarke, *supra* note 35.

48 Kim Nielsen, Response to panel, Berkshire Conference on the History of Women, University of Toronto, 23 May 2014.

49 S Taylor, "The Right Not to Work: Power and Disability" (2004) 55:10 Monthly Rev, online: <http://www.monthlyreview.org/0304taylor.htm>.

PART 2

Debates in Disability Studies

4

Dancing with a Cane
The Public Perception of Franklin Delano Roosevelt's Disability

ANNE FINGER

Franklin Delano Roosevelt, who was the president of the United States from 1932 until his death in 1945, skilfully managed the public perception of a disability, navigating the treacherous shoals that public figures traverse as they seek to present a narrative about their personal disability. The posthumous "rehabilitation" of FDR as a disabled icon points to both the value and downside of an uncomplicated reclaiming of a historical figure as "one of us."

In the summer of 1921, Roosevelt contracted a paralytic illness, which he and his doctors believed to be poliomyelitis – or infantile paralysis, as it was then commonly called.[1] As an aside, I should mention that an article in the *Journal of Medical Biography* makes a compelling case that Roosevelt in fact had Guillain-Barré syndrome.[2] Whatever the medical cause of his condition, Roosevelt believed himself to have the disease, as did others: socially, Roosevelt had polio. A wealthy man from a patrician background, he had been assistant secretary of the Navy and an unsuccessful candidate for the American vice-presidency, and he was regarded as a rising star in the Democratic Party before he became ill.[3]

In *Elegy for a Disease: A Personal and Cultural History of Polio* (2006), I discuss how diseases accrue narratives, narratives that change over time, while looking specifically at polio, the disease that so shaped my life, and Roosevelt's. The historian Charles E. Rosenberg notes: "Disease serves as a structuring factor in social situations, a social actor and mediator. This is an ancient truth. It would hardly have surprised a leper in the twelfth century, or a plague victim in the fourteenth."[4] Nor, need I add, would it surprise those affected today by Ebola – whether people with the disease, healthcare workers, or those fearful of it – and those who find themselves cast either as "innocent victims" of AIDS or "lethal carriers" of HIV.

One of Roosevelt's early concerns as he struggled with the acute effects of his illness and the impact of what threatened to be a game-changing disability was that the public not see him as an "invalid" or a "cripple." His aides and doctors spun the story of his illness as serious but not "permanently crippling," and early newspaper reports emphasized that he was "slowly nearing recovery."[5] From the start of his disability, FDR and those around him understood that he needed to stage-manage the public perception of his illness.

Sociologist John B. Kelley, in speaking of the initial despair that can follow a disability, said, "We know exactly what we have become," alluding to the lowered social status of disabled people (personal communication). Like whiteness, heterosexuality, and maleness, "ability" is a category that at first blush appears to be so transparent that to ask what it means seems so obvious as to border on the nonsensical. But in fact, all of us, disabled and nondisabled, have spent a lifetime learning about disability, wherever we are placed on the divide. Roosevelt certainly knew that if he were seen as a "cripple," it would effectively end his political career. However, to go through a life-altering illness and to come out on the other side – to be one who has overcome, recovered, triumphed – was another story altogether. Throughout the remainder of his life, he skilfully used a strategy of showing himself as having "recovered" from his disease, minimizing the extent of his disability, performing nondisability, and finding means of alternative embodiment and performing masculinity, which disability imperilled. Further, such strategies reshaped the narrative of the disease: rather than being a disease associated with immigrant filth, as it had earlier been seen in the United States, it became a disease one could triumph over, a builder of character. At Roosevelt's side as he managed his public persona was Louis Howe, his long-time aide and confidant. Howe, who had been facially disfigured as the result of a childhood bike accident and was described as being "gnomelike," "looking like a singed cat," and the "third ugliest man in New York," surely understood what was involved in managing physical difference.[6]

Although Roosevelt did occasionally use a wheelchair – both the cumbersome wood-and-wicker chairs of that time period and a kitchen chair outfitted with wheels – architectural barriers at that time made use of such a chair as a means of everyday locomotion nearly impossible. Roosevelt also occasionally used crutches, although most often – at least when not in public – he was carried about by his African American valets, a topic to which I will later return.

When Roosevelt entered the narrative of polio, the disease had been framed as a scourge of young children. It was also thought to be spread outwards from the slums, where immigrants were assumed to live in filthy conditions that bred disease. Medical historian Naomi Rogers titled her exploration of the 1916 polio epidemic, the first major polio epidemic in the United States, *Dirt and Disease*. (Her subtitle, *Polio before FDR*, suggests the importance that Roosevelt's polio would play in the national discourse about poliomyelitis.) In the summer of 1916 – for reasons that are still not well understood, polio almost invariably flared up in the summer – a polio epidemic broke out, centred in New York City.[7] Throughout the month of June, cases slowly increased, although concern about the disease was largely limited to public health officials. By July, the number of new cases had increased to nearly fifty a day, and it wasn't long before polio was causing panic throughout the city. After rumours started that cats carried the disease, thousands of owners turned out their animals, who yowled at the doorsteps of their former homes and scrounged for food. Children were barred from movie houses, and some – largely the offspring of the wealthy – were evacuated from the city, with train stations mobbed by those seeking to escape. Those fleeing – who were sometimes spoken of in the press as "refugees" and "fugitives" – could find themselves forced back, for fear that they might carry the plague. Around one New Jersey town, "[p]olicemen were stationed at every entrance to the city – tube, train, ferry, road and cowpath – with instructions to turn back every van, car, cart, and person laden with furniture."[8] A newspaper cartoon from that summer showed a neatly dressed white girl, labelled "New York Child," standing on a suburban street while others dashed away from her – the only figure coming towards her is a policeman with a raised truncheon. The mix of emotional reactions to those infected or suspected of being infected with a disease recalls the response to the Ebola epidemic: the mix of dread, sympathy, panic, and rage that greeted those seen as possible carriers.

Although the Ellis Island Quarantine Station, vigilant against disease and disability, reported in 1916 that cases of polio had not been seen among immigrants, nor were there any reports of the disease in Italy, Italian immigrants found themselves scapegoated as the source of the contagion. Early twentieth-century Italian immigrants originated primarily from the rural south of Italy and brought their peasant habits with them to New York – for instance, sometimes not segregating nonhuman and human animals, so that roosters, goats, pigs, and monkeys – used by organ grinders – cohabited with people in city tenements. Immigrants resisted the good-hearted and superior "native Americans" – used in this period to refer to those of solid northern European stock – who came into their neighbourhoods to clean them up, to teach the ignorant foreigners how to care for their children, and to enforce quarantine and hospitalization orders promulgated during the polio epidemic – orders that were often stubbornly resisted.[9] Hospitals seemed particularly frightening to southern Italians, who saw them as places for the isolated and despised. You could curse an enemy by saying, "May you die in hospital."[10] The New York epidemic, occurring in the country's largest metropolitan area, received widespread media coverage. Further, those who survived other infectious diseases usually bore no outward marks of what they had been through – smallpox, of course, was one exception – while many of those who recovered from polio were left permanently disabled, keeping the memory of the epidemics alive.

Given this history, Roosevelt not only needed to combat his public perception as an invalid or a cripple, but he also needed to change the narrative of the disease itself. In this new narrative, polio would no longer be a disease of filth, stewed into virulence in slums and tenements, reaching out from there to infect the pure and noble. Instead, it became a disease that one triumphed over by pluck, hard work, and courage.

The town of Warm Springs, Georgia, and the allied National Foundation for Infantile Paralysis played key roles in this reframing of the disease. In October 1924, Roosevelt journeyed for the first time to Warm Springs, a sleepy town with a ramshackle hotel, the Meriwether Inn, near a mountain-fed hot spring with mineral-rich waters. Almost certainly, when Roosevelt arrived, he was not consciously thinking about remaking polio: like many of the recently disabled who had exhausted the available medical treatments, he was taking the advice of those who offered hope in some form, often any form.[11] He had heard about a young man who had undergone physical therapy in the waters of Warm Springs and was able to walk with two canes. Roosevelt began a similar regimen and, with the owners of the hotel, devised a plan for Warm Springs to become a centre for polio rehabilitation. A local newspaper reporter wrote an article entitled "Franklin D. Roosevelt Will Swim to Health," which was syndicated and widely printed across the country.[12]

People disabled by polio flocked to Warm Springs – although accommodations were primitive and hardly set up for wheelchair users and others with mobility impairments – drawn by the promised miracle of the healing waters, but most likely kept there by the air of camaraderie and freedom. As Hugh Gregory Gallagher put it in *FDR's Splendid Deception,* "[t]he oppressive hostility of the Victorian hospital routine, the pain of body bracing and muscle stretching, had been replaced overnight by a world of sunlight and warm water, laughter, encouragement and hope."[13] Roosevelt worked out physical therapy regimes for the patients – they called him "Doc Roosevelt" – and word spread that, with therapeutic diligence and mineral water, polio was being overcome at Warm Springs. That the "triumph" was usually partial was less widely admitted. One long-time resident wrote that disabled visitors "improve[d] in every respect. One came with crutches and a brace and left with a cane only. Others came in wheelchairs and *nearly* put them aside that summer."[14] Roosevelt eventually bought the Warm Springs property and lobbied hard to get orthodox medical organizations to endorse the work going on there. The image of polio as a disease that could be defeated by diligence and grit grew in the public mind.

The perception of polio had so changed that, by the 1940s, when Bentz Plagemann got polio and went to Warm Springs, he was told quite earnestly by his physical therapist, the redoubtable Miss Plastridge – was ever anyone so aptly named? – "'Only a particular group of people contract polio ... It indicates a highly organized central nervous system, which usually means talent, or special ability of some kind.'" She reinforced this lesson when he said he found the women at Warm Springs beautiful and ventured aloud that that was because he had seen so few "American girls," having been serving in the US Navy. "But they are beautiful ... You must remember that polio strikes the most fit; the healthiest, the gayest, the most brilliant."[15] Polio had completed its journey from being a plague to being a tragedy that could nonetheless mark one as special; from being a mark of Cain to being, in the words of early twentieth-century novelist Mary Webb, a "precious bane."[16]

By the early 1930s, Roosevelt was presenting himself as a man who had largely recovered from polio: certainly this was true in that he was stronger and more agile than he had been after the initial attack. What was also true was that he remained significantly disabled and went to great lengths to hide any public presentation of the reality of his impairment. Sometimes his efforts were relatively straightforward. For instance, prior to his first run in 1932 for the US presidency, he had himself examined by three doctors – including a "brain specialist" – selected by the director of the New York Academy of Medicine.[17] The medical reports – which emphasized his overall robust good health and high spirits – were given to journalist Earle

Looker, who although nominally a Republican was nevertheless close to the Roosevelt camp. Looker reported on this evaluation in *Liberty Magazine*, adding, "Insofar as I have observed him, I have come to the conclusion that he seemed able to take more punishment than many men ten years younger. Merely his legs were not much good to him."[18]

It should be noted that Roosevelt's political career occurred during the heyday of the eugenics movement. Although polio was clearly not a genetic disability, the understanding of which disabilities were inherited and which were not was hazy at best among scientists, and even more so in the public mind. Serious suggestions were put forth in this period about those with innately weak constitutions being prone to infectious disease, and the notions of "fitness" and "unfitness" contained moral, psychological, and mental dimensions. It is not surprising, therefore, that a "brain specialist" was one of the medical experts called on to examine Roosevelt and pronounce on his fitness for office.

In order to get to win the presidential election, there were rituals that had to be performed, one of which was walking – or perhaps I should say "walking," because FDR's performance was far more complex and difficult than what is usually understood by that term. He would sometimes walk to podiums with a cane in one hand and his son James holding his other arm, propelling him along. He gripped so tightly that James's arm was sometimes bruised as a result.[19] He also needed to perform physical ruggedness: Nine days after winning the Democratic nomination for the presidency in 1932, he sailed, along with three of his sons, up the coast to New England, a press boat filled with reporters and photographers behind them. He thus presented himself as active, in motion, not a stranded, helpless cripple.[20]

When Roosevelt was photographed with an assistive device, it was invariably a cane. (Often such photographs are cropped so that they do not show his wide-legged stance, which gave him extra balance, or that his other hand is behind him, gripping something sturdy to keep him upright.) A cane, after all, can mark its user as debonair and urbane. Roosevelt became so identified with his cane that there is an exhibit at Warm Springs of canes that were given to him, often as gifts by foreign dignitaries – most of them obviously quite incapable of supporting a walker.[21]

Despite care taken with his image, the knowledge that the president was disabled was widespread. During the controversy in the late 1990s over whether Roosevelt should be depicted in his wheelchair at the memorial to him in Washington, DC, Blynn Garnett wrote to the *New York Times*: "I was 10 years old when Franklin D. Roosevelt died, and I knew that he used a wheelchair. His enemies, who referred to him as 'that cripple in the White House,' knew. My family lived in a working-class neighbourhood in northern Manhattan, with no private pipeline to Washington." The writer continued: "Perhaps a covert bargain was struck: F.D.R. pretended people thought he could walk; the people pretended to believe him." Gallagher compared the shared illusion to the story told in "The Emperor's New Clothes": "The nation *wanted* to believe its Emperor was clothed, and it simply would not hear otherwise."[22]

There are many first-person accounts of the surprise visitors to the White House experienced at seeing the president picked up and carried like a child. As James Tobin reports in his *The Man He Became*, "Whenever I spoke with someone who remembered the 1930s and 1940s, I would ask if he or she knew at the time that FDR was crippled. Everybody said they knew. But some people said this: 'We didn't know how crippled he was.'" Tobin found the same thing in contemporary source material, where many were shocked at the extent of his disability when they saw the president in person. Others said: "We knew, but we forgot about it." "We knew, but we didn't think of him that way."[23] If I had a nickel for every time I heard, as a child growing up with polio in the 1950s, "Roosevelt had polio" – well, I would have a lot of nickels.

Once elected to the presidency, Roosevelt had the assistance of the Secret Service, the agency charged with protecting the president, in carrying out his sleight of hand – or perhaps "sleight of leg" would be a more apt term. If he needed to be lifted out of a car, it was done in a garage or behind a plywood screen. The podiums at which he spoke had to be bolted to the floor so they would not topple over when he leaned his full weight on them – once, during his initial run for the presidency, this wasn't done, and both FDR and the podium crashed onto the floor. Although press photographers were present at the event, no pictures were taken of him: there was an understanding between Roosevelt and the press corps that no photographs would reveal the extent of his disability. If someone broke this unspoken agreement, the Secret Service would seize the film of the person who photographed Roosevelt transferring or being carried.[24] Once he was elected to the presidency, "[s]turdy, permanent ramps for the President's use were constructed at the Capitol, the War State Navy Building (now the Executive Office Building), the farther reaches of the White House offices, and St. John's Church across Lafayette Square."[25] While there is at least one photograph of one of these ramps in the FDR Library, photographs of them were not published in contemporary newspapers, nor were they written about.

As well as keeping explicit images of the extent of his disability from the American public, Roosevelt and his supporters also recast the story of his impairment as one of overcoming. Disability requires a narrative, an answer to the question, sometimes asked directly, "What happened to you?" Part of Roosevelt's narrative was to present himself as a disabled person who had "overcome" – whatever that means – his disability: in other words, I had polio but I swam in the waters of Warm Springs and worked hard and it made me a better person. Often, this narrative would be explicitly voiced by his wife, Eleanor Roosevelt, who variously said that "Franklin's illness gave him strength and courage he had not had before. He had to think out the fundamentals of living and learn the greatest of all lessons – infinite patience and never-ending persistence"[26] and that "[i]f the paralysis couldn't kill him, the presidency won't."[27] This narrative is still being told, most recently in James Tobin's 2013 *The Man He Became: How FDR Defied Polio to Win the Presidency*. While it would be a disservice to reduce Tobin's complex and well-researched book to an easy formula, the narrative trope of "disability made him a better person," one of the central arguments in Tobin's work, is stated in his prologue:

> Without the polio virus and what it did to FDR, the history of American life since the 1920s would not be what it has been. It is a truism to say Roosevelt overcame polio to become president. It is just as accurate to say that Roosevelt would not have become the president he became – probably would not have been president at all – had it not been for the germ that infected him.[28]

I would argue that, although Roosevelt's personal experience with disability may have had a role in shaping "the president he became," the influence of mass movements pushing him significantly to the left proved more decisive in shaping the presidency of a man who had been a middle-of-the-road politician. In the words of the late Paul Longmore, "Great movements give rise to great leaders."[29]

The work of reshaping the narrative had to be ongoing. In January 1938, vaudeville and radio star Eddie Cantor coined the phrase "March of Dimes" – a play on the popular television newsreel "March of Time" – when he urged radio listeners to send dimes to the White House for the fight against polio. Cantor said, "The March of Dimes will enable all persons, even the children, to show our President that they are with him in this battle against this disease."[30] The response was overwhelming – the business of the White

House nearly came to a halt as bag after bag of mail – weighted down with dimes – was delivered to the executive offices, and official letters were lost in the piles. The dimes came in "fixed with gummy tape, baked into cakes, jammed into cans, imbedded in wax and glued to profiles of the President."[31] The president was not a victim of the disease, but a fighter against it, mobilizing Americans into battle.

Another fundraiser was the annual President's birthday balls, which were held across the country from 1934 until Roosevelt's death, from New York's Waldorf-Astoria to mining towns in Alaska and even in Japanese American internment camps during the Second World War, raising money for the battle against polio. Posters for the balls did not show Roosevelt's disabled body, of course, but often did include silhouetted figures of children with crutches, and the caption "Dance So that Others May Walk." Roosevelt's disabled presence lurked in the shadows: the birthday balls and the March of Dimes were ways of talking about the thing that could not be talked about, or could only be talked about sideways.

Disability imperils masculinity. As Russell Shuttleworth and his colleagues write, "[a] much-cited point by those who study the intersection of gender and disability is that masculinity and disability are in conflict with each other because disability is associated with being dependent and helpless whereas masculinity is associated with being powerful and autonomous, thus creating a lived and embodied dilemma for disabled men."[32] This conflict, of course, is not lived out only by disabled men; in the case of FDR, it was lived out by the nation as a whole. The iconic image of Roosevelt with his fedora tipped back and his cigarette holder raised high creates an image of jaunty potency. Freud tells us that sometimes a cigar is just a cigar, but I think that this cigarette is not just a cigarette. It was an open secret that Roosevelt had had an affair with Lucy Mercer[33] and was rumored to have an ongoing relationship with Missy LeHand, one of his secretaries.[34] The affair with Mercer, which had occurred while she was serving as Eleanor Roosevelt's social secretary between 1914 and 1918, ended – at least temporarily – when Eleanor discovered love letters from Mercer to her husband. The revelation of her husband's infidelity ended the sexual relationship between Roosevelt and his wife. Later, in the 1940s, the affair began again, with Mercer – who had subsequently married – visiting the White House under the pseudonym Mrs. Paul Johnson.[35]

The relationship with LeHand and the revived affair with Mercer notwithstanding, Hugh Gregory Gallagher argues in his book *FDR's Splendid Deception*, which details the lengths to which Roosevelt went to hide the extent of his disability, that FDR was celibate from the time of his becoming disabled until his death. The evidence he offers is rather flimsy, relying largely on statements from Roosevelt's son James that his father did not have intercourse after his disability; but offspring are notoriously unreliable narrators when it comes to their parents' sexual lives. Gallagher also states that, "[a]lthough the evidence is not overwhelming in support of FDR's celibacy, it is at least significant that there is no piece of evidence, large or small, which counters such a conclusion." But after all, physical evidence of presidential philandering is hardly common, Monica Lewinsky's semen-stained blue dress notwithstanding. Gallagher does note that, "[w]here FDR lived, there lived Missy – whether at Warm Springs, in the governor's mansion, or in the White House." Further, he states that LeHand stopped dating during the time she was involved with Roosevelt; that in the cottage they shared at Warm Springs, she had to walk through his bedroom in order to get to their shared bathroom; and that in the governor's mansion, she and FDR had adjoining bedrooms with a connecting door – with Eleanor sleeping down the hall.[36] Not to be overly Clintonesque – during Bill Clinton's grand jury interrogation about his relationship with Monica Lewinsky, he famously said, "It depends on what the meaning of the word 'is' is" – but such evidence suggests that one's assessment of FDR's sexual life may depend on one's definition of the word "celibate." Perhaps, having a mistress with whom he did not actually complete what is sometimes called "the sex act," he may have been a disabled person who, unable or unwilling to fit into normative sexuality, nonetheless claimed a sexual life.

The actual relationship between Missy LeHand and Roosevelt is largely a moot point: he was widely believed to have had such an affair. This is a case where a whispering campaign about a politician's illicit sexual life may actually have been to his benefit, allowing him to be seen as fully masculine. I grew up in a family in which we didn't believe in God, we believed in Roosevelt. At the secular Sunday school in Hamilton, New York, set up by faculty wives of Colgate professors so that their offspring would have a quasi-religious education, we crocheted squares that would be sewn together to make blankets for Algerian refugees (this was during the anticolonial war of the 1950s); learned about the Bible, although we were told that perhaps the burning bush that Moses beheld was not actually on fire – it may just have been that a vivid sunset behind it made it look *as if* it were on fire; and heard about the Appalachian coal miners' shacks, bare of all ornament save for a picture of FDR nailed to the wall. At the family dinner table, I heard my father talk about Roosevelt's mistress, although at the age of eight I wasn't exactly sure what a "mistress" was (it sounded enticing and naughty and vaguely French, and was one of those words that caused my mother to say, in a voice half-mournful and half-reproving, "Jack!").[37]

One of the ways in which Roosevelt deflected attention from his disabled body was by becoming his voice, particularly in his weekly "fireside chats." The recording of a clip from Roosevelt's first inaugural address, in which he stated, "The only thing we have to fear is fear itself," has become emblematic of him and, indeed, of the Depression itself. Eight days after his 1933 inauguration, Roosevelt took to the airwaves to explain his decision to declare a "bank holiday" in order to put a brake on the panicked runs on banks. He spoke in a folksy, down-to-earth yet authoritative style. Humorist Will Rogers praised him for speaking about the banking crisis so that he "made everyone understand it, even the bankers." Rogers continued to praise Roosevelt as the "first Harvard man" to know enough to speak plainly. "Compared to me," Rogers said, "he's almost illiterate."[38] He meant it as a compliment – patrician, well-educated Roosevelt was able to talk directly to his listeners, in an intimate, engaging manner. Roosevelt's use of his spoken voice was, of course, a masterful use of modern media, but it was also a way of creating an alternative embodied presence that was not just strong and resonant but almost beyond the natural in its ability to cross time and space. The identification of FDR with his voice was so pervasive and so emblematic that one of the statues at the Roosevelt Memorial in Washington, DC, shows a man in a wooden chair leaning forward in a posture that is almost reverent towards a cathedral radio, listening to one of Roosevelt's fireside chats. So closely was Roosevelt identified with his voice that when he ran for his unprecedented third term, opposition political buttons read not just "No Roosevelt Dynasty" and "Out! Stealing Third," but, significantly, "No More Fireside Chats."[39]

Often, the tendency of FDR to minimize his physical condition has been presented as a feature of his psychology, a tendency towards denial on his part. In fact, there is strong evidence that Roosevelt enjoyed the company of other disabled people, as witnessed by the time he spent at Warm Springs, where he was surrounded by others who had polio.[40] When he no longer needed to dance the dance of ability, he seemed glad to give up its rigours. Addressing a joint session of Congress to report on the Yalta Conference on 1 March 1945, having recently been inaugurated for his fourth term, and knowing that he would certainly not run for a fifth, he began by saying, "I hope that you will pardon me for an unusual posture of sitting down during the presentation of what I want to say, but I know that you will realize that it makes it a lot easier for me in not having to carry about ten pounds of steel around on the bottom of my legs." When he finished his sentence, the member of Congress burst into applause – perhaps everyone was relieved that the elaborate feints and sallies of dancing around his disability could at last come to an end.[41]

When it opened in 1997, a memorial to FDR in Washington, DC, aroused enormous controversy by failing to show his disability; in 2001 a statue was added depicting Roosevelt in his wheelchair.[42] Picasso has said, "Every act of creation is first an act of destruction." While this act has reclaimed Roosevelt as an iconic figure for the disabled community, it has done so by writing out of history the African American men who acted as Roosevelt's everyday means of mobility. It is hard to imagine a statue of one of Roosevelt's servants carrying him: such an image would underscore the failure of New Deal liberalism to resolve – or even significantly grapple with – racism. For example, the US Army remained segregated until 1948; and Roosevelt himself signed Executive Order 9066, calling for the internment of Japanese Americans.

In preparing this chapter, I wrote to the Roosevelt Presidential Library, seeking names and photographs of these men, who had been so integral to Roosevelt's functioning, imagining – foolishly, I now realize – that there would be 8 x 10 glossy photos of them, short biographies. I got back an email that gave me the names of Irwin McDuffie, George Fields, a man identified only as "Caesar," "a Puerto Rican, who begged for the job but suffered a nervous breakdown on it," and finally, Arthur Prettyman, described as follows by Roosevelt's distant cousin (and perhaps his lover) Margaret Suckley: "Though very black, his features are refined & rather Jewish. He is a little portly, & walks with great dignity."[43] The email included a blurry photo in which Arthur Prettyman appears in the background (personal communication). Clearly, the tensions around race and disability, the intersections and conflicts, remain hidden in this recovering of Roosevelt as a disabled person.

Roosevelt managed the public perception of his disability by forging a new narrative. It depicted him as having triumphed over and been made stronger by polio, as a strongly masculine presence who had not been feminized by disability, and as a heroic figure seeking to return to the world of the able bodied, both on a personal level and through his fundraising for the March of Dimes. As we anticipate the biography of the disabled labour activist E.T. Kingsley mentioned in the introduction to the present volume, it will be interesting to see how the personal, social, and political circumstances, so different from those of FDR, shaped his narrative of disability. And, as the foregoing discussion of Roosevelt suggests, we may wish to consider what we may find ourselves losing sight of when we claim Kingsley as "one of us."

NOTES

1 "F.D. Roosevelt Ill of Poliomyelitis," *New York Times* (16 September 1921) 1.
2 Armond S Goldman et al, "What Was the Cause of Franklin Delano Roosevelt's Paralytic Illness?" (2003) 11 J of Medical Biography 232.
3 James Tobin, *The Man He Became: How FDR Defied Polio to Win the Presidency* (New York: Simon & Schuster, 2013) at 37.
4 Charles E. Rosenberg, "Framing Disease: Illness, Society, and History" in Charles E. Rosenberg & Janet Golden, eds, *Framing Disease: Studies in Cultural History* (New Brunswick, NJ: Rutgers University Press, 1992) at xviii.
5 Tobin, *supra* note 3 at 100.
6 Tobin, *supra* note 3 at 55.
7 Tony Gould, *A Summer Plague: Polio and Its Survivors* (New Haven, CT: Yale University Press, 1995) at 3–28.
8 *Ibid* at 7.
9 Naomi Rogers, *Dirt and Disease: Polio before FDR* (New Brunswick, NJ: Rutgers University Press, 1992); Alan M Kraut, "Plagues and Prejudice: Nativism's Construction of Disease in Nineteenth- and Twentieth-Century New York City" in David Rosner, ed, *Hives of Sickness: Public Health and Epidemics in New York City* (New York: Museum of the City of New York, 1995) 65.
10 Richard Schickel, "A Stardom Doomed by Expectation," *Los Angeles Times* (11 May 2003), online: <http://articles.latimes.com/2003/may/11/books/bk-schickel11>.
11 Christopher James Rutty, *"Do Something! Do Anything!" Poliomyelitis in Canada, 1927–1962* (PhD thesis, University of Toronto, 1995) [unpublished]; Edward J Sass, George Gottfried & Anthony Sorem, *Polio's Legacy: An Oral History* (Lanham, MD: University Press of America, 1996).
12 Gregory Cleburne, "Franklin D. Roosevelt Will Swim to Health," *Atlanta Journal Sunday Magazine* (26 October 1924) 7.
13 Hugh Gregory Gallagher, *FDR's Splendid Deception: The Moving Story of Roosevelt's Massive Disability – And the Intense Efforts to Conceal It from the Public*, rev ed (Arlington, VA: Vandamere Press, 1994) at 40.
14 Fred Botts, unpublished memoir, quoted in *ibid* at 42 [emphasis in original].
15 Bentz Plagemann, *My Place to Stand* (New York: Farrar, Straus, 1949) at 137, 167.
16 Mary Webb, *Precious Bane* (London: J. Cape, 1928).
17 Betty Houchin Winfield, *FDR and the News Media* (New York: Columbia University Press, 1994) at 20.
18 Earle Looker, "Is Franklin D. Roosevelt Physically Fit to Be President? A Man to Man Answer to a Nation-Wide Challenge" *Liberty* (July 1931), quoted in Tobin, *supra* note 3 at 293.

19   Gallagher, *supra* note 13 at 142.
20   "Roosevelt to Run Campaign at Sea for Week," *New York Times* (8 July 1932) 1.
21   Online: <http://www.vukelicfamily.com/G21.JPG>.
22   Gallagher, *supra* note 13 at 96.
23   Tobin, *supra* note 3 at 8.
24   Gallagher, *supra* note 13 at 94.
25   *Ibid* at 96–97.
26   Rosemarie Garland-Thomson, "The FDR Memorial: Who Speaks from the Wheel-chair?" *Chronicle of Higher Education* (26 January 2001), online: <http://m.chronicle.com/article/The-FDR-Memorial-Who-Speaks/22439>.
27   Gallagher, *supra* note 13 at v.
28   Tobin, *supra* note 3 at 7.
29   From his address at the *Americans with Disabilities Act* twentieth anniversary celebration in San Francisco, online: <http://lflegal.com/2010/08/paul-longmore/?>.
30   March of Dimes, online: <http://www.marchofdimes.org/mission/eddie-cantor-and-the-origin-of-the-march-of-dimes.aspx>.
31   Victor Cohn, *Four Billion Dimes* (Minneapolis: Minneapolis Star and Tribune, 1955) at 53, cited in Tony Gould, *A Summer Plague: Polio and Its Survivors* (New Haven, CT: Yale University Press, 1995).
32   Russell Shuttleworth, Nikki Wedgwood & Nathan J Wilson, "The Dilemma of Disabled Masculinity" (2012) 15:2 Men and Masculinities 174.
33   Charles McGrath, "No End of the Affair," *New York Times: News of the Week in Review* (20 April 2008).
34   Doris Kearns Goodwin, *No Ordinary Time: Franklin and Eleanor Roosevelt. The Home Front in World War II* (New York: Simon & Schuster, 1994) at 154–55.
35   Michael E. Ruane, "What Was for FDR's Eyes Only Is Now for Yours," *Washington Post* (29 July 2010), online: <http://www.washingtonpost.com/wp-dyn/content/article/2010/07/28/AR2010072805917.html>.
36   Gallagher, *supra* note 13 at 136–37.
37   Later, my younger sister, a lesbian, took great delight in needling my then-homophobic father – he later saw the error of his ways – when the passionate love letters between Eleanor Roosevelt and Lorena Hickok were revealed in 1978: "Oh! I want to put my arms around you, I ache to hold you close. Your ring is a great comfort. I look at it & think 'she does love me, or I wouldn't be wearing it!'" "So, Dad, Eleanor Roosevelt was a dyke," she said, to his great consternation. (Letter excerpt from Rodger Streitmatter, ed, *Empty without You: The Intimate Letters of Eleanor Roosevelt and Lorena Hickok* [Cambridge, MA: DaCapo Press, 2000] at 10.)
38   Jonathan Alter, *The Defining Moment: FDR's Hundred Days and the Triumph of Hope* (New York: Simon & Schuster, 2006).
39   Online: <http://www.yjstore.com/WENDELL-WILLKIE-NO-ROOSEVELT-DYNASTY-1940-POLITICAL-CAMPAIGN-PIN_p444827.html>; Online: <http://www.collectorsquest.com/collectible/7119/out-stealing-third>; Online: <http://www.loriferber.com/no-more-fireside-chats-button.html>.
40   Susan Richards Shreve, *Warm Springs: Traces of a Childhood at FDR's Polio Haven* (New York: Houghton Mifflin Harcourt, 2008) at 19.

41 Online: <http://millercenter.org/president/fdroosevelt/speeches/speech-3338>.

42 David Stout, "Clinton Calls for Sculpture of Roosevelt in Wheelchair," *New York Times* (24 April 1997), online: <http://www.nytimes.com/1997/04/24/us/clinton -calls-for-sculpture-of-roosevelt-in-wheelchair.html>.

43 Geoffrey C. Ward, ed, *Closest Companion: The Unknown Story of the Intimate Friendship between Franklin Roosevelt and Margaret Suckley* (New York: Simon & Schuster, 2012).

5

Disability in Motion
Aesthetics, Embodiment, Sensation, and the Emergence of Modern Vestibular Science in the Nineteenth Century

MARK WALTERS

Seasickness has afflicted humankind since ancient times – indeed, the words "nausea" and "nautical" are etymologically linked. However, it was not until the late nineteenth century that the exact mechanism for seasickness, and the physiology of the inner ear more generally, became known. In this chapter, I sketch some of the history of late nineteenth-century work on balance, reconstructed from primary documents and scholarly histories of otology. I argue that the recognition of disability and the categorization of certain persons (those labelled as "deaf-mutes") as "disabled" were key components of unlocking the inner ear's role in regulating balance. In addition, I argue that the emergence of vestibular science indicates a potential for fascinating and productive work at the intersection of disability studies, sound studies, and the history of the senses. I suggest that such work might yield critical models for revaluating our understanding of what it means to hear, or to live in the world as sensory beings.

The Anatomy and Physiology of the Inner Ear: Current Understandings
The physiology of the middle and inner ear comprises three separate organ systems – first, the tympanic system, which transfers the vibrations of the tympanic membrane through a series of tiny bones (the incus, malleus, and stapes) into vibrations in the fluid of the cochlea; second, the cochlear system, a snaillike enclosure that transduces these fluid vibrations into electrical impulses, which are transferred as signals down the cochlear nerve; and third, the vestibular system (including the

semicircular canals and otoliths), which accounts for balance and orientation of the head in space.

I focus on the vestibular system for most of this chapter, and so it makes sense to examine its role a little more closely. Its semicircular canals are three hollow bones, each of which corresponds to one of the planes in standard Euclidean space. These bones are filled with fluid and contain a thin membrane that senses the movement of the head through the inertia of the fluid in a given canal.[1] Scott McCredie draws an analogy between the function of these canals and that of the air-bubble level used by carpenters and masons. The latter contains a long, straight edge, at the centre of which is a fluid-filled vial that also contains a bubble of air; by resting the straight edge along a timber or piece of masonry, the builder can easily judge whether a construction is perfectly horizontal.[2]

The second organs within the vestibular system are the otoliths (although not shown in Figure 5.1, these would be contained in small cavities just to

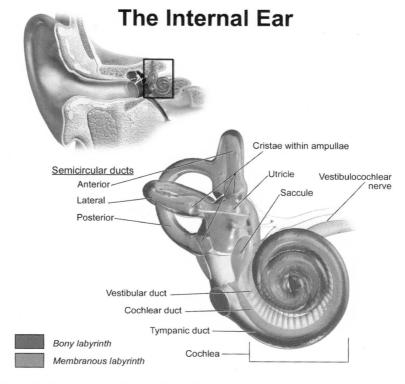

The Internal Ear

Cristae within ampullae

Semicircular ducts
  Anterior
  Lateral
  Posterior

Utricle

Saccule

Vestibulocochlear nerve

Vestibular duct
Cochlear duct
Tympanic duct
Cochlea

Bony labyrinth
Membranous labyrinth

Figure 5.1 The anatomy and physiology of the inner ear. | Blausen.com staff, "Blausen gallery 2014." *Wikiversity Journal of Medicine,* DOI:10.15347/wjm/2014.010. Creative Commons Attribution 3.0.

the right of the stapes). Otoliths (literally, ear-rocks) are tiny, fluid-filled sacs that contain miniscule crystals of chalk. As the head moves in space, the crystals accelerate at a slower rate than the fluid. Nerves register this lag in acceleration when these tiny crystals press on membranes within the cavities where they are housed. These otolithic sensations feed into nerves that are connected directly to the eyes, and these nerves adjust eye movements nearly instantaneously, compensating for micro-movements of the head; this is known as the vestibulo-ocular reflex.[3] Otolithic reflexes thus allow a person's eyes to remain focused on some object while his or her head moves. This allows a person, for example, to be able to read road signs from the seat of a moving car. It is just one way in which balance is very directly and physiologically multimodal and precognitive: the inner ears and eyes effectively work as a single organ, registering sensory input and reacting accordingly by reflex.[4]

Troubling Common Sense: Critically Reimagining the Sensory Body

All three of these organ systems – the tympanic system, the cochlear system, and the vestibular system – share the same anatomical space and are all identified as part of the inner ear; biomedical scholarship going back at least a century points to why this might be so from an evolutionary standpoint. And yet, recent critical work emerging from authors of sound studies on the role of the ear in nineteenth-century social relations tends to focus on the former two systems while virtually ignoring the last. Taking two examples in a small field of scholarship, Jonathan Sterne's *The Audible Past* constructs the story of sound in modernity (roughly 1870–1925) as one of "tympanic apparatuses" – machines or devices that use some kind of membrane to transduce sound impulses into electrical ones, and vice versa.[5] Alternatively, Veit Erlmann's *Reason and Resonance* focuses intensively on evolving understandings of the form and function of the cochlea and tympanic system over the eighteenth, nineteenth, and early twentieth centuries, yet mentions the vestibular system only in passing.[6] Only Scott McCredie's *Balance: In Search of the Lost Sense* – which presents an immensely fascinating (though neither historically rigorous nor critically dense) survey of the history of nineteenth- and twentieth-century research into the vestibular sense and its relation to sound, balance, and the body – offers details about the vestibular system and its connection both to hearing and to bodily comportment and balance.[7] (I credit McCredie far more than I cite him – this chapter would not be possible without his work.)

I contend that the seemingly odd disavowal of the vestibular system – both in sound studies and in most current academic scholarship on the ear, hearing, and sound – is an artifact of a longstanding, broad social consensus on what properly constitutes the role of the ear in sensory life. Put more simply, the ear is about sound (narrowly understood), and therefore those parts of the ear that are not directly involved in perceiving sound (narrowly understood) are not, scholarly speaking, parts of the ear at all. I further contend that this sensory atomism – which still carries validity today – had social impacts that both supported and impeded the development of vestibular science in the nineteenth century: impeded, because there persisted through the experiments I describe below an insistence on understanding any structures in the ear as having to do with hearing; supported, because the nineteenth century saw the institutionalization and segregation of people whose hearing was abnormal or nonfunctional ("the deaf"), thus making it possible for researchers to notice that balance disorders or abnormalities were more common within the deaf population than the nondeaf one.[8] This finding, in turn, allowed late nineteenth-century researchers to make the case that aural structures were somehow related to balance.

Going further, I suggest that vestibular science provides ground for sound studies and disability studies scholarship to combine in a very fruitful way. What if, as sound and disability scholars, we posit another way of understanding the human sensorium as it relates to sound? What if we were to begin from the assumption that what we believe sound to be is just a narrow slice of what sound is or could be? What if we were to acknowledge that physical aspects of our world that exist outside of the sensing body may influence our bodies in multimodal, complex ways that defy our common-sense sensory epistemologies?

Here I draw an obvious analogy to our experience of light: the bodily experience of colour is clearly different from the bodily experience of sunburn. From the "common-sense" perspective, we would say that colour and sunburn are different sensory phenomena – they are different bodily experiences, and therefore belong in different epistemological categories. However, we now know that our eyes are capable of sensing one tiny slice of what we now understand to be a much broader electromagnetic spectrum. Beyond the narrow band of visible light, our body is still capable of experiencing electromagnetic radiation – as heat (infrared) or as sunburn (ultraviolet). So, "light" is not just light. In the same way, I suggest that, perhaps, "sound" is not just sound.

In other words, rather than understanding hearing and balance as separate phenomena (because the body experiences them differently), I suggest that we understand both as reactions to the same physical process – specifically, more or less regular disturbances in the physical medium in which the body is immersed. If we thus proceed from an obvious question – "Why are the vestibular, cochlear, and tympanic organs so intimately connected within the body?" – to a critical re-evaluation of what sound sensation *is* and *means*, we point to new ways we can and should do a history of sensation as it relates to sound, sonic phenomena, and the body.

Three Models for Balance and Embodiment

Academic work on balance and embodiment generally falls into one of three models. These models are important to my project because they repudiate longstanding assumptions: that the sensory body is universal (each body is like all others), that the sensory body is fixed or "hardwired" (the sensory body does not change, adapt, or learn), and that the sensory modalities of the body are distinct and are attuned to the world in certain limited ways. Instead, various scholars suggest that the senses and the divisions between sensory modalities are culturally relative, learned, malleable, manifold, and complex. Thus, while we are biologically predisposed to sense sound, the exact ways in which we understand and interpret this sensory input vary widely across times, cultures, and bodies. In the following discussion, I refer to work in the history, philosophy, and anthropology of the senses, and recent work on disability and the senses. Then, using two case studies, I sketch how this work points to a potentially productive deficit in our historical scholarship on balance and embodiment.

One: Syntactic "Drift" in the History of the Senses

The first model for balance is what I call the syntactical, a term I borrow from scholars in both sound studies and the history of the senses. The syntactical model is perhaps best explained by Shakespeare scholar Bruce Smith. In "Listening to the Wild Blue Yonder," Smith asks us, "How did Shakespeare and his contemporaries order the sounds they heard and made? How did they use these sounds to position themselves in the world?"[9] At the root of Smith's investigation is the notion of a "sensory syntax" (an idea he borrows from acoustic ecology, specifically the work of Barry Truax[10] and R. Murray Schafer[11]). A sensory syntax, like a linguistic syntax, is a set of rules about what constitutes the elemental units of sensation and about how these elemental units are ordered into larger wholes. Thus, although we encounter the "same" objects in the world that Shakespeare and his contemporaries did (be these texts or sounds), Smith asserts that Shakespeare's culture had different ways of interpreting these objects – Shakespeare and his contemporaries, for example, "heard" written materials in ways that we generally do not. Smith thus observes that it should be possible to encounter written texts multimodally: "Texts not only represent bodily experience; they imply it in ways they ask to be touched, seen, heard, even smelled and tasted."[12] What is important, according to Smith, are the phenomenological aspects of a given object – that is, how that object is understood to connect to certain sensory capacities of the body – within a given culture.

This syntactical model is also at the root of Alain Corbin's "sensory balance," a fact made very clear by Corbin in his work on the history of the senses:

> Is it possible to discern retrospectively the nature and presence in the world of people in the past through an analysis of the hierarchy of the senses and the particular balance established between them at a particular moment in history within a given society? Is it possible to detect those hierarchies, and so identify the purposes which presided over this organization of the relations between the senses?[13]

Like Smith, Corbin thus sees the sensorium as culturally relative – sensation is largely learned rather than innate. Each historical moment and location, Corbin asserts, has its own norms and understandings of the proper configuration of the senses, including "modalities of attention, thresholds of perception, significance of noises, and configuration of the tolerable and intolerable."[14] According to Corbin, it is one task of the historian to take into account these varying modalities, thresholds, and significances, because they shift from moment to moment and from culture to culture. I suggest there is a tremendous amount to learn from Smith and Corbin as sound scholars and disability scholars.

Two: Strange Proportions and Aesthetic Embodiment

The second model for balance and embodiment is what I call the aesthetic/indexical. This model uses formal representations from the musical, visual, or plastic arts in order to construct the normal body and dictate what "balance" can and should mean, in terms of both the body's comportment and the proper configuration of its sensory relationships. Both of the major works I cite here – the late Tobin Siebers's *Disability Aesthetics* and Joseph Straus's work on modernist classical music – are avowedly indebted to scholarship on disability and embodiment.

Balance is central to Siebers's *Disability Aesthetics*, though the word
is almost never used. Siebers's essential argument is that there exists a
tension between classical aesthetics – with its reliance on formal rules,
harmony, and balance, and its concomitant glorification of a singular or
formally "perfect" body – and what Siebers calls "disability aesthetics":
"Disability aesthetics prizes physical and mental difference as a significant value in itself. It does not embrace an aesthetic that defines harmony,
bodily integrity, and health as standards of beauty ... [I]t drives forward
the appreciation of disability found throughout modern art by raising
an objection to aesthetic standards and tastes that exclude people with
disabilities."[15]

Siebers finds strong historical precedent for disability aesthetics, even
going so far as to propose that "beauty always maintains a sense of disability ... It is often the presence of disability that allows a piece of artwork to
endure over time."[16] Though Siebers never uses the word "balance," his relationship to the concept is clearly expressed in a quote he borrows from
Francis Bacon and uses twice in his book: "There is no exquisite beauty,
without some strangeness in the proportion." Siebers shows how Nazi art of
the 1930s was obsessed with "perfect" formal balance: "Strangeness in proportion ... is eschewed in Nazi art because its goal is to portray a new human
being whose embodiment of beauty and health results in an almost obscene
regularity of features and body parts."[17]

Another recent scholar to explicitly connect sound and balance is the mu-
sicologist Joseph Straus, whose work notes the connections between musical counterpoint and notions of balance within the normal body. For Straus,
classical music (roughly defined as nineteenth- and early twentieth-century
art music) uses harmonic balance (that is, the distribution and arrangement
of notes within a given musical work) to tell a story about physical balance
(that is, the proper comportment of the body in reaction to its physical
environment):

> In all the literature on musical symmetry, there is an emphasis on balance,
> on the physical sense of symmetrical balance around a fulcrum, of a body in
> a physically balanced state. In this context, deviations from inversional sym-
> metry are felt as physical disruptions that unbalance the musical body – that
> create the threat or the reality of a disability – which the music must deal with
> in some way. Inversional symmetry and symmetrical balance thus create the
> possibility for musical narratives that depend on a contrast of normative and
> non-normative bodily states.[18]

According to Straus, experiments in musical aesthetics thus index changing or revolutionary understandings of bodily abnormalities, including disabilities. A stronger reading of Straus's work might suggest that music's aesthetic value lies precisely in its ability to index such abnormalities.

Such aesthetic representations are important for two reasons. First, they do political work – they tell us not how bodies are, but rather how they should be. This is perhaps most explicitly clear in Siebers's work, which contrasts Nazi art and the "aesthetics of human disqualification" on the one hand, with disability aesthetics and an artistic embrace of radically variant and disabled bodies on the other. At the same time, such representations (like the bodies they represent) are both highly varied and highly malleable – they index not "the body," but "bodies," and they can also index volatilities or instabilities in the ways that bodies can and should be "balanced." Siebers thus parrots a common aphorism among disability scholars: "nondisabled bodies are all alike, while disability takes a thousand unique and different forms."[19] To the extent that balance implies equivalency with respect to some centre or norm, imbalance registers itself as abnormal.

Three: Aesthetic Formalism versus "Reincarnated" Aesthetics
The third model I point to I call the "reincarnated aesthetic" model. This is (again) strongly based on Siebers's work; this model suggests that it is incumbent upon critical theorists to work in the interests of social justice, even when such interests threaten to undermine long-cherished social institutions. The dearest and most dominant assumptions of Western aesthetics since Kant – including, most importantly, the notion of a universal aesthetic subject and the decoupling of form from content – work to legitimize certain kinds of bodies and delegitimize others. And so, while the opening of Siebers's book illustrates how the history of art has been largely dependent on images of disability or bodily abnormality, the final chapter constitutes a close interrogation of the textual bias of academics and the ideological and aesthetic assumptions that such a bias reifies. Like Siebers, I note that the bias of (textual) reading, of formalism, and of classical aesthetics are all the same: they draw us away from a world of sensuous and confused bodily experience and towards a world of formal rules and clear, definitive epistemic categories. For Siebers, this bias is best demonstrated in scholars' need to linguistically "control" visual images of disability and difference:

> The preference for reading is only a metaphor, I understand, but it is a metaphor with a reason because it undergirds the linguistic prejudices defining

our favourite critical methods ... Perhaps the impulse to read an image is a
measure of the desire to control it. Images too complex to be read refuse
this control, and they challenge the authority of reading as a privileged activity because they demonstrate a surplus of meaning untranslatable into
linguistic terms.[20]

Siebers is not the only recent scholar to advocate for a new kind of
aesthetics that privileges messy sensory experience over classical formalism and textual supremacy. The cultural anthropologist David Howes has
suggests that contemporary scholarship take note of the scholarly potential that might be unleashed, were aesthetics to return to its pre-Kantian,
pre-formalist roots:

In its modern [classical] incarnation (or more accurately, disincarnation),
aesthetics has to do with the appreciation of the formal relations intrinsic to
a work of art, and is divorced from that work's content ... Aesthetic perception thus depends on a dual process of sensory demarcation and the elision
of non-intrinsic sensations so that the viewer may come to appreciate the
"organic unity" of a given work of art, be it a painting or a symphony.[21]

Howes' main thrust is to reverse the logic of form over content, in order
"to recuperate the original idea behind the 'science of sense perception' as
defined by Baumgarten." Such an aesthetics would be largely synesthetic and
intersensorial (or as Baumgarten would have it, "confused"[22]), and would
privilege the kinds of experiences bodies *do* have over the kinds of experiences they *should* have. Obviously, disability scholars would have a clear
ideological interest in such a project; I believe that sound studies scholars
could also benefit from such an aesthetic "reincarnation."

Advocacy for Action: Disability Scholarship and Sound Studies

With respect to this new, reincarnated aesthetics, sound studies scholars are
playing catch-up. Thus, Sterne's *Audible Past* opens with a particularly
striking example of aesthetic (and literal) disincarnation. In Sterne's first
chapter, we are presented with the ear phonautograph, a device created by
Bell and Blake in 1874.[23] The device used an excised human ear affixed to a
stylus, enabling the tympanic membrane to be used in "tracing" sound. As
Sterne notes, this device is fascinating as a cultural artifact because it helps
construct sound as a particular "*effect* in the world."[24] But a deeper point that
Sterne makes – at least implicitly – is that this effect is understood as

bearing on the ear *only* as part of a tympanic-electric transducer. Sterne thus defines sound with respect to modernism, atomizing sound as a sense and literally excising any part of the ear that does not fit.

While I contend that Sterne's version of sonic history is immensely valuable, I also believe that we should remain critical of the tacit (and largely uninterrogated) work that it does in teaching us what we (think we) already know about sensation and modernism. There are other, more critical histories of the senses and modernism waiting to be written. Returning to the analogy of our experience of sunburn and colour: light is not just "light," just as sound is not just "sound." Understanding light and sound in broader ways may reveal connections between what we otherwise understand to be discrete, separate sensory modalities, and looking for evidence that late nineteenth-century researchers might have been trying to redraw or redefine the senses might yield fascinating results. Using the vestibular system and the emergence of vestibular science as a test case, beginning with a broad understanding of sound may help explain why the vestibule – which has nothing to do with hearing *qua* hearing – is so intimately entangled with the organs that do. Such a treatment of sound and balance as both phenomenologically and physiologically linked seems bizarre because it threatens common epistemologies about the way the sensory body is ordered. Thus the connection of such work to disability studies (via Siebers et al) should seem clear: disabled bodies defy translation, overflow with excessive meanings, and threaten commonly held beliefs about the proper relationship not only between sensory modalities but also of the sensory body to its world. Disabled bodies throw the body's sensory capacities "out of balance." My hope is that a cursory survey of two cases from the nineteenth century will suggest that we have much work to do in "reincarnating" the history of the senses.

A Brief Prehistory of Modern Vestibular Science

Medical professionals often make the distinction between "anatomy," which describes the form of parts of the body, and "physiology," which describes the function of these parts. Anatomical descriptions of the vestibular system go back at least as far as Galen, who described the organs of the inner ear as akin to the fabled labyrinth of Crete. However, the physiology of the labyrinth was grossly misunderstood until well into the nineteenth century.[25] Given this centuries-long history of investigations into the ear, why was this organ of balance not understood as such until roughly a century ago?

I believe this misunderstanding has to do with Western scholarship's longstanding tendency towards an insistence on sensory atomism – thus, while hearing loss was easily localizable to the ear, balance or vertiginous disorders were harder to "locate" within the body. The experience of vertigo, like the images of disability that Siebers confronts us with, "defies translation." Vertigo is a nauseatingly multisensory, full-body experience. Thus both classical and Renaissance texts in the West attributed vertiginous disorders to a neurological problem and grouped these disorders with those such as epilepsy, lethargy, and mania – disorders of the mind, not the body. Even J.E. Purkyne, a Czech doctor who specialized in research on sensation and whose 1820 work dealt specifically with nystagmus and vertigo "believed, as did other physicians of his time, that the senses of motion and acceleration were mediated by cutaneous pressure receptors or alterations in blood flow, and that all vertiginous disorders were due to cerebral or cerebellar pathology."[26] By the end of the nineteenth century, the anatomy of the inner ear had been well documented, but the function of the vestibular labyrinth was still assumed to play a role in hearing, and vertiginous disorders were still "located" in the brain.[27] Even as late as the early twentieth century, some disagreement remained regarding the vestibular labyrinth's role in sensation and balance, and some scholars clung to the increasingly unpopular idea that the labyrinth's primary function had more to do with hearing than with balance.[28]

The first anatomist generally credited with identifying the proper function of the vestibular system was the Frenchman Marie-Jean-Pierre Flourens. In 1824 and 1830, Flourens published the results of several experiments in which he had stimulated or destroyed the semicircular canals in small animals (pigeons and rabbits). He determined that doing so seemed to affect both balance and the movements of the eyes but had no noticeable effect on hearing.[29] Oddly enough, this discovery seems to have been either ignored or overlooked for three decades, until another Frenchman, Prosper Ménière, recalled Flourens's experiments while seeking a treatment for the balance disorder that now bears Ménière's name.

From the beginning, contemporary vestibular science was built upon disability – beginning with Flourens's disabling of pigeons and rabbits and continuing through Ménière's search for a way to "cure" the debilitating effects of chronic vertigo and William James's observations of deaf-mutes. From the mid-nineteenth century onward, the development of vestibular science would be at least partially dependent upon social classifications of disability and the social segregation of disabled people. Again, this is no accident, given the ways in which the emerging vestibular science, like sensory disability, troubled commonly accepted divisions between the senses.

Bodies off Balance: Prosper Ménière and Vestibular Science

The history of science is often the history of eponyms, and nineteenth-century otology is no exception. But, while Prosper Ménière's preeminence among nineteenth-century otologists has remained well established in literature published since his death, ongoing debate remained, and remains, about the particulars of what, exactly, he discovered. Thus one scholar, writing sixty years after Ménière's death, called his most famous medical case a "myth," in the sense that the case itself did not seem to accurately demonstrate the pathology that Ménière claimed as the basis for his work on vestibular disease and balance.[30] There is evidence to suggest that Ménière himself did not recognize any significant connection between vertigo and hearing loss (at least not publicly) until 1861, thirteen years after he published his first academic work – a translation of a textbook on hearing loss in which he had footnoted a case of "labyrinthine hemorrhage resulting in sudden deafness."[31] Thirteen years later, Ménière would return to this footnote, using it as a "case study" that was borne out in other such cases in which vertigo emerged in conjunction with deafness.

I claim that Ménière's seeming inability or unwillingness to note the correspondence of vertigo and hearing loss in the decade before his death marks him as a product of a particular historical moment. The inertia Ménière faced – against his own assumptions and (later) those of his colleagues – was at once productive of and dependent upon sensory atomism and the aesthetic formalism that dominated the nineteenth century. To borrow a phrase from Marx (via Susan Stewart): "the forming of the five senses is a labour of the entire history of the world down to the present."[32] Writing nearly a century after Ménière's death, an apologist would note that "Ménière had no reason to describe the vertigo in the original report, since the topic discussed dealt exclusively with hearing impairment, and the mention of vertigo was superfluous."[33] Again, because balance is a multimodal disorder, most researchers in Ménière's generation maintained that balance was located in the brain, not the ear, and that balance disorders were therefore a psychological problem, not a physiological one. Ménière would spend the last year of his life defending his claim within a medical community that was largely hostile to it, before dying in early 1862.[34]

Interlude: Deafness, Disability, and Segregation in Nineteenth-Century America

In the wake of Ménière's death, research into balance and vertigo experienced something of a renaissance. Surprisingly, one of the most important aspects of this renaissance was the degree to which it was co-constituted with the creation of disability as a social category. Vestibular research often involved deaf subjects, and it is likely that the research would not have been as successful as it was without the social segregation of deaf people.

While there have certainly always been people who could not perceive sound, deafness as a social or cultural category seems to be very recent. In *Enforcing Normalcy*, Lennard Davis shows how the rise of print literacy in Europe in the eighteenth century led to the emergence of deafness as a cultural category, because deaf people had a specifically inflected relationship to visual texts and the oral/aural ways in which these texts were expected to be read. From here, Davis notes that in the nineteenth century, the deaf would collectively be subsumed into Deaf culture – a kind of diasporic nationality:

> Douglas Baynton shows us that by the nineteenth century, the Deaf were regarded as foreigners living in the United States, a kind of fifth column in society resisting nationalization. Baynton quotes from the oralist publication the *American Annals of the Deaf and Dumb* which in 1847 described the deaf not as afflicted individuals but as a "strongly marked class of human beings" with "a history peculiar to themselves."[35]

The social fact of deafness was made manifest in social relations – including segregation and intermarriage, alternative forms of education, and institutionalization – that constructed the deaf as a category. In other words, by 1850, "deaf-mutes" in America were a socially segregated and stigmatized group with their own collective identity. Interestingly, it was this social fact of deafness and the segregation of deaf-mutes into asylums that helped one researcher, William James, to recognize a peculiarity shared by deaf-mute people: specifically, their resistance to nausea brought on by motion – deaf-mutes did not get seasick. James would recall Ménière's work and, through the late 1870s, he would conduct a series of experiments on institutionalized deaf-mutes, in which he tested their sense of balance. The results of these experiments would help lead to our current understandings of the role of the vestibular apparatus as the organ of equilibration.

Turning a Deaf Ear: William James, Deaf-Mutes, and Vertigo

William James was a Harvard professor, trained in philosophy and forerunner of both modern psychology and phenomenology. As an affluent New Englander, James was frequently a passenger on ocean-going ships, where seasickness was a common ailment. It was on one of these voyages that James noticed a group of deaf-mutes, who seemed immune to the seasickness that was pervasive among other passengers. This observation, coupled with James's work in asylums for the deaf, provided anecdotal evidence that guided his investigations into the connections between hearing and balance:

> The number of deaf-mutes who are afflicted with disorders of locomotion seems never to have attracted the attention of physiologists, *although it has long been notorious in asylums*. The connexion of these disorders with the loss of the semicircular canal sense becomes now a most interesting problem, into which I have begun to inquire ... The evidence I already have in hand justifies the formation of a tentative hypothesis, as follows: *The normal guiding sensation in locomotion is that from the semicircular canals.* This is co-ordinated in the cerebellum (which is known to receive auditory nerve fibers) with the appropriate muscles, and the nervous machinery becomes structurally organized in the first few years of life. If, then, this guiding sensation be suddenly abolished by disease, *the machinery is thrown completely out of gear, and must form closer connexions than before either with sight or touch.* But the cerebellar tracts, being already organized in another way, yield but slowly to the new co-ordinations now required, and *for many years make the patient's gait uncertain, especially in the dark.*[36] [My emphasis]

James's writing here is remarkable for a number of reasons. First, he showed how tacit, informal knowledge about deaf bodies and their relationship to balance was an outgrowth of the formation of communities of deaf people within asylums. Again, before the nineteenth century and the recognition of the deaf as a "strongly marked class of human beings," such tacit knowledge would not have been possible. Second, James specifically constructed balance as multimodal – in his work, balance was understood as bearing relation to hearing (as James was studying deaf-mutes), sight (as locomotion becomes "uncertain, especially in the dark"), touch, and muscle memory. Third and most strikingly, James also suggested that balance is learned (i.e., is *not* innately known by the body), and is learned differently (and relearned continually) by each individual. The relation of all of these sensory modalities to one another is peculiar to each individual body – thus the analogy to "machinery ... thrown out of gear" as a more or less temporary, intermediate condition of the newly disabled body. Deaf people can balance themselves, while newly deafened people often cannot. Thus James's description of the deaf body is pregnant with meaning for current disability and sound studies scholars.[37]

James's experimental findings were referenced in a number of works in the decade subsequent to their publication, and they would become a driving force in the development of modern vestibular science. James's findings appeared in George Parker's "On Vertigo," and were used to refute a tentative claim made by Michael Foster in his entry "Hearing and Muscular Sense" in his *Textbook of Physiology* (1876), a standard work used to train British and American medical students at the time:

> [Dr. James] examined a number of deaf mutes to see how far vertigo could be caused in them by rapid rotation. Out of 200 healthy students of Harvard taken for the purpose of comparison, only one was free from giddiness after rotation in a swing with the eyes closed: whereas of the deaf mutes (519 in number) 186 remained perfectly free from the feeling, and 134 were only slightly affected ... Another curious fact was, that of 15 deaf mutes who had been to sea, only one had suffered from sea-sickness ... I think we must confess, after Dr. James's experiment, that there is no reason to think vertigo can be caused after destruction of the auditory nerve by anything like rotation which does not affect sight or the muscular sense.[38]

As illustrated by Parker (again, one publication out of many), James's work represented a turning point in vestibular research – a turning point that connected balance and hearing and suggested that the senses functioned in a highly manifold, synesthetic way. This, I believe, is ground that is still largely uncharted within both our cultural and medical histories.

Mad Verticals: Mach, Gravity, and Auditory Origins

James's work with deaf-mutes offered compelling evidence, from a social and experimental perspective, for the entanglement of hearing and balance. At roughly the same time that James was making his observations, three European researchers were each making similar discoveries, independently of one another. Through experiments carried out in 1873–74, Alexander Crum-Brown, Josef Breuer, and Ernst Mach would each show unique aspects of the entanglement between hearing, balance, and the other senses.[39] Here I will focus on Mach's work, bearing in mind that Mach himself acknowledged the debt he owed to Breuer and others.

According to Mach, the ideas for these experiments came to him travelling on a train:

> I was rounding a sharp railway curve once when I suddenly saw all the trees, houses, and factory chimneys along the track swerve from the vertical and assume a strikingly inclined position. What had hitherto appeared to me perfectly natural, namely, the fact that we distinguish the vertical so perfectly and sharply from every other direction, now struck me as enigmatical. Why is it that the same direction can now appear vertical to me and now cannot? By what is the vertical distinguished for us?[40]

Mach returned to his lab, where in 1873 he proceeded to build an apparatus to figure out the role of acceleration in human orientation. This new device consisted of a series of three interlocking wooden frames, with a chair for the test subject at the centre. The outer frame was fixed; the middle frame was placed on a pivot (A-A in Figure 5.2), allowing it to be rotated. The innermost frame could also be rotated around a vertical pivot and was

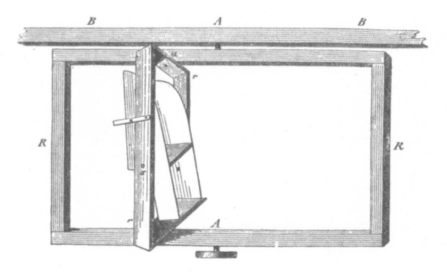

Figure 5.2 Mach's apparatus for testing perception of acceleration. | Ernst Mach, "On Sensations of Orientation" (1897) 8:1 Monist 81 at 83.

placed on a track so that its centre ("aa" in Figure 5.2 – visible above the pivot and in the shadow of the central frame) could be fixed at varying distances from the pivot of rotation (A-A). The experimental subject was placed in a large paper box, so as to deprive him of all visual and tactile information other than that which the apparatus produced.

What Mach observed was striking. If the subject were placed at a distance from the axis of rotation (A-A) and rotated, he would perceive the earth's gravitational pull to be at a tilt corresponding to the combination of gravity and the centrifugal force generated by the apparatus. The subject would thus insist that the paper box was being tilted when it was not, and would register this observation objectively using a pointer.[41] What Mach had discovered was a phenomenon that would become a major concern forty years later, when early airplane pilots would suffer an epidemic of what came to be called "ear deaths": "our balance system was designed for one thing: two-legged travel on Earth's terra firma ... But when we venture into the air, gravity no longer seems constant; moving through the three dimensions of space, the brain can be led to misinterpret centrifugal force – the pull caused by turning and climbing and diving – as gravitational force."[42]

Having found that humans – including Mach himself – could be severely disoriented or "tricked" into feeling sensations that were not real, by means of this and similar apparatuses, Mach attempted to trace the evolutionary origins of balance back through other creatures. Like Flourens, Mach began using small creatures (mice, birds, and rabbits), placing them within a "cyclostat" – an enclosure that could be rotated rapidly in order to observe the effects on the animals.[43]

Twenty years later, Mach would concur with Breuer on another key idea: evolutionarily speaking, the sense of hearing was very recent. The sense of balance – which had only recently been connected to aural structures at all – was actually the ear's primary, primordial function. Mach based this on both his own observations of crustaceans and birds and his reading of contemporary publications by Breuer, James, and others from across the sciences:

> In the lower animals the analogue of the labyrinth is shrunk to a little vesicle filled with a liquid and containing tiny crystals, auditive stones, or otoliths, of greater specific gravity, suspended on minute hairs. These crystals appear physically well adapted for indicating both the direction of gravity and the direction of incipient movements ...
>
> If we will but reflect how small a portion of the labyrinth of higher animals is apparently in the service of the sense of hearing, and how large, on

the other hand, the portion is which serves the purposes of orientation ... the view is irresistible suggested which Breuer and I ... expressed, that the auditive organ took its development from an organ for sensing movements by adaptation to weak periodic motional stimuli.[44]

In other words, the sense of hearing in higher animals was a refinement of the ear's older, more primary functions – using changes in pressure to provide feedback on a given creature's movements and orienting the body with respect to gravity.

Ernst Mach and Decentring the Sensory Universe

Mach's later writings, especially "The Analysis of the Sensations" and "On Sensations of Orientation," mark a shift away from objective measurement and towards an analysis of subjective experience. These writings intermingle a number of observations from Mach and others, including those of Flourens and James:

> [James] found that many deaf and dumb people on being ducked under water, whereby they lose their weight and consequently have no longer the full assistance of their muscular sense, utterly lose their sense of position in space, do not know which is up and which is down, and are thrown into the greatest consternation – results which do not occur in normal men. Such facts are convincing proof that we do not orientate ourselves entirely by means of the labyrinth, important as it is for us.[45]

Mach took James's experiments as "proof that we do not orientate ourselves entirely by means of the labyrinth" in the sense that balance is as much learned or situational as it is physiological or innate. In other words, each (particular) body balances in its own (particular) way. As further evidence of this idea, Mach cited case studies of humans and other creatures who learned to navigate their worlds in ways that defied normal sensory logics, including crustaceans and a blind cat that Mach worked with in the lab.

Mach's assertions in "On Sensations of Orientation" perform three simultaneous decentrings: first, because they are built upon an elision of human and nonhuman sensory experience, they exhibit a strong move away from human exceptionalism. Second, these writings reconceptualize bodies (both human and nonhuman) as varied and variably adapted to their environments. Finally, Mach's work pointed to the apotheosis of Copernican development in ways of thinking about human perceptions and observations of the universe. In his work, Mach sees human perception itself as a result of processes in the physical universe rather than as a way of accurately measuring such processes. Thus, he writes:

> Everyone who disbelieves in sensations of movement should be made acquainted with these phenomena [referring to the disorientation experienced by his subjects in the "paper box" experiment]. Had Newton known them and had he ever observed how we may actually imagine ourselves turned and displaced in space without the assistance of stationary bodies as points of reference, he would certainly have been confirmed more than ever in his unfortunate speculations regarding absolute space.[46]

Here, Mach was anticipating two of the twentieth century's most revolutionary upheavals: relativity's shift away from absolute space and time, and the turn away from scientific objectivism signalled by phenomenology. What had begun seven decades before with Flourens, as an investigation into the anatomy and physiology of the inner ear in lower creatures, had helped set the stage for deeper, more skeptical inquiry about both the nature of sensation and its limits in helping humanity understand its place within the universe.

NOTES

1 Tutis Villis, "Vestibular System and Eye Movements" (2013) *Brain Notes for Medical Students*, online: <http://www.tutis.ca/NeuroMD/L8Ves/Ves.pdf>.
2 Scott McCredie, *Balance: In Search of the Lost Sense* (New York: Little, Brown & Co, 2007) at 246.
3 Villis, *supra* note 1.
4 *Ibid.*
5 Jonathan Sterne, *The Audible Past* (Durham, NC: Duke University Press, 2003).
6 Veit Erlmann, *Reason and Resonance* (Brooklyn, NY: Zone Books, 2010).
7 McCredie, *supra* note 2 at 243.
8 Here I use "deaf," rather than "Deaf," in order to emphasize the nascent character of what would become the Deaf community and to emphasize deaf-ness as a social relation determined (in this particular case) by those who occupied and acted on behalf of a privileged "norm."
9 Bruce Smith, "Listening to the Wild Blue Yonder" in Veit Erlmann, ed, *Hearing Cultures* (New York: Berg, 2004) at 21.
10 Barry Truax, *Acoustic Communication,* 2d (Santa Barbara, CA: Praeger, 2000).
11 Murray R Schafer, *The Soundscape* (Rochester, VT: Destiny Books, 1993).
12 Smith, *supra* note 9.
13 Alain Corbin, "Charting the Cultural History of the Senses" in David Howes, ed, *Empire of the Senses* (New York: Berg, 2004) 128 at 129.

14   *Ibid* at 130.
15   Tobin Siebers, *Disability Aesthetics* (Ann Arbor: University of Michigan Press, 2010) at 19.
16   *Ibid* at 4–5.
17   *Ibid* at 32–33.
18   Joseph Straus, "Inversional Balance and the 'Normal' Body in the Music of Arnold Schoenberg and Anton Webern" in Neil Lerner & Joseph Straus, eds, *Sounding Off: Theorizing Disability and Music* (New York: Routledge, 2006) 257.
19   Siebers, *supra* note 15 at 32.
20   *Ibid* at 122.
21   David Howes, "Hearing Scents, Tasting Sights: Toward a Cross-Cultural Multi-Modal Theory of Aesthetics" (Paper delivered at the Art and the Senses Conference, 2006, Oxford, UK) [unpublished].
22   Alan Dunn & Allen Singer, "Alexander Gottlieb Baumgarten" in Alan Singer & Allen Dunn, *Literary Aesthetics: A Reader* (Malden, MA: Blackwell, 2000) 154.
23   Sterne, *supra* note 5 at 31–35.
24   *Ibid* [emphasis in original].
25   Joseph E Hawkins & Jochen Schacht, "Sketches of Otohistory" (2005) Audiology & Neurotology 185.
26   Lawrence Lustig & Anil Lalwani, "The History of Ménière's Disease" (1997) 30 Otolaryngologic Clinics of North America 917.
27   *Ibid* at 924–29.
28   *Ibid* at 933.
29   Hawkins & Schacht, *supra* note 25 at 186.
30   Dan McKenzie, "Ménière's Original Case" (1924) J Laryngology & Otology 446.
31   Lustig & Lalwani, *supra* note 26 at 927.
32   Susan Stewart, "Remembering the Senses" in David Howes, ed, *Empire of the Senses* (New York: Berg, 2005) 59.
33   Lustig & Lalwani, *supra* note 26 at 928.
34   *Ibid.*
35   Lennard Davis, *Enforcing Normalcy* (New York: Verso, 1995) at 83.
36   William James, "Sense of Dizziness in Deaf-Mutes" (1881) Mind 412.
37   George Parker, "On Vertigo" (1885) 7 Brain 514 at 520–21.
38   *Ibid.*
39   V Henn, "E. Mach on the Analysis of Motion Sensation" (1984) 3:3 Human Neurobiology 145.
40   Ernst Mach, "On Sensations of Orientation" (1897) 8:1 Monist 79 at 81.
41   Henn, *supra* note 39 at 146.
42   McCredie, *supra* note 2 at 124.
43   Hawkins & Schacht, *supra* note 25 at 187.
44   Mach, *supra* note 40 at 92–95.
45   *Ibid* at 90.
46   *Ibid* at 84.

"Of Dark Type and Poor Physique"
Law, Immigration Restriction, and Disability in Canada, 1900–30

JEN RINALDI AND JAY DOLMAGE

This chapter provides an overview or genealogy of Canadian policies and practices of immigration restriction that were based on evolving eugenic ideas of race and disability in the early part of the twentieth century. We fold together legislative histories, archival documents, and popular texts to investigate the ways that new categories of race and disability were constructed and reinforced as immigration into Canada accelerated between 1900 and 1930. These policies and practices, it will be shown, were powerfully influenced by ideas about the Canadian environment and the forms of labour needed to reshape and subsist in this environment, but they were also profoundly influenced by at times shocking ideas about race and genetics. This history is thus imbricated with Canadian trade interests and colonialism, including settler colonialism, as well as eugenic philosophies influenced by industrialism and agriculture. The chapter provides an important backdrop, which gives context not only for the other labour and social movement histories in this collection, but also for current Canadian immigration laws and policies.

Our research brings together disability studies, legal studies, and rhetoric, with emphases on both legal history and archival research to investigate the peak era of Canadian immigration in the early part of the twentieth century, focusing on the ways that racial and disability categories were used to exclude, deport, and reject immigrant groups and individuals. Thus, a keyword for this overview is "eugenics." Charles Davenport, an American cited by many as the eugenics movement's greatest proponent, defined the movement as "the science of the improvement of the human race by better breeding."[1] Yet alongside these genetic goals, immigration restriction gave eugenicists an opportunity to construct an improved national body by excluding undesirable races. To do so, eugenicists suggested that certain racial and ethnic groups were disabled, biologically inferior.[2] For instance, in Canada, eugenicists such as C.K. Clarke suggested that "feeble-minded" immigrants from certain parts of Europe "invariably mated with the mental weaklings in their own class as partners, thus perpetuating a race of defectives."[3] This threat fuelled Clarke's increasingly vehement calls for immigration inspection and restriction at the Canadian borders between 1909 and his death in 1924.

Popular history tends to tie eugenics to Nazi Germany, yet historians have shown that the US Immigration Restriction League and the American Eugenics Society were hugely influential organizations that established rhetorics of eugenics in the United States long before the Nazi program, and in fact served as exemplars. Canadian historians tend to isolate Canadian eugenics mainly to forced sterilization programs, which began in the late 1920s and were most popular in the West. Yet Canada had its own extremely influential but often overlooked eugenics movement beginning at the turn of the twentieth century, one with clear connections across the country and across the Atlantic. Beginning in the early 1900s, and rooted in the geographies of immigration, Canada developed its own public figures, texts, discourses, spaces, and visual rhetorics of eugenics.

As Janice Cavell and others have shown, Canada always had the eugenic aim of preserving "Canada's predominantly British character."[4] Yet this developed into more negative eugenic goals and restrictions. One effect was the rhetorical darkening and disabling of the non-British immigrant in the public mind. William Lyon Mackenzie King wrote in 1908 that the idea "that Canada should remain a white man's country is believed to be not only desirable for economic and social reasons but highly necessary on political and national grounds."[5]

Despite this history, relatively little has been done to study Canadian eugenics, immigration restriction, or the confluence between these movements. In what follows, we first map out the implementation of laws explicitly restricting immigration of specific racial, ethnic, and/or religious groups. We link these laws to eugenic public discourse that insinuated the undesirability of these groups along genetic lines. By doing so, we reveal the public face of eugenic immigration restriction in Canadian history. But we also offer a few specific archival examples of the ways that eugenics functioned as an extra-legal, behind-the-scenes, but nonetheless powerfully influential everyday sentiment or rhetoric that shaped Canadian immigration history.

Early Canadian Immigration Law: Anti-Asian Eugenics

Following Confederation, the 1867 *British North America Act* (later the *Constitution Act, 1867*) included two provisions relevant to immigration: section 91(25), which conferred on the federal government exclusive authority over naturalization (or the acquisition of Canadian citizenship) and aliens (immigrants who had not or not yet been naturalized as citizens); and section 95, which ensured both federal and provincial jurisdictions over immigration law.[6] Beyond this Act, there were few restrictions on immigration until the dawn of the twentieth century.[7]

These restrictions materialized in response to what Timothy Caufield and Gerald Robertson call "a climate of growing suspicion and fear over the rising tide of immigrants to Canada, particularly from Eastern and Southern Europe and the Orient."[8] Anti-Asian sentiment, or alarm over the "Yellow Peril,"[9] could be found in both Parliamentary rhetoric and street rioting, and resulted in the *Chinese Immigration Act* of 1885. Under section 4 of this federal statute, Chinese immigrants were each required to pay a fee upon entering Canada, something later called a head tax.[10] Payment of the tax meant the immigrant would be issued a certificate of entry. Chinese persons already living in Canada had the option, though were not legally required, to pay a smaller fee for a certificate of residence.[11] These certificates could be produced as evidence of compliance with the statute. Originally the Act required immigrants to forfeit their certificates should they leave the country for an extended period of time and repay upon their return, although the parameters of this rule were challenged in court.[12] With successive legislative amendments, the head tax was $100 by the year 1900, then raised to $500 in 1903.[13]

This tax remained in effect for twenty years thereafter, until the 1923 *Chinese Immigration Act* excluded Chinese immigrants entirely, except under extremely narrow circumstances. According to section 5 of the statute, "the entry to or landing in Canada of persons of Chinese origin or descent irrespective of allegiance or citizenship, is confined to the following classes":[14] diplomats, Canadian citizens born of Chinese parents who temporarily left the country, merchants, and students. The Act significantly reduced Chinese immigration, far more effectively than the head tax had done. These federal strategies had the effect of separating families: the head tax resulted in family patriarchs immigrating to and working in Canada until they could afford the head tax for each family member; employment exclusion and low wages functioned as roadblocks until legislation made it altogether impossible for residents to send for their families.[15]

In addition to federal immigration law, provinces took up tactics to exclude Asian immigrants from employment. These strategies included the 1903 amendment to the British Columbia *Coal Mines Regulation Act*, the second attempt of its kind. The 1890 amendment under section 4 read: "No boy under the age of twelve years, and no woman or girl of any age, and no Chinaman, shall be employed in or allowed to be for the purpose of employment in any mine to which this Act applies."[16] The amendment was challenged and struck down in court,[17] but in 1903 the BC legislature tried again. The new language in the statute read as follows: "No Chinaman or person unable to speak English shall be appointed to or shall occupy any position of trust or responsibility in or about a mine subject to this Act, whereby through his ignorance, carelessness or negligence he might endanger the life or limb of any person employed in or about a mine."[18] The language employed indicated that immigrants were untrustworthy or irresponsible and were seen as unfit for the work because they might jeopardize the lives and health of deserving citizens and employees.

Such sentiments were also embedded in the 1914 case *R v Quong Wing*,[19] which challenged Saskatchewan legislation that denied immigrant business-owners the right to hire white women. Under section 1 of the legislation in question:

> No person shall employ in any capacity any white woman or girl or permit any white woman or girl to reside or lodge in or to work in or, save as a bona fide customer in a public apartment thereof only, to frequent any restaurant, laundry or other place of business or amusement owned, kept or managed by any Japanese, Chinaman or other Oriental person.[20]

Plaintiff Quong Wing, a café owner from Moose Jaw, Saskatchewan, challenged the statute on the grounds that it was outside the province's authority to limit his business activities. The Supreme Court of Canada ruled that the pith and substance of the law was actually meant to regulate working conditions for white women, which was within provincial jurisdiction.[21] The statute remained in effect until 1947,[22] protecting white women for decades from the mythic Chinaman.

Indeed, reflected in exclusionary laws that regulated immigration and immigrants, as well as in the discourse conducted by political and judicial authorities to develop these laws, was a depiction of the Asian population as "depraved, degenerate, and conniving drug addicts who sought to undermine white society by seducing and ruining white women."[23] In an 1882 debate in the House of Commons, Sir John A. Macdonald claimed that the Chinese "would not be a wholesome element for this country,"[24] on the grounds that they were an inferior race, incapable of assimilation. He noted that Asian men entering Canada were leaving behind their wives in their countries of origin, a phenomenon later exacerbated with the imposition of a head tax. The resultant bachelor population stoked fears of "a mingling of the races."[25] These concerns persisted in a 1902 Royal Commission report on Chinese and Japanese immigration, which was presented in a 1903 Senate debate.[26] The report explored associations with opium dealing and human sex trafficking, and quoted anti-Asian sentiments. For example, Frances Kate Morgan, a teacher in a Chinese Girls' Home, opined: "I know [unrestricted immigration] is bad for the country. I see no signs of the Chinese adopting our mode of life; I think they are a menace to the public from their way of living." And railway superintendent Joseph Hunter claimed that "the presence of a transient population is inimical to the best interests of the country."[27] Fear of racial mingling seemed to entail only the mingling of immigrant men and white women, for head tax legislation since 1887 exempted women of Chinese origin as long as they married non-Chinese Canadian residents.[28] Female immigrants could more successfully assimilate, it would seem, because they could not compromise white patrilineal lines; and women who married into white households no longer embodied the stereotype of the transient or wayward immigrant.

While racism of the early 1900s especially targeted Chinese immigrants, South Asian populations also encountered legal obstacles. In 1914, when the *Komagata Maru* arrived at Vancouver's shoreline with 376 passengers from India, they were detained and then deported. Because the ship had travelled from India with stopovers in China and Japan, it had violated the "continuous journey rule." This rule, found in section 30 of the *Immigration Act,* prohibited "the landing in Canada of any specified class of immigrants who have come to Canada otherwise than by continuous journey from the country of which they are natives or citizens and upon through tickets purchased in that country."[29] Thus, immigrants travelling to Canada from distant countries were not permitted entry if they travelled by ships that stopped at ports along the way.

In *Canada v Singh*,[30] *Komagata Maru* passenger and British citizen Munshi Singh challenged the legality of his detention, and in so doing challenged the constitutionality of the *Immigration Act*'s recently developed regulation. His case and subsequent appeal were dismissed on the grounds that the federal government had complete authority to craft exclusionary immigration law:

> Under the authority so conferred, Canada has a right to make laws for the exclusion or expulsion of aliens ... and it seems to me plain beyond question that Canada has a right also to make laws for the exclusion and expulsion from Canada of British subjects whether of Asiatic race or of European race, irrespective of whether they come from Calcutta or London.[31]

This was not to say that British subjects hailing from London had to fear barriers in immigration law. The ruling went on to justify turning away "Hindu aliens," notwithstanding their British citizenship: "It is plain that upon study of the question, the Hindu race, as well as the Asiatic race in general, are, in their conception of life and ideas of society, fundamentally different to the Anglo-Saxon and Celtic races, and European races in general."[32] So, while the continuous journey rule made no explicit mention of race, the plainness of racial difference justified its legality.

As Andrew Parnaby and Gregory S. Kealey argue, anti-Asian immigration laws that expanded "Category Asian" to include citizens of British colonies (the authors cite what are now Bangladesh, India, Pakistan, and Sri Lanka) were tricky to accomplish: "unlike the Chinese and Japanese, [South Asian immigrants] were British subjects and possessed all the rights and freedoms associated with that status."[33] While laws since 1907 denied South Asian immigrants political rights and excluded them from employment opportunities,[34] no law comparable to the Chinese head tax or the *Chinese Immigration Act* applied to them.[35] But the continuous journey rule contained the promise of a crafty solution, one of several developed in Canada during this timeframe,[36] by imposing what was arguably an impossible condition on travellers from South Asian colonies.

Race and Contamination

Overlaying this history is a negative and eugenic framing of the immigrant body as a site and source of contamination – of evil, deficiency, or disease.[37] That was certainly how the Asian body so feared in the early 1900s was framed, and this view only expanded as new and different groups of immigrants began to seek a new home in Canada. Such a framing is haunted by and entangled with disability. For instance, in a historical analysis of early twentieth-century US "ugly laws" – antivagrancy ordinances that themselves emerged from eugenic projects and sought to protect public spaces from unsightly disease and deformity – Susan M. Schweik demonstrates that legal constructions of othered embodiments at the time lumped together the immigrant with the mendicant, the criminal, and the sick. Citing Diana Courvant, she characterizes the intersection of race, poverty, and disability as a confluence of rivers: "different currents but not entirely different matter of substance."[38] Therefore, socio-legal histories of race and disability can be read together, through one another, to articulate the varied and complex contours of eugenics.

Restrictions pertaining to the physically and mentally infirm were built into Canada's original immigration legislation of 1869;[39] and the 1886 *Immigration Act* established screening and quarantine processes, where failure to report the medical conditions of inspected steamship passengers resulted in financial penalties.[40] In 1902, the statute was amended to prohibit the entry of immigrants "suffering from any loathsome, dangerous or infectious disease or malady."[41] When debating the amendment in the House of Commons, Member of Parliament Frank Oliver held that "the first consideration [in immigration standards] should be the intellectual as well as the physical quality of those immigrants."[42]

In the 1906 iteration of the statute, under sections 26–28, the following persons constituted classes prohibited from entering Canada and to be turned away on Canadian shorelines: physically and mentally disabled persons, or anyone "who is feeble-minded, an idiot, or an epileptic, or who is insane, or has had an attack of insanity within five years; [who is] deaf, or dumb, blind or infirm";[43] persons with diseases that are "loathsome ... contagious or infectious and which may become dangerous to the public health or widely disseminated";[44] and impoverished persons, or anyone "who is a pauper, or destitute, a professional beggar, or vagrant, or who is likely to become a public charge ... or has become a charge upon the public funds."[45] The silver lining of an exception under section 26, that disabled persons were admissible as long as they had families willing and able to provide permanent support, was left out of the 1910 amendments in cases of mental defect.[46] As Valentina Capurri has further explored, with the passage of this statute, persons with mental deficiencies and "loathsome or infectious diseases" were automatically and absolutely barred from entering the country.[47]

Passengers would be deemed members of prohibited classes, particularly those classes related to health status, after inspections. Following earlier practices under quarantine acts, sections 21–23 of the 1906 *Immigration Act* required medical inspections upon arrival, and those immigrants who did not receive a stamp of approval from the inspecting medical officer were refused entry and detained.[48] These amendments were introduced to the statute under Frank Oliver, by then minister of the interior, whose approach to immigration could be described as a closed-door policy on the basis of cultural origin. He advocated for legislative reform "to give the department in control of immigration greater authority to deal with immigrants who, for one reason or another, may be properly subjected to restriction on their landing in Canada."[49] Government officials were extended broad and absolute discretionary power to manage immigration, invested in boards of inquiry that were stationed at each Canadian port.[50] Throughout his tenure, Oliver would continue to expand the reach of port gatekeepers and tighten borders in order to, in his own words, "weed out and send back the undesirable."[51]

The legislating of medical inspections did encounter jurisprudential challenges. In *Re Chin Chee*,[52] the case's namesake had been a Vancouver resident for over ten years before visiting China, his country of origin. When he returned to Canada by steamship, the port medical officer subjected him to an examination and diagnosed him with trachoma, a contagious bacterial condition that can cause blindness. Chin Chee contested his detainment and the court ruled in his favour, deeming it unreasonable to extend the term "passenger" under immigration legislation to include long-established permanent Canadian residents returning home from travels. In the 1907 case *Ikezoya v Canadian Pacific Railway Company*,[53] four ship passengers from Japan to Vancouver who were inspected upon arrival were recommended for deportation: three were found to have trachoma, and a fourth was a child who "might become a public charge owing to the condition of its eyes."[54] The plaintiffs successfully petitioned for the right to have port medical officer examinations reviewed.

Notwithstanding case law that imposed limits to medical inspections, politicians still defended the screening process and argued for its expansion, evidenced in Eugene Paquet's remarks in the House of Commons:

> Let us adopt the most rational methods in the selection of our immigrants. Let us vote the necessary amounts to organize on the best footing our medical system of inspection; let us give to our medical inspectors the required

help; let us build isolation hospitals; let us receive in becoming and proper fashion those who are admitted into the great Canadian family circle. These immigrants, *if they are properly selected* ... will love Canada, our laws, our institutions, and will help in the development of our agriculture, our commerce and our industries.[55]

This impassioned call in the House to support medical inspection infrastructure would be echoed again and again, even a decade later when Rodolphe Lemieux expressed concern over hurried medical examinations of immigrants: "The result was that unfortunately a poor class of immigrant was sometimes admitted. I was startled the other day to see the figures of the feeble minded in the province of Manitoba."[56] Dissatisfied politicians suggested there be inspections on ships en route to Canada, and even in countries of origin prior to departing for Canada. As Ena Chadha notes in her review of House of Commons transcripts, calls for more complex and careful inspection processes were frequently raised in the early twentieth century, on the grounds that people of poor mental and moral fibre were slipping through the cracks; she observes, "the debates reveal the overwhelming frustration of lawmakers decrying lax immigration screening procedures."[57]

But alarm bells were sounded over the need for more caution and care only to ensure that fewer immigrants were admitted into the country, that is, that more be routed out for their undesirability and turned away at ports. The list of prohibited classes was broad in scope, and medical officials' diagnoses of disease or defect could be rendered based on scant evidence. Unless court challenges were issued, as was the case in *Chin Chee* and *Ikezoya*, lawmakers demanding reform meant only for there to be stricter standards and did not address inspections that yielded detention and deportation orders.

Tightening and Expanding the Borders

Medical inspections were spectacles that strongly influenced the first experience of Canada for most arriving aliens. In the years of peak immigration between 1900 and 1930, the inspection process at Canadian immigration stations empowered inspectors to recognize defective bodies through just a glancing appraisal, what Anne-Emmanuelle Birn calls "snapshot diagnosis."[58] These snapshot inspections were used at Pier 21 in Halifax, but such inspections were also undertaken very explicitly at the Grosse Île quarantine station on the lower St. Lawrence River, to ensure that no "defective" or contagious immigrants made their way to Quebec City. Similar processes were in place at the Partridge Island and Middle Island quarantine stations in New Brunswick and the William Head station on Vancouver Island, though these have not been studied in depth.

At these inspection stations, a key criterion for rejection or deportation was the (perhaps intentionally) vague clause "All immigrants who are unable to satisfy the agent or Inspector-in-charge either that they have independent means of support or that they are suited to farm work and intend to engage in such work, are liable to be excluded."[59] Circulars among immigration agents beginning in 1909 detail how this clause was to be implemented.[60] Yet nearly a decade later, in 1918, agents admitted this clause was an ongoing "source of considerable confusion."[61] Their solution was to make an ad hoc amendment to the clause in pen and ink, and then communicate this nonbinding amendment via circular among immigration agents. The correction suggested that agents "may relax" this liability for exclusion "if satisfied that the immigrant is in all other respects an acquisition to Canada."[62] Then, "this amendment shall be exercised in the cases of immigrants of only the following races: English, Scotch, Irish, Welsh, French, Belgian, Scandinavian, Dutch and Swiss." "Finnish" was later added by hand.[63] E. Blake Robertson, the assistant immigration inspector at the time, suggested that, "The countries in which immigration effort is carried on, or is to be carried on, should be enumerated; otherwise the inspectors will not understand clearly what is meant."[64] What this meant was that, in fact, the clause had always been intended to be applied only to immigrants from nondesired countries, and would be interpreted as such. The agents – in essence – decided that only immigrants from certain countries could engage in the work needed to stay in Canada. Thus, immigrants from all other countries were disabled, rhetorically. If an immigrant was from one of the countries in Robertson's informal list, and thus desirably "raced," according to their calculus, inspectors could use their discretion to allow landing in Canada; if not, then no discretion could be used at all. This list was never legally added to the clause – yet before 1918 the list certainly existed implicitly as part of the nature of the code, and after 1918 Robertson made it an explicit aspect of the code's application, albeit scribbled in by hand. These circulars can still be found in the Immigration Fonds (or collection of archival documents) at Library and Archives Canada (LAC).

Canadian restrictionists also effectively used law that made possible the deportation of immigrants for up to two years after their arrival, stretching the inspection process out and redistributing responsibility across a range of social institutions. Under section 33 of the 1906 iteration of the *Immigration Act,*[65] immigrants who had committed a crime "involving moral turpitude" or had been committed to a hospital or charitable institution within two years of arriving in Canadian were targeted. Municipal officials were responsible for reporting these cases to the minister of the interior, who would order deportations, whenever possible at the expense of the immigrant in question: the Immigration Fonds at LAC are full of negotiations between agents, agencies, steamship lines, and individuals regarding who was to be held to account for the cost of these deportations. In fact, these particular archival records are dominated by correspondence between Canadian National (the major steamship line at the time) and immigration officials about who is to blame for an "undesirable" immigrant landing in Canada. This debate led to much more stringent inspection at foreign ports before potential immigrants could even board a ship. As Angus McLaren has shown, this practice led to over ten thousand persons forbidden entry to Canada in the 1920s – a number that was "still not enough" to quell the concerns of eugenicists.[66]

Still dissatisfied with even this temporal and geographical extension for inspection and refusal or deportation, Uriah Wilson in the House of Commons cited Dr. C.K. Clarke's recommendation that the two-year window be doubled and offered his own opinion that there should be no time limit for deporting immigrants who became public charges: "If people come into this country who are not able to take care of themselves, who have to be sent to an insane asylum, or other places, to be supported by the public, I do not see why we should retain them at all."[67] Wilson was among a vocal chorus of early twentieth-century Canadian lawmakers who expressed concern over the inadequacy of initial medical inspections. This two-year leeway period for deporting immigrants would remain, designed to catch and expel those who could pass as nondisabled at the examination stage of the immigration process. As Wilson's testimony in the House of Commons made clear, support for these deportations was considerable.[68]

In this way, eugenics proponents effectively used and sanctioned specialized public spaces and institutions to enforce immigration restriction. There were dozens of cases of public officials across the country writing to immigration agents, complaining of having to deport individuals just weeks after they had arrived because inspection itself had been "deficient." In one publicized instance, the Toronto School Board wrote to immigration officials complaining that nearly one thousand students "recommended for classes for the mentally subnormal" were either born outside of Canada or to parents born outside of Canada, and many were "so sub-normal that they should have been noticed readily at the ports of entry."[69] These complaints were repeated in a *Toronto Globe* article from 12 November 1925, with the title "Immigration Barrier Is Not Tight Enough."[70] Importantly, as Geoffrey Reaume has shown, "people labeled 'mentally defective' covered a wide variation in human expressions and appearances that were deemed unacceptable" – including mad people, "racialized and ethnic minorities, females, and [the] working class."[71] A tightened border, then, could be used to reject and remove a wide variety of "undesirable" bodies. The stated basis for this removal might be their own, or their parents', country of origin. But the real reason for the rejections and deportations was rooted in ableism.

Complaints from newspapers and public officials like those from the Toronto School Board led to legislative changes but also a tightening at the border, and this is evident throughout the archival record of immigration agent correspondence. For instance, when there was concern that officials might be allowing in the wrong sort of biological stock, an official reminded his inspectors that "we would rather discourage five good members of a family than take in one who was subnormal."[72] In another example, immigration official Peter Bryce justified the deportation of a young girl named Daisy Fetch by writing that, although her deportation would cause "a great deal of inconvenience for her relatives ... you will understand that our action is taken solely in the interest of this country and for the protection of future generations."[73] When a woman deemed insane ended up at a mental hospital in Saskatchewan as a "public charge," a letter circulated to immigration officials chastising them, and reminding them that it was not the cost of caring for the woman that was the foremost concern. Instead, the emphasis was placed on the "menace in the future to this country from the progeny of such persons."[74] Again, this eugenic rhetoric invoked the idea that certain bodies were in effect a contagion, and did so to reinforce the selective power of the border, from the immigration stations on each coast to the social institutions in between, while expanding the timeframe for deportation. In such archival stories, we also see the extra-legal networks in place to enforce eugenic sentiments that may not have been policy but certainly became practice.

The Eugenic Construction of Intellect

Eugenic language also shaped Canadian immigration policy. One important facet of this language was the category of the "feeble-minded," used as a catch-all or "wastebasket term" in Canada as well as the United States. As historian Robert Menzies shows, between the 1920s and the outbreak of the Second World War, more than five thousand people were deported from Canada based on the "feeble-minded" diagnosis, a practice "bolstered by theories of eugenics and race betterment, and drawing on public fears about the unregulated influx of immigrants ... nourished by the flood of nativist, rac(ial)ist, exclusionist, eugenicist, and mental hygenist [sic] thinking in Canada during this period."[75] In this way, eugenics proponents effectively used a specific discourse and language to enforce immigration restriction. That language is woven into political archives that predate Menzies's historical analysis, illustrating the breadth of the history of eugenics rhetoric. In a 1919 House of Commons debate, Michael Steele raised concerns over immigrants arriving in Canada and spreading feeble-mindedness:

> I think we shall find that a very large number of such people are in our hospitals for the insane throughout the country, a burden that is laid upon this country, that will continue for years to come and that will grow in cost to Canada, because we know that these feeble-minded people, if they are not confined in some institution, multiply very rapidly.[76]

The burden of responsibility that immigration law imposed is a recurring theme in Parliamentary transcripts, found also in Paquet's statement that "on our shoulders rests the burden of establishing European civilization within our immense territory," and claims that feeble-mindedness – bred freely among undesirable immigrants – posed a threat to this mandate: "Deficients and feeble-minded persons are too frequently admitted in our country. Oftentimes they become criminals, patrons of our jails and hospitals. Should they remain at large, then their descendants will bear the imprint of degeneracy."[77] So the term "feeble-mindedness," that subset of conditions under the general category of mental deficiency, was complex, with notions and fears of poverty, criminality, and racial contamination folded in.

The invention of the term "moron" then became another important weapon for immigration restriction. This term was invented by American Henry Goddard in 1910, and the classification was key to research he performed on immigrants at Ellis Island beginning in 1913. As Anna Stubblefield has argued, Goddard's invention of this term as a "signifier of tainted whiteness" was the "most important contribution to the concept of feeble-mindedness as a signifier of a racial taint," through the diagnosis of the menace of alien races, but also as a way to divide out the impure elements of the white race.[78] The moron was seen as, in the words of Goddard's contemporary and sometimes colleague Margaret Sanger, "the mental defective who is glib and plausible, bright looking and attractive."[79] This person "may not merely lower the whole level of intelligence in a school or in a society, but may ... increase and multiply until he dominates and gives the prevailing 'color' – culturally speaking – to an entire community."[80] The moron was seen as a high-functioning feeble-minded individual, capable of "passing" as normal and of being attractive to normal individuals. The moron was often constructed as highly sexualized and thus could be held up as an even greater menace to the gene pool. In Canada, eugenicist C.K. Clarke wrote the unpublished novel *The Amiable Morons* to drum up Canadian worry about this newly designated danger. The novel warned of "the evil consequences of importing insane and defective immigrants [and] was circulated to members of the federal cabinet in Ottawa."[81] According to his biography, "this led to the amended Immigration Act of 1919 which extended the list of prohibited persons."[82] Clarke later spent a month in St. John's, "personally supervising the landing of some four thousand immigrants and instructing the inspectors on how to inspect them."[83] All of this is recounted in a celebratory tone in Cyril Greenland's 1966 memorial profile of Clarke.

In this way, eugenics had its own public champions in Canada, and eugenic ideas became popular. Terms like "moron," though still very young, filled public discourse and fomented public fear of immigration. McLaren argues that for Canadian eugenicists, their final "chief success" was not necessarily even the drastic increase in restriction and deportation focused on specific groups of immigrants after 1919. Instead, it was "in popularizing biological arguments."[84] That is, eugenic immigration restriction not only reshaped the Canadian body, but it also reshaped how Canadians thought about bodies and minds, as well as the environments from which they came and into which they were coming.

Climactic Suitability and Labour

While anti-Asian legislation was often explicitly exclusionary, tactics like the continuous journey rule made exclusion possible without citing races by name; so too did strategies developed to implicitly mark black bodies as undesirable. Alongside the continuous journey rule (which was by then under section 38(a)), section 38(c) of the 1910 *Immigration Act* allowed the government to prohibit the landing of immigrants "belonging to any race deemed unsuited to the climate or requirements of Canada."[85] This section of the legislation was expanded in 1919 to prohibit the following immigrants:

> [Those] deemed unsuitable having regard to the climatic, industrial, social, educational, labour or other conditions or requirements of Canada or because such immigrants are deemed undesirable owing to their peculiar

customs, habits, modes of life and methods of holding property, and because of their probable inability to become readily assimilated.[86]

Decades later, the *Immigration Act* of 1952 still allowed agents to exclude immigrants on the basis of "climatic suitability." In short, this practice solidified the sense that only certain sanctioned races were biologically matched to the Canadian environment, even as settlers were drastically altering that very same environment in ways that were making it toxic to the peoples who had actually been living on the land for generations. For instance, James Daschuk's recent *Clearing the Plains: Disease, Politics of Starvation, and the Loss of Aboriginal Life* looks at how the arrival of disease interacted with the ecological change and harm brought first by the fur trade and later by large-scale agriculture to sow the seeds of the historical and contemporary health disparities between Aboriginal peoples and settlers in "Canada."[87] Regardless, the notion that some bodies were suited to immigrate to, live in, and work in Canada has always shaped immigration law.[88]

In the early part of the twentieth century, the Canadian government, with the help of Canadian National (CN), a major rail and steamship line, was also promoting immigration *into* the country. That is, Canada was promoting the immigration of desired people from desired countries, and was constructing a tailored identity for Canada in the process. The state did so by going overseas to recruit. As one agent wrote in the 1922 Canadian Department of Immigration *Annual Report,* "our agents would be equipped as missionaries of Canada, carrying propaganda to the smallest town and remotest Hamlet."[89] Canada's two most highly regarded photographers, William Topley and John Woodruff, were paid to take photographs of Canada that could then be used in "magic lantern slide shows" and lectures that would promote the country to potential immigrants from the United States and western Europe.[90] Many of the photos were of summer landscapes – crops, gigantic apples and huge tomatoes, men at work in farm fields, choice livestock. The images made clear arguments about the Canadian environment, and about the labour desired and needed in Canada. This focus on the fecundity of the land turned these shows into spectacles of settler colonialism, promising this land to preferred immigrant groups.[91] Lecturers, when they delivered the magic lantern shows, also addressed negative myths about Canada. For instance, the cold winter was reframed as having "done an enormous good in keeping out the Negro races and those less athletic races of southern Europe."[92] The myth of threatening "natives" was addressed by showing pictures of Aboriginal youth "under control" at residential schools. Preferred ethnic groups were showcased in photos taken in the moments after they had passed successfully through Pier 2, Pier 21, or another immigration station. An image of a "deformed idiot" has also been found among photos used in these slide shows, suggesting that agents also wanted to show prospective immigrants the types of bodies and minds that were not welcome.

The magic lantern shows, their valorization of the Canadian landscape as a place of robust production, as well as their placement of potential immigrant bodies on farms, tied into evolving immigration law. Recall, for instance, this vague clause: "All immigrants who are unable to satisfy the agent or Inspector-in-charge either that they have independent means of support or that they are suited to farm work and intend to engage in such work, are liable to be excluded."[93] Circulars among immigration agents beginning in 1909 detail how this clause was to be implemented and, as mentioned above, developed their own clear categories of desirable ethnic and racial groups.[94]

The delineation between "racial" groups was stark, but so was the circularity and informality of the process itself – the fate of entire groups was determined in letters between a few men, hastily typed up and revised in pen and ink. Repeatedly, these important decisions were made, excluding entire racial and ethnic groups, in ways that were justified by extremely flawed eugenic ideas about what type of body could or should be allowed into Canada. For instance, in March of 1927, a group of seven Macedonian immigrants was issued certificates in Zagreb by the Canadian officer there, F.W. Baumbgartner. When they arrived in Canada on 24 March, they were rejected for being "of dark type and poor physique."[95] This description alone speaks to the idea that the category of "poor physique" most often hinged on other ethnic or racial factors. No one could formally be rejected for being of "dark type," and yet yoking this characteristic to "poor physique" created grounds for exclusion. This shows just one way in which Canadian immigration linked racial types with insinuations of biological deficiency. Here, the idea also was that only those with a satisfactory physique were suited to the labour, climactic, and environmental demands of Canada.

In this case, Baumbgartner was essentially blamed for having issued certificates to this group of men. He responded by offering the CN continental superintendent, as well as Canada's deputy minister of immigration, a lesson on political history, geography, and race. He promised that no passenger with skin of even a "slight degree dark shade" would be given a certificate.[96] He then went on, in great detail, to discuss the regions from which each of these men came, defending the stock from these regions as "good woodmen" or as having a "deep seated democratic spirit."[97] Baumbgartner did admit that "ethnographic conditions" in many of these regions were "extremely complicated," and he even made an effort to parse these complications. He concluded that "the selection is not easy and [neither is] the rejection of the apparently for Canada undersirable [sic] types ... but a severer selection is possible."[98] In these definitions and clarifications, we can see the ways that certain regions of the world were being mapped as zones of environmental and embodied undesirability.

CN responded by issuing instructions to its overseas agents that no certificates were to be given to any passengers from southern Serbia or Dalmatia, "or to any immigrant slightly dark in colour."[99] Baumbgartner's lesson on race also resulted in CN suggesting to F.C. Blair, the acting deputy minister of immigration, that "it will always be difficult to define precisely the degree of colour which should bar an applicant." Dr. Black, the CN representative, then also, perhaps defensively, suggested that, "in the examination of these immigrants, it is sometimes necessary to inspect the skin underneath the clothing as in many cases the arms, neck, and face are somewhat dark owing to exposure."[100]

In these ways, agents manufactured shades of nonwhiteness, using darkness to symbolize genetic inferiority and using the inferiority to rescind whiteness. A result was that "black colour" and "dark races" became powerful tools for eugenic immigration restriction. Although long neglected, many further examples of this can be found in the Canadian archival record. For instance, when a young woman named Louise Abbott was rejected and deported from Canada for being "feeble-minded," the nationality on her medical certificate was marked as "negro."[101] Pier 21 historian Jan Raska recounts the similar case of Rebecca Barnett, who faced deportation in 1907 and was labelled "[u]ndesirable (insane) (black)."[102] In short, while other medical cards listed nationality by country, if one was "black" or a "negro," such a designation superseded country of origin, or made nationality immaterial, and at the same time was linked to mental and physical inferiority.

Opportunistic eugenic uses of the concept or label of disability have always operated as a key or central theme within Canada's colonial history. Undesirable bodies were held up at the border in service of the desire for a particular type of colonial Canadian, the valorization of certain forms of Canadian labour, and the preservation of a sense of the Canadian environment, which itself was rapidly changing in the period as result of settler colonialism.

This rhetorical history can and should also be mapped upon contemporary debates. Modern eugenic rhetoric, while not as overt as turn-of-the-century sentiment, continues to inflect citizenship debates and to shape both race and disability. The 2001 *Immigration and Refugee Protection Act* (IRPA), still in effect, outlines admissible immigrant classes, including an economic or skilled working class.[103] Persons admissible under this class qualify according to a points-based system that assesses, among other factors, education level, language proficiency, and work experience – arguably markers of privilege that would require some means to accumulate.

As Judith Mosoff indicates, Canadian immigration statistics reflect a preference for foreign nationals admitted on economic over humanitarian grounds.[104] While race is no longer explicitly cited as an exclusionary criterion in immigration law, policy, or practice, historic racial and colonial relations have shaped a world where poverty continues to intersect with race; so, while our politicians may no longer fill Parliamentary transcripts with lamentations and warnings about undesirable ethnicities (notwithstanding antiterrorism measures and reactions to Ebola epidemics),[105] there remain distinctive racial trends in those bodies that are disqualified from admission into the country based on quantitative assessments.

Those who enter Canada as temporary foreign workers or as workers without legal status remain vulnerable in the employment sector, not because there are laws that directly cast out specific derogated groups, but because of an absence of regulation. A silence that speaks volumes, this absence has resulted in deplorable living conditions, pay below minimum wage standards, and barriers to accessing or outright denial of insured healthcare services and compensation for workplace injury for these temporary workers.[106] Foreign bodies remain an expendable resource for labour, admissible only as long as they are useful. In the case of undocumented immigrants whose status exacerbates their experience of exploitation and the framing of their labour as expendable – manifest in the work they take up under sweatshop conditions – the legal response has entailed raids and mass deportations.[107]

Should foreign nationals not qualify under the economic class, they might still enter the country as dependants, under the family class.[108] This means that an immigrant admitted under the class of skilled worker can sponsor a spouse, child, or family relation who has a condition that requires service support. Still, dependants often remain inadmissible on health grounds, as long as their health condition can be constructed as posing a danger to public health or safety, or "might reasonably be expected to cause excessive demand on health or social services."[109]

Laws around the language of excessive demand have led to legal challenges: in a Supreme Court of Canada ruling over two related cases, *Hilewitz v*

Canada and *De Jong v Canada*,[110] David Hilewitz's and Dirk De Jong's permanent residence applications were denied on the IRPA grounds that their
intellectually disabled children could require social assistance in the future.
They contested the respective decisions and the Supreme Court of Canada
ruled in their favour, in part flagging a shift from categorical immigration
exclusion on the basis of disability to case-by-case assessments, but also and
largely because the two appellants indicated they could cover costs of care
and thereby not impose excessive demands on Canadian social and medical
infrastructure.

That Hilewitz and De Jong entered the country not as skilled workers but
as investors or entrepreneurs (a class that requires a sizable financial investment in Canadian business and is no longer listed in the IRPA) is worth noting, for recent deportation orders reported in media outlets have involved
persons or families of persons who risked imposing an excessive demand
or economic burden on the Canadian healthcare system or other social
services.[111] This practice of admitting immigrants with disabilities or health
problems on the condition that families vow to cover costs of medical care
can be dated back to as early as the 1906 iteration of the *Immigration Act,*
the statute responsible for first expanding the category "defective."[112] Roy
Hanes goes so far as to claim that "Canadian immigration legislation from
the mid-19th Century to the present day has consistently labeled people
with disabilities as non-desirable."[113] Moreover, a person marked by disability has throughout the history of restrictionist immigration law been discur-
sively situated in a relationship of dependency in order to qualify for admission into the country. As Robert Menzies argues, "while the mentally and
cognitively afflicted are no longer singled out for prohibition in Canadian
law, the code words of dependency and risk have become convenient discursive substitutes for lunacy and feeble-mindedness."[114] It is estimated that
two million Canadian immigrants undergo mental and physical examination each year; approximately four thousand are deported each year, and
this number is "almost certain to include an abundance of people deemed
psychiatrically ill" or physically unfit.[115] The accuracy and impact of such
attribution must be interrogated.

Further, issues of immigration were central to the 2015 Canadian federal
election. When Stephen Harper mentioned "old stock" Canadians during
a nationally televised debate, many commentators linked this to the history of eugenics: stock is an implicitly (or perhaps explicitly) eugenic term,
with allusions to genetics, and "old stock" most often means white, western European immigrants.[116] Presumably, "old stock" Canadians are not

"of dark type and poor physique," and Harper – whether unwittingly or intentionally – was appealing to anti-immigrant sentiment. In particular, "old stock" creates a discursive division: conveying the idea that there are good and bad immigrants, and that good immigrants come from particular parts of the world, a belief that we hope to have shown has deep roots in Canadian immigration (and eugenics) history.

Harper's government was also criticized for revoking healthcare coverage for refugees, many of whom we can assume could be disabled by war, travel, hunger, and poverty. This all occurred across the backdrop of a Syrian refugee crisis. When the Liberals defeated Harper and won a majority, one of their first acts was to reinstitute this healthcare coverage and to work on an arrangement to land a large number of these Syrian refugees.[117] Almost immediately thereafter, Donald Trump won the American presidency, and his racialized immigration rhetoric promised to change the landscape for refugees and immigrants across North America, with some Canadian political leaders on the right aligning with Trump, while others attempted to carefully allay his rhetoric. How Canadian lawmakers will respond in the coming years is yet to be seen. Doubtless, the history recounted here is crucially important to remember. Immigrant and refugee bodies have clearly become a rhetorical pivot, providing further evidence that current immigration policy is inflected by the history of eugenics, and that this history must be further studied as we interrogate our present and future policies.

NOTES

1 Charles B. Davenport, *Heredity in Relation to Eugenics* (New York: Henry Holt and Co., 1911) at 1.
2 Nancy Ordover, *American Eugenics: Race, Queer Anatomy, and the Science of Nationalism* (Minneapolis: University of Minnesota Press, 2003); Marouf A Hasian, *The Rhetoric of Eugenics in Anglo-American Thought* (Athens: University of Georgia Press, 1996).
3 Ian Robert Dowbiggin, *Keeping America Sane: Psychiatry and Eugenics in the United States and Canada, 1880–1940* (Ithaca, NY: Cornell University Press, 2003) at 619.
4 Janice Cavell, "The Imperial Race and the Immigration Sieve: The Canadian Debate on Assisted British Migration and Empire Settlement, 1900–30" (2006) 34:3 J Imperial and Commonwealth History 345.
5 William Lyon Mackenzie King, *Report by W.L. Mackenzie King, C.M.G., Deputy Minister of Labour, on Mission to England to Confer with the British Authorities on the Subject of Immigration to Canada from the Orient and Immigration from India in Particular* (Ottawa: S.E. Dawson, 1908) at 7.
6 *Constitution Act, 1867*, 30&31 Vict, c 3, s 91(25), 95.

7 Ninette Kelley & Michael Trebilcock, *The Making of the Mosaic* (Toronto: University of Toronto Press, 1998).

8 Timothy Caufield & Gerald Robertson, "Eugenic Policies in Alberta: From the Systematic to the Systemic?" (1996) 35 Alta L Rev 64; see also Angus McLaren, *Our Own Master Race: Eugenics in Canada, 1885–1945* (Toronto: McClelland & Stewart, 1990).

9 Evelyn Kallen, *Ethnicity and Human Rights in Canada* (Don Mills, ON: Oxford University Press, 2010); Canadian Race Relations Foundation (CRRF), "Canada's Immigration Policies: Contradictions and Shortcomings," online: <www.crr.ca>.

10 *Chinese Immigration Act 1885*, SC 1885, c 71, s 4.

11 *Ibid* s 10, 13.

12 See *Canada v How* (1919), 27 BCR 294; *R v Fong Soon* (1919), 26 BCR 450.

13 Victor Lee, "The Laws of Gold Mountain: A Sampling of Early Canadian Laws and Cases that Affected People of Chinese Ancestry" (1992) 21 Manitoba Law Journal 301.

14 *Chinese Immigration Act 1923*, SC 1923, c 33, s 5.

15 Lee, *supra* note 13.

16 *Coal Mines Regulation Act 1877*, SBC 1877, c 84, as amended SBC 1890, c 33, s 1.

17 *Union Colliery Company of British Columbia v Bryden*, [1899] AC 580.

18 *Coal Mines Regulation Act 1877*, SBC 1877, c 84, as amended SBC 1903, c 17, s 2.

19 *R v Quong Wing* (1914), 49 SCR 440 [*Quong Wing*].

20 *An Act to Prevent the Employment of Female Labour in Certain Capacities*, SS 1912, c 17, s 1.

21 *Quong Wing, supra* note 19.

22 Lindsay Ferguson, "Constructing and Containing the Chinese Male: *Quong Wing v. The King* and the Saskatchewan Act to Prevent the Employment of Female Labour" (2002) 65 Sask L Rev 549.

23 *Ibid* at 13.

24 *House of Commons Debates*, 4th Parl, 4th Sess (12 May 1882) at 1477.

25 *Ibid*; see also Ferguson, *supra* note 22 at 6.

26 *Senate Debates*, 9th Parl, 3rd Sess (19 March 1903).

27 Canada, *Report of the Royal Commission on Chinese and Japanese Immigration*, Sess 1902 (Ottawa: SE Dawson, 1902) at 224.

28 Lee, *supra* note 13.

29 *Immigration Act*, RS 1906, c 6, s 30, as amended RS 1908, c 33, s 30.

30 *Canada v Singh* (1914), 20 BCR 243 [*Singh*].

31 *Ibid* at para. 16; see also *Canada v Cain*, [1906] AC 542.

32 *Singh,* supra note 30 at para 99.

33 Andrew Parnaby & Gregory S Kealey, "The Origins of Political Policing in Canada: Class, Law, and the Burden of Empire" (2003) 41:2/3 Osgoode Hall LJ 211 at para 21.

34 Valerie Knowles, "Forging Our Legacy: Canadian Citizenship and Immigration, 1900–1977," online: <www.cic.gc.ca>.

35 At least until 1930, when an Order in Council was issued under the authority of the *Immigration Act*: "From and after the 16th August, 1930, and until other wise ordered, the landing in Canada of any immigrant of any Asiatic race is hereby prohibited."

(*Immigration Act*, RSC 1927, c 93, s 38, SOR/50–583, dated 16 September 1930). See also John P McEvoy, "Rand on Conflict of Laws: An Independent Voice" (2010) 34:1 Man LJ 173 at para 67.

36   Also of note, without developing formal legal prohibitions in Canada, a gentleman's agreement (called the Hayashi-Lemieux Agreement) was arrived at with the Japanese government in 1908, according to which Japan would restrict quotas of immigrants travelling to Canada. See Parnaby & Kealey, *supra* note 33.

37   See K Paupst, "A Note on Anti-Chinese Sentiment in Toronto before the First World War" (1977) 9 Can Ethnic Studies 54; Susan M Schweik, *The Ugly Laws: Disability in Public* (New York: New York University Press, 2009).

38   Schweik, *supra* note 37 at 61.

39   *An Act Respecting Immigration and Immigrants*, SC 1869, c 10; see also Judith Mosoff, "Excessive Demand on the Canadian Conscience: Disability, Family and Immigration" (1999) 26 Man LJ 149.

40   *Immigration Act 1886*, RSC 1886, c 65.

41   *An Act to Amend the Immigration Act*, RSC 65, c 14, s 24.

42   *House of Commons Debates*, 9th Parl, 2nd Sess (29 April 1902) at 3740; see also Ena Chadha, "'Mentally Defectives' Not Welcome: Mental Disability in Canadian Immigration Law, 1859–1927" (2008) 28:1 Disability Studies Quarterly, online: <http://dsq-sds.org/article/view/67/67>.

43   *Immigration Act*, RSC 1906, c 19, s 26.

44   *Ibid* at s 27.

45   *Ibid* at s 28.

46   *Immigration Act*, RS 1910, c 27.

47   *Ibid* at ss 3(a)–(b); see also Valentina Capurri, "The Medical Admissibility Provision vis-à-vis the Charter of Rights and Freedoms" (2012) 16:1 Left History 91.

48   *Immigration Act*, RSC 1906, c 19, ss 21–23.

49   *House of Commons Debates*, 10th Parl, 2nd Sess (19 June 1906) at 3712.

50   K Tony Hollihan, "'A Brake upon the Wheel': Frank Oliver and the Creation of the Immigration Act of 1906" (1992) 1 Past Imperfect 93.

51   *Edmonton Bulletin*, 7 February 1910; cited in Hollihan, *supra* note 50 at 107.

52   *Re Chin Chee* (1905), 11 BCR 400.

53   *Ikezoya et al v Canadian Pacific Railway Company* (1907), 12 BCR 454.

54   *Ibid* at para. 3.

55   *House of Commons Debates*, 11th Parl, 1st Sess (10 May 1909) at 6137, emphasis added.

56   *House of Commons Debates*, 13th Parl, 2nd Sess (1 April 1919) at 1071.

57   Chadha, *supra* note 42 at para 34.

58   Anne-Emanuelle Birn, "Six Seconds per Eyelid: The Medical Inspection of Immigrants at Ellis Island, 1892–1914" (1997) 17 Dynamics 281.

59   Letter, Robertson to Cory, Ottawa, 13 December 1918, Ottawa, Library and Archives Canada (LAC) (Immigration Fonds, RG 76, vol 642, file 947852, pt 1) [Robertson to Cory].

60   See Jay Dolmage, "Grounds for Exclusion: Canada's Pier 21 and Its Shadow Archives" in Susan Ashley, ed, *Diverse Spaces: Examining Identity, Heritage and Community within Canadian Public Culture* (Cambridge, UK: Cambridge Scholar's Press, 2013) 100.

61 Robertson to Cory, *supra* note 59.
62 *Ibid.*
63 *Ibid.*
64 *Ibid.*
65 *Immigration Act*, RSC 1906, c 19, s 33.
66 McLaren, *supra* note 8 at 64.
67 *House of Commons Debates*, 11th Parl, 2nd Sess (14 March 1910) at 5519.
68 See Chadha, *supra* note 42; Penny L Richards, "Points of Entry: Disability and the Historical Geography of Immigration" (2004) 24 Disability Studies Q, online: <http://dsq-sds.org/article/view/505/682>.
69 Pearse to Egan, 27 October 1925, LAC (Immigration Fonds, RG 76, vol 269, file 228124, pt 14).
70 "Immigration Barrier Is Not Tight Enough," *Toronto Globe* (12 November 1925).
71 Geoffrey Reaume, "Disability History in Canada: Present Work in the Field and Future Prospects" (2012) 1:1 Can J Disability Studies 35 at 52.
72 Unattributed correspondence, 1926, LAC (Immigration Fonds, RG 76, vol 269, file 228124, pt 10–12).
73 Bryce to unnamed official, 4 May 1926, LAC (Immigration Fonds, RG 76, vol 269, file 228124, pt 14).
74 Jolliffe to Clarke, 4 May 1926, LAC (Immigration Fonds, RG 76, vol 269, file 228124, pt 14).
75 Robert Menzies, "Governing Mentalities: The Deportation of 'Insane' and 'Feebleminded' Immigrants out of British Columbia Confederation to WWII" in Chris McCormick, ed, *Crime and Deviance in Canada: Historical Perspectives* (Toronto: Canadian Scholars Press, 2005) 135 at 135–36.
76 *House of Commons Debates*, 13th Parl, 2nd Sess (1 May 1919) at 1974.
77 *House of Commons Debates*, 12th Parl, 3rd Sess (9 March 1914) at 1440.
78 Anna Stubblefield, "Beyond the Pale: Tainted Whiteness, Cognitive Disability, and Eugenic Sterilization" (2007) 22:2 Hypatia 162.
79 Margaret Sanger, *The Pivot of Civilization* (New York: Brentano's Press, 1922) at 210.
80 *Ibid.*
81 Cyril Greenland, *Charles Kirk Clarke: A Pioneer of Canadian Psychiatry* (Toronto: University of Toronto Press, 1966) at 21.
82 *Ibid.*
83 *Ibid.*
84 McLaren, *supra* note 8 at 61.
85 *Immigration Act*, RSC 1910, c 27, s 38(a)(c).
86 *Ibid* at s 38(c).
87 James Daschuk, *Clearing the Plains: Disease, Politics of Starvation, and the Loss of Aboriginal Life* (Regina, SK: University of Regina Press, 2012).
88 Further, the process of immigration itself was designed to create disabling conditions, tracing these intentions upon certain bodies. The environmental conditions of the regions of the world from which immigrants came were also mapped as zones of environmental and embodied undesirability.
89 Canada, Canadian Department of Immigration and Colonization, *Annual Report, 1922* at 25.

90 These images are credited to the "Topley Studio" or to Woodruff, but we know that at times Woodruff worked in Topley's studio, so the credit is difficult to truly discern.

91 If we take there to be a key distinction between settler colonialism and other forms of colonialism: that the land is the key resource at stake.

92 W Hennessy Cook, Lantern slide lecture, "If England Only Knew," LAC (RG 76, vol 560, file 808468, pt 1).

93 Robertson to Cory, *supra* note 59.

94 *Ibid.*

95 Baumbgartner to England, 22 July 1927, LAC (Immigration Fonds, RG 76, vol 623, file 938332, pt 2).

96 *Ibid.*

97 *Ibid.*

98 *Ibid.*

99 Black to Blair, 6 September 1927, LAC (Immigration Fonds, RG 76, vol 623, file 938332, pt 2).

100 *Ibid.*

101 Louise Abbott Medical Certificate, 24 March 1925, LAC (Immigration Fonds, RG 76, vol 269, file 228124, pt 13).

102 Jan Raska, "Facing Deportation: The Curious Cases of Rebecca Barnett and Rebecca Grizzle," *Canadian Museum of Immigration at Pier 21* (blog), online: <http://www.pier21.ca/blog/jan-raska/facing-deportation-the-curious-cases-of-rebecca-barnett -and-rebecca-grizzle>. Raska and other Pier 21 historians have been engaged in work to try to recognize and represent the eugenic roots of Canadian immigration history.

103 *Immigration and Refugee Protection Act*, RSC 2001, c 27, s 12(2).

104 Mosoff, *supra* note 39.

105 "Conservatives Pass Controversial Anti-Terror Bill Bill C-51," *Toronto Star* (6 May 2015), online: <https://www.thestar.com/news/canada/2015/05/06/conservatives-pass -controversial-anti-terror-bill-bill-c-51.html>; Erin Anderssen & André Picard, "Canada's Ebola-Related Visa Restrictions Criticized for Being at Odds," *Globe and Mail* (10 November 2014), online: <http://www.theglobeandmail.com/life/health-and -fitness/health/canadas-visa-restrictions-criticized-for-being-at-odds-with-ebola -science/article21517101/>.

106 Anette Sikka, Katherine Lippel & Jill Hanley, "Access to Health Care and Workers' Compensation for Precarious Migrants in Quebec, Ontario and New Brunswick" (2011) 5:2 McGill JL & Health 203.

107 "CBSA Rushes Deportation of Men Rounded up in Racial Profiling Anti-immigrant Raids," *No One Is Illegal*, online: <http://toronto.nooneisillegal.org/node/871>.

108 *Immigration and Refugee Protection Act*, RSC 2001, c 27, s 12(1).

109 *Ibid*, s 38(1).

110 *Hilewitz v Canada; De Jong v Canada*, [2005] 2 SCR 706.

111 "Deported, Disabled U.K. Citizen Arrives in Britain," *CBC News* (20 January 2009), online: <http://www.cbc.ca/news/canada/manitoba/deported-disabled-u-k-citizen -arrives-in-britain-1.845793>; Kenyon Wallace, "Family Faces Deportation over Son's Autism," *Toronto Star* (9 June 2011), online: <http://www.thestar.com/news/canada/ 2011/06/09/family_faces_deportation_over_sons_autism.html>.

112 Roy Hanes, "None Is Still Too Many: An Historical Exploration of Canadian Immigration Legislation as It Pertains to People with Disabilities," *Council of Canadians with Disabilities*, 2013, online: <http://www.ccdonline.ca/en/socialpolicy/access-inclusion/none-still-too-many>.

113 *Ibid.*, para. 80.

114 Menzies, *supra* note 75 at 172.

115 *Ibid.*

116 Peter Edwards, "'Old Stock Canadians' Comment Gives Chills to Professor," *Toronto Star* (18 September 2015), online: <http://www.thestar.com/news/canada/2015/09/18/old-stock-canadians-phrase-chills-prof-ignites-twitter.html>.

117 Louise Elliot, "Syrian Refugee Plans Has Officials 'Working Around the Clock,' McCallum Says," *CBC News* (7 November 2015), online: <http://www.cbc.ca/news/politics/canada-mccallum-syrian-refugee-plan-1.3307788?cmp=rss>.

PART 3

Legal Debates

7

Battling the Warrior-Litigator
An Exploration of Chronic Illness and Employment Discrimination Paradigms

ODELIA R. BAY

Working at a law firm often demands fierce commitment and many hours of hard work. But workplaces that valorize a workaholic mentality become sites of alienation for those people who cannot adhere to such ideals. While there has been ample critique of the disadvantages perpetuated by this model for parents and caregivers, and in particular women, there have been relatively few conversations expanding the analysis to disabled workers, in general, and people who experience chronic illnesses, in particular.

It has been more than twenty years since the Canadian Bar Association's first report on the status of women lawyers in Canada. *Touchstones for Change: Equality, Diversity and Accountability* painted a picture of a profession in need of a radical makeover.[1] The report outlined the challenges women face within a "white, male, elitist"[2] legal profession and highlighted issues concerning employment opportunities, career development and advancement, accommodation for family caregiving, and sexual harassment.[3] Two decades later, the subject of gender balance within the profession is still a hot topic. Recent conversations focus on how the nature of legal work drives women away and the ways in which men should adapt to take on their fair share of caregiving responsibilities at home.[4]

These debates serve as examples of how women continue to battle against the stereotypical idea of the model lawyer: the "warrior-litigator," a term I borrow from a group of Ontario women lawyers and use throughout this chapter to denote a kind of workaholic performance standard.[5] This warrior norm, along with the issues concerning women and work, extends to the corporate world more broadly and drives debate about whether a woman must be the warrior and "man up" or "lean in" to succeed.[6]

Comparatively, there is relatively little discussion about what it means to work in a competitive setting as a disabled person.[7] The conversations are fewer still when the disability is the result of a chronic illness – that is, a health condition that is not acute but rather lasts over an extended period of time.[8] As is elaborated on throughout this chapter, Susan Wendell divides the world of disability into the "healthy" and the "unhealthy" disabled.[9] This way of thinking about kinds of disability helps to illustrate the particular challenges facing those who are disabled because of illness.[10] Chronically ill people may face a number of barriers when it comes to competing in a world of work that demands a high level of devotion to career. Because of this, the warrior trope is not only useful in highlighting gender-based bias in professional workplaces like law firms, but it can also be used to highlight disability-based bias, particularly when it comes to chronic illness. Using private legal practice as an example, this chapter argues that, when it comes to accommodating people with chronic illnesses in the workplace, the disability paradigm, while helpful, fails to fully and adequately capture the barriers faced by these workers. In part, this is due to a lack of visibility that affects how these workers are perceived, as well as conceptual hierarchies of disablement and an emphasis on a social model of disability that do a disservice to those with chronic health conditions. As a result, incorporating some aspects of the gender and caregiver antidiscrimination paradigm – which promotes flexibility, caregiving, and work-life balance as social goods rather than individual goods – can help to more adequately illuminate the stigma these workers face and lead to more dynamic solutions.

The purpose of this chapter is to advance a new way of looking at the problem of chronic illness and work to set the stage for more effective solutions. The first section sets out some context by exploring the dynamics of chronic illness within the realm of disability generally and legal practice more specifically. The analysis is expanded to look at issues of accommodation, career advancement, and retention in a legal setting and beyond. The second section demonstrates how chronic illness is not fully covered by contemporary perspectives concerning disability and accommodation. I lay out how a conceptual hierarchy of disability – that is, how we have come to imagine and understand disability – results in the marginalization of people with chronic illnesses and the ways this is reflected in the law. The third section argues for a shift in how we imagine and adapt to chronic illness in the workplace. It looks to the gender and family status discrimination and accommodation paradigm, and in particular at how human rights law has expanded to protect caregiving and work-life balance for parents. Finally, the chapter concludes with ideas about how the law's approach to gender and family status accommodation offers some useful concepts that help to move the law forward for chronically ill workers.

Chronic Illness and Work

While the numbers are difficult to track due to variances in data collection and analysis,[11] a 2007 study found that 13 percent of 20–39-year-olds and 37 percent of 40–59-year-olds reported having at least one chronic health condition.[12] The diagnosis rate for such conditions appears to be climbing, perhaps by as much as 14 percent annually.[13] In part, this is a natural consequence of Canada's aging population, but there is also some indication that a number of chronic conditions are generally increasing in terms of prevalence and severity.[14] Because of the rising rate of chronic illness, the need to address these kinds of disabilities in our workplaces is also growing.

Chronic illnesses represent a unique class of disability, in part because they are often invisible, but also because they may require accommodations that are distinct from the physical and environmental changes we have come to expect as necessary for the paradigmatic example of a person who uses a wheelchair, for example. Because the dominant social model sees the problems associated with disability as located outside of the individual and created by society – an analytical framing that has been critical in advancing social responses to disability – it would follow that the right environmental changes allow for the disabled person to be the warrior-worker. As is explained below, however, this approach does not work in the context of chronic illness.

A focus on chronic illness and work within the legal profession brings with it certain predispositions. First, there is an implicit assumption that work and employment are good or at least important.[15] Second, given the relatively privileged position of lawyers – in terms of average income and general social standing as middle-class professionals – there are also class biases inherent in the focus.[16] Third, and perhaps most importantly, the full range of disability experiences, invisible or otherwise, is not reflected in the analysis. It is worth noting that many people who are visibly disabled face tremendous barriers, attitudinal and otherwise, when seeking and maintaining work thus pushing many into poverty.[17] People who appear disabled cannot avoid discrimination by covering their impairments and passing as nondisabled.[18]

Given the above, what follows is some discussion about chronic illness as a disability; how this class of disability disadvantages workers (for my purposes, particularly those working as lawyers); and why the law and social institutions recognize that they have a right to work.

Chronic Illness as Disability

The term "chronic illness" refers to a wide range of health conditions. What these illnesses have in common is that they are characterized by their duration or frequency of symptoms. Unlike an acute illness, a chronic illness persists over an extended period of time. This definition encompasses a wide range of diseases, such as those that are incurable, like lupus or diabetes; those that last for very long periods of time before resolving, like Lyme disease; those that are potentially terminal but can be slowed with treatment, like HIV and some forms of cancer; and those that affect a person over his or her lifetime but fluctuate in terms of degree of debilitation, like certain autoimmune disorders and mental illnesses.[19] Each condition has its own set of symptoms and resulting impairments that may vary over time and be difficult to predict. Every individual experience is different. Generally, however, others may not immediately regard these people as different or disabled – or initially discriminate against them on this basis – because they do not bear any visible markings of their illness.

Yet, some common experiences differentiate these people as a class with- in the broader rubric of disability. In the discussion below, I borrow from the work of Susan Wendell, who, as we have seen, provides a useful framework by contrasting the "healthy" disabled with the "unhealthy" disabled.[20] The former category refers to people with physical or functional limitations who are otherwise healthy. The latter covers people with chronic conditions attributable to some loss of health. Wendell defines chronic conditions as those that "are understood to be illnesses that do not go away by themselves within six months, that cannot reliably be cured, and that will not kill the patient any time soon."[21] In addition, many disability activists and theorists are careful to note that disability is a social construct, and therefore located outside of the body, while illness is not socially created but rooted in the body of a person who is ill.[22] As is discussed more below, these factors have an impact on how others view people with a chronic illness.

While not a universal truth, many people with chronic conditions belong in the category of disabled – if not permanently, then periodically. This is because many chronic conditions can lead to various impairments, often related to symptoms like pain or fatigue. When they are not accounted for and accommodated, these impairments become obstacles to full social participation. This view accords with Canadian antidiscrimination law, which is broad enough to encompass within the definition of disability health conditions and impairments that may fluctuate over time, even during periods of remission or relief of symptoms.[23]

When Lawyers Are Chronically Ill

The following section largely references legal practice; however, the issues and resulting discrimination are not unique to the world of legal work.[24] Thus, the discussion expands beyond law at points to reflect the wider employment context.

Legal practice can take a number of forms. Still, traditional private practice continues to be regarded as particularly prestigious and influential. Rightly or wrongly, many young law graduates view the prospect of landing a job with one of Canada's big Bay Street law firms as the stuff of dreams and compete accordingly. These firms are private partnerships that rely on hourly billing. In a way, billable hours is piecework with units of production measured in terms of the number of hours a lawyer puts in on a client's file. These firms are also demanding environments that valorize a workaholic mentality at the expense of flexibility and accommodation.[25] In terms of employees, they seek a form of warrior-litigator: someone who is fiercely committed, fearless, intensely focused and hardworking, and seems to have boundless energy.[26] In the 1990s, the typical lawyer was described as the "male breadwinner available to work almost unlimited hours by relying on a wife to take care of home and family."[27] This person is also likely nondisabled and white.[28] He is designed to fit comfortably within the traditional law firm.[29] And, as the discussion here demonstrates, he is as alienating a concept for chronically ill lawyers as he is for many female lawyers.

Many of the large Bay Street firms say that they accommodate disability and gender-related caregiving needs through things like alternative work schedules and flex-time policies, as well as performance evaluations that combine billable targets with other criteria.[30] These types of measures are required by the duty to accommodate under statutory Canadian human rights law, which places a robust responsibility on Canadian employers.[31] The legal duty mandates accommodation up to the point of undue hardship[32] and aims "to achieve full participation and equal opportunities for persons with disabilities in the workplace."[33] Law societies also place an additional obligation on lawyers not to discriminate on the basis of disability when hiring or working in a professional capacity with other lawyers and staff.[34] But the reality does not measure up. While the current legal and extra-legal policy frameworks should be sufficient, they do not serve to render visible the forms of employment discrimination faced by lawyers with chronic illnesses.

Very little information has been gathered about the experiences of lawyers with disabilities in general, never mind the particular experiences of those with chronic illnesses. Even when such studies are done, the numbers may not reflect the true extent of the problem. This is because people with invisible disabilities, like chronic conditions, either choose not to report because of confidentially concerns or do not identify as disabled.[35] The Law Society of British Columbia notes this in stark terms: "[T]he reality [is] that many lawyers have learned that identifying themselves as 'disabled' is a faster way to job loss than employee theft – getting lawyers with disabilities to self-identify was extremely difficult."[36]

In terms of legal practice, most of the material I rely on for the summary below comes from reports conducted by law societies in Ontario[37] and British Columbia.[38] None of these studies delineate between the "healthy" and "unhealthy" disabled. Although there is no special consideration of chronic conditions as a class of disability, it is clear from the reports that these issues were considered. In addition to these documents, I also look to another scholarly examination of disability and legal work incorporating a gender lens. American lawyer and academic Carrie Griffin Basas uses narrative to draw on her own experiences and presents a qualitative assessment of interviews with thirty-eight disabled women working as lawyers in the United States. Again, Basas does not single out chronic illness as a separate category of disability, but it is clear that a number of those people interviewed in her study belong within this group.[39]

A close reading of the available material noted above begins to reveal several trends in law common to other sectors of employment.[40] Lawyers with chronic illnesses have difficulty receiving adequate accommodations, and, even when they are appropriately accommodated, their careers may be stunted because of structural issues like mechanisms for evaluations based on billable hours and stereotype and stigma associated with chronic illness. If the warrior is the ideal, the worker with a chronic illness becomes the damsel: dependent, needy, and even melodramatic.

Appropriate Accommodation

Whether it is because of pain, fatigue, or some other symptom, chronic illness may require a person to work flexible or reduced hours or to telecommute. These accommodations may be needed on either an ongoing or occasional basis because of a flare up, as a means of preventing the exacerbation of symptoms, or for medical treatment. A chronic condition may require that a person account for and budget energy and the feeling of well-being as if they were limited resources.[41] Unlike installing a ramp for a person using a wheelchair or computer software to aid someone who is blind, accommodations for chronic illness are not generally one-offs – in other words, these are not actions that can be taken once to provide an ongoing or long-term solution. They are also measures needed by people who otherwise appear nondisabled and healthy, yet whose health conditions fluctuate over time, occasionally diminishing their ability to perform at a level that meets warrior-litigator expectations.

In general, lawyers working in law firms are less likely to receive the above kinds of accommodations when compared to their legal colleagues in nonprivate practice, such as those who work in governmental or nongovernmental organization settings, as in-house counsel, or on their own as solo practitioners.[42] When accommodation is requested, lawyers with disabilities report that they feel resented and perceived as weak, less valuable, inefficient, and incompetent.[43]

These findings accord with conclusions reached by those studying other sectors of employment. Because laws concerning disability accommodation vary between jurisdictions, it is helpful to look to other Canadian writing on the topic. A recent study of academics with multiple sclerosis seeking accommodation in university workplaces found that, for a number of reasons, workers with chronic illnesses tend to try to use "back door" methods of arranging accommodation as opposed to official or formal channels.[44] The authors give three reasons for this behaviour. First, workers often perceive risks of stigmatization and discrimination associated with disclosing an illness. Second, while employers have a duty to accommodate disability, the extent of this duty is unclear – if not vague – making formal requests complex and cumbersome. And third, even when an office dedicated to disability accommodation exists, participants say they must continually educate staff and fight to have their needs met.[45]

In her study, Basas talks about a phenomenon she calls "self-accommodation" among disabled women lawyers. This happens, she says, when "attorneys with disabilities implement strategies and create reasonable accommodations on their own to be able to work or to work more effectively."[46] For Basas, however, this "self-accommodation" means more than unofficial and informal measures in any particular job. It also extends to decisions regarding career advancement, including "selecting jobs that are disability-friendly" and "becoming their own bosses through entrepreneurialism."[47]

Career Advancement and Retention

Even when lawyers with chronic illnesses are accommodated, they may find that they are given lesser files or that they face additional barriers to financial and career advancement.[48] As noted above, some of this is attitudinal. Requesting accommodation in terms of work flexibility means that a lawyer may face stigma and a devaluing of his or her work. The other problem has to do with the common metric used to evaluate a lawyer's value to a practice: billable hours, or measurable time that can be charged to a client – again, a kind of piecework, albeit in units of time as opposed to product. Those who can work substantially more hours are privileged over those who cannot, all the while giving a false sense of fairness or neutrality.[49] As one disabled lawyer puts it, the use of billable hours "provides a false impression of objectivity and devalues talent."[50]

Alternatively, some lawyers with chronic illnesses find that they are forced to abandon a job altogether. A law firm's inability or unwillingness to accommodate health-related needs may push a lawyer to exit private practice.[51] Others report that remaining closeted makes staying within the competitive firm environment untenable.

> In their motivation to have a career as a lawyer, respondents reported a pattern of hiding their disabilities if possible and putting up with lack of accommodation, lack of support and even harassment in both law firms and government offices. This strategy commonly fails, and sooner or later the individual burns out and/or is let go. The most common choice at this point is to set up in solo practice or withdraw from the profession.[52]

More than half of the lawyers who took part in the British Columbia study say that discrimination "eventually led to loss of employment, marginalization into solo practice or early retirement."[53]

Again, other research corroborates these sentiments. A recent examination of the employment trajectories of people with chronic illnesses in the United States found some discouraging trends.[54] Workers in a variety of sectors often find long-term illness negatively impacts their careers in several ways: plateauing, redirecting, retreating, and self-employment.[55] Plateauing – that is, remaining in a position without the opportunity for advancement – is the most common of the four career paths. Others react to career barriers by choosing either to redirect their career objectives towards other kinds or work, or to retreat by making "a conscious choice to decrease their work effort."[56] Finally, some look to "opting-out of the career game" via self-employment.[57] There is nothing inherently bad about being less am-bitious or choosing any particular career path over another. The negative aspect of these moves has more to do with the fact that some workers feel pushed off a desired path and made to take a different employment route. Interestingly, the author of this study finds that these workers are caught in a kind of accommodation limbo: they do not need the kinds of permanent, physical accommodation required by the "healthy" disabled, yet short-term sick leave designed to address the needs of people with acute illnesses does not offer the long-term solutions they require.[58]

Logically, issues impacting advancement and retention also affect remu-neration in the form of both salary and related benefits. While there are no Canadian numbers, the America Bar Association has reported that the mean salary for a lawyer with a disability is about 85 percent of the mean salary of all law graduates.[59] As well, because many benefits may be tied to hours of work, also known as active service, people with reduced hours may also lose things like access to flex-time, benefits coverage, sick leave accrual, vacation pay, pension plan participation, severance pay calculations, raises and bonuses, and seniority accrual.[60]

It is worth noting that there has been some improvement in the recog-nition by law societies of the professional capacity of lawyers with chron-ic conditions. For example, those people hoping to be called to the bar in British Columbia are no longer required to answer a medical fitness ques-tion that began by stating that "[t]he practice of law is often rigorous, de-manding a high level of physical, mental and emotional health."[61] People hoping to be called to the bar were then made to disclose information about particular diagnoses and whether they had "ever failed to follow the recom-mendation of a medical or mental health professional."[62] Still, as recently as 2009, the province's law society was found to have systemically discrimi-nated against those with mental illnesses by requiring disclosure of certain conditions without sufficient proof that those conditions had any bearing on the ability to practise law.[63]

Chronic Illness and the Cracks in the Disability Antidiscrimination Paradigm

On its face, discrimination directed towards workers with chronic illnesses might appear to make good business sense. A competitive workforce is a productive workforce. Economic interests implicit in running a law firm – or any other business – create pressures not to accommodate someone with a chronic illness who may not always be up for a demanding workload. After all, if one worker has less stamina than another, or has other competing demands on his or her time, then why shouldn't an employer hire someone else who does not require accommodation and all of the associated costs?

As noted above, Canadian human rights law requires that, notwithstanding economic incentives, employers must accommodate certain employees, and a refusal to do so up to the point of undue hardship, even if rationally justified, is illegal. Law professor and labour arbitrator Michael Lynk sets out three reasons why the duty to accommodate disability is recognized as a priority in Canada: "[A]t the heart of the accommodation duty is the recognition that employment is central to the aspirations and self-esteem of Canadians; that disability is in part a social construct that can be significantly alleviated with political will; and that the social and economic value of an inclusive workplace substantially outweighs the actual costs of accommodation for all parties."[64]

Arguments about the importance of work have also been made from the feminist perspective. American scholar Vicki Schultz argues that paid employment forms the foundation for equal social citizenship, provides a means for community contribution and membership, and allows for the formation of identity and aspirations.[65] Indeed, human rights legislation provides that, "all individuals should have an opportunity equal with other individuals to make for themselves the lives that they are able and wish to have."[66] For many of us in Western society, jobs are central to our life aspirations as well as formative in terms of how we see ourselves and how others see us. Because of this relationship, people should not only have a right to work but also to determine what work they do, and should be permitted to advance in their careers and professions.[67]

Yet, having acknowledged the importance of work and the necessity for accommodation, the discussion in the preceding section demonstrates that people with chronic illnesses are not exactly welcome employees. The following is an exploration of why chronic illness does not fit comfortably within the disability paradigm and how this affects antidiscrimination and accommodation law.

A Conceptual Hierarchy of Disability

The international symbol for access – a stylized blue-and-white representation of a person in a wheelchair – speaks volumes about how society generally tends to conceive of disability. It is the quintessential portrayal: a body "confined to a wheelchair," to borrow an oft-used and hated phrase. In our collective consciousness, disability often entails physicality, permanence, and predictability.[68]

Based on this way of thinking, it is possible to imagine that paradigmatic disability cases centre on issues like modifying railway cars so that they are accessible to wheelchair users,[69] or ensuring that American Sign Language interpretation is available in hospitals.[70] While there are certainly economic arguments to be made with respect to the costs of accommodation, the needs appear to be more or less fixed and, once addressed, allow for a person's full participation.[71]

These narrow notions dovetail with the prevailing model of disablement. According to the social model, disability is rooted in societal attitudes and environments; therefore, the obligation to remove barriers is placed on society and owed in the form of citizenship rights to those people who are disabled. As a school of thought, the social model was born out of activism and the disability rights movement. Michael Oliver, the English academic credited with the original terminology and theorizing, explains: "[The social model] does not deny the problem of disability but locates it squarely within society. It is not individual limitations, of whatever kind, which are the cause of the problem but society's failure to provide appropriate services and adequately ensure the needs of disabled people are fully taken into account in its social organization."[72] The social model differs from the medical model, which situates disability in the individual bodies of those people who are impacted and puts the burden on "abnormal" individuals to modify themselves or even disappear from view.[73]

Canadian courts have, by and large, embraced the social model of disability.[74] The Supreme Court cites the work of professor Jerome Bickenbach, who describes the social model as follows: "[H]andicaps are socially constructed phenomena brought about by attitudes toward people with disabilities which, once embedded in social practices and institutions, sustain the disadvantageous social condition of people with disabilities."[75] He goes on to explain:

> An investigation into the theoretical significance of this dimension of disablement must, indeed, be premised on two interlocking claims: that handicaps are socially constructed and that *accounts* of handicaps are socially constructed. In other words, the question of whether handicaps exist, and what form they take, is not a purely empirical issue: it is an issue that derives its significance from normative assumptions about proper and improper responses to human differences. Thus, handicaps are not only social constructs; one can make them disappear by altering one's account of political morality.[76]

By removing responsibility for exclusion from the individual and placing a demand on society at large for civil and human rights, the social model has proven to be an important tool in the disability rights movement.[77] In theory, this model should also provide space for people with chronic illnesses. Because disablement under this frame may also be a matter of attitudinal barriers, society bears the onus for accommodating difference. For example, according to this view, employers should take responsibility for adjusting work to fit people's needs and capacities regardless of the root cause.

The problem, however, is that understanding disability strictly as a matter of social construction presents some challenges in terms of the ability of the chronically ill to fit comfortably within the disability rubric. This is because there is a kind of pressure to divorce disability from impairment and view it as something external to the person impaired. Feminist disability scholar Carol Thomas draws on feminist epistemologies that place personal experience at the centre of theoretical analysis and political gain.[78] She explains that, "from the point of view of disabled individuals, 'lived experience' is such that disability and impairment effects interact, and meld together in a holistic fashion."[79] Fiona Sampson, who has studied and written about the intersection of disability and gender, points out that a strict adherence to the social model of disability runs the risk of oversimplifying the "bio-medical realities" of disability.[80] This oversimplification especially impacts people who are impaired by virtue of chronic illness.

For example, Jill Humphrey's research demonstrates that the social model leads to the creation of a group ethos privileging those who are visibly disabled, while marginalizing those who are not, thus creating a cycle of exclusion.[81] She concludes: "[T]he social model as operationalised ... has both reified the disability identity and reduced it to particular kinds of impairments – physical, immutable, tangible and 'severe' ones – in a way which can deter many people from adopting a disabled identity and participating in a disability community."[82]

Recalling Susan Wendell's "healthy" and "unhealthy" disability dichotomy, we know that illness and the associated impairments cannot be made to "disappear," to borrow Bickenbach's turn of phrase, as a matter of shifting political ethics. Yet, it is possible for these people to experience a form of erasure from the category of disabled. People with chronic illnesses are not often visibly identifiable as such and may be more or less impaired depending on the day. This means that they fail to fit comfortably within the stereotypical disability box described above. It also means that, consciously or unconsciously, there is a tendency to question the validity of their impairments.

Because "unhealthy" disabled people experience fluctuations in illness and impairment and may be able to pass as nondisabled, they are often regarded as well and face the challenge of having to remind employers, coworkers, and others of the difficulties they face.[83] Wendell describes how hard it was for her to communicate the fact of her disability to friends and colleagues:

> It was easier to identify myself as disabled to myself than it was to identify myself as disabled to others ... The problem was that when I had recovered enough strength to return to work part-time, I no longer *looked* very ill although I still fought a daily battle with exhaustion, pain, nausea, and diz-. ziness, and I used a cane to keep my balance. I was struggling, and since people could not see that I was struggling, I was constantly explaining to them that I was struggling, that I could no longer do things that I had done before, and that I did not know when or even if I would ever be able to do them again. I simply wanted my friends and the people I worked with to recognize my limitations and to accept, as I had, that they might be permanent, but it is hard to describe the invisible reality of disability to others.[84]

Wendell paints a picture of a person who must deal not only with health-related impairments but also with the challenge of trying to convey the reality of her circumstances to others who might easily presume a greater level of health or ability based on the fact that she appears to be fine. The result of this misconception may be that she consistently fails to meet the expectations of others or measures created without regard to her condition or need for accommodation. It is difficult to explain this disconnect as anything but a recipe for failure.

As the next section demonstrates, because chronic illnesses are less visible than other forms of disability, they are less likely to be viewed as real and the affected individual may be seen as less deserving of accommodation.

The Failings of the Disability Model

The tendency to create a kind of conceptual hierarchy of disability, with invisible and chronic illness pushed to the margins, is also reflected in the way courts and tribunals view these conditions in an antidiscrimination context. Gender and disability scholar Sampson points to the case of *Granovsky v Canada (Minister of Employment and Immigration)*[85] as an example of the conceptual disability hierarchy at play in judicial decision making and how the law prioritizes those people with permanent disabilities over those with chronic or episodic conditions.[86]

On its face, *Granovsky* appears to be a case about entitlement to a social benefit scheme. Sampson sees it as a kind of accommodation case.[87] The claimant, Allan Granovsky, injured himself in a work-related accident. The result of this event was an intermittent and degenerative back condition that made it impossible for him to work for periods of time, and then possible at other times. Because of this condition, he was employed on and off over a twenty-one-year period. Eventually, Granovsky found himself too disabled to work – his periodic, temporary disability had become a permanent one – and he made a claim for disability benefits under the Canada Pension Plan. The problem was that his intermittent condition meant he had not satisfied the contribution requirements necessary to be eligible for the benefits. According to the *Canada Pension Plan Act*,[88] a "drop out" exception exists so that people who are unable to make the requisite contributions because of permanent disabilities may still qualify for benefits. Granovsky looked to the equality provisions of the *Canadian Charter of Rights and Freedoms*[89] to challenge the fact that the temporary nature of his disability left him unable to take advantage of the same exception.

The conceptual hierarchy of disability, described above, comes through in the Court's unanimous determination that the legislation was not discriminatory. Instead of comparing Granovsky to nondisabled workers who then become permanently disabled, the Court compares workers with chronic conditions to permanently disabled workers, thus forcing a kind of race to the bottom that asks which group of disabled people is worse off and more deserving of accommodation.[90] In doing so, Justice Binnie, who writes the decision for the Court, masquerades as the champion of the disabled while dismissing those who do not match the stereotype. Sampson offers the following critique:

> The problematic nature of the hierarchy of disadvantage analysis in *Granovsky* was compounded by the impossibility of reaching qualitative or quantitative conclusions about the relative disadvantage associated with temporary vs. permanent disability, or congenital vs. acquired disability. Binnie J. concluded that Mr. Granovsky and those who experience temporary disabilities that develop into permanent disabilities, are "better off" and "more fortunate" than those who have permanent pre-existing disabilities. This is a very controversial conclusion for the Court to adopt. No

accurate determination can be made with respect to the relative severity of a pre-existing permanent disability vs. a newly acquired disability. Those who are disabled from birth may adjust to their disability naturally with a fair degree of ease as a child. Those who develop disabilities as adults may experience more difficulty adapting to new limitations and challenges. It seems incredibly presumptuous of the Court to conclude that one disadvantaged group is "better off" than another.[91]

In this decision, the sometimes or occasionally disabled lose in a battle against the always disabled and must forego accommodation. It is absurd that disability becomes some kind of status attained through birth or permanent injury, rather than something that can be acknowledged, and accommodated, during particular periods of impact. Disability is not an aggregate concept to be measured over the course of someone's lifetime.

One of the more striking passages in the decision is Justice Binnie's evocation of famous "supercrips," a trope that portrays disabled people as exceptional because they are able to exceed the bar of normalcy and thus displace any social responsibility for disablement.[92] He writes:

An individual may suffer severe impairments that do not prevent him or her from earning a living. Beethoven was deaf when he composed some of his most enduring works. Franklin Delano Roosevelt, limited to a wheelchair as a result of polio, was the only President of the United States to be elected four times. Terry Fox, who lost a leg to cancer, inspired Canadians in his effort to complete a coast-to-coast marathon even as he raised millions of dollars for cancer research. Professor Stephen Hawking, struck by amyotrophic lateral sclerosis and unable to communicate without assistance, has nevertheless worked with well-known brilliance as a theoretical physicist. (Indeed, with perhaps bitter irony, Professor Hawking is reported to have said that his disabilities give him more time to think.) The fact they have steady work does not, of course, mean that these individuals are necessarily free of discrimination in the workplace. Nor would anyone suggest that, measured against a yardstick other than employment (access to medical care for example), they are not persons with daunting disabilities.[93]

Justice Binnie seems to be saying that even those people with "daunting disabilities" can work just as hard as, or harder than, everyone else. The implication is that not doing so is a choice rather than a fact of life. And, by extension, those who choose to do otherwise are less committed to their jobs; the opposite of the warrior-worker.

Perhaps it is this attitude, the idea that commitment and effort are a matter of choice, that accounts for failures in accommodating the chronically ill worker. Add to this conception, again, the fact that the person's disability is not visible or consistent, and the worker appears to be less willing and thus less deserving. For example, it seems to be acceptable that some people with chronic illnesses may be expected to endure a high level of disbelief about their condition. While the Supreme Court decision in *Honda v Keays*[94] is most often cited as an authority for the calculation of notice periods upon dismissal from employment, it also speaks volumes about how the Court regards employer skepticism of employees who seek accommodation. Kevin Keays, who was diagnosed with chronic fatigue syndrome, was terminated following a period of absences due to his illness. He provided his employer with medical documentation from his doctor, but the employer did not see this as sufficient proof and instead insisted that he meet with company doctors. Keays felt he was being set up and refused, leading to his termination. In the end, the Supreme Court held that the employer's actions were not unusual, and perhaps were even justifiable. At any rate, its conduct did not warrant the aggravated or punitive damages awarded by the lower courts, and these amounts were set aside.

Also, while not the absolute rule, in the vast preponderance of cases concerning workers who reduce their hours of work from full-time to part-time to manage illness, it is acceptable to deny them benefits and other perks regardless of any demonstration of undue hardship to the employer that could possibly result from such costs. This denial is permitted despite the fact that the change in workload is, in fact, an accommodation measure. As noted above, this situation may have an impact on things like access to flex-time, benefits coverage, sick leave accrual, vacation pay, pension plan participation, severance pay calculations, raises and bonuses, and seniority accrual, to name but a few of the related issues. Paradoxically, it is the chronically ill worker who may benefit most from these measures.

In his treatise on employment and the duty to accommodate, Kevin MacNeil explains that the denial of these forms of benefits has been justified by comparing the disabled worker to the absent but nondisabled employee to find that there is no discriminatory treatment.[95] As one arbitrator noted, "entitlement to benefit[s] ... turns on attendance at work, not on handicap. In other words, everyone is treated the same way, based upon attendance, regardless of handicap."[96] This kind of comparison, however, fails to account for the reasons people may work part time in the first place. For some, it may be a matter of choice; for others, it may result from forms of structural disadvantage that have the effect of curtailing choice. In any event, the comparison is unfair to the chronically ill employee whose disability is unaccounted for in the comparison, an exercise that does not require much stretch of the imagination when the condition is already invisible.[97]

Looking to Gender and Family Status to Fill the Gaps

If we understand that the role of antidiscrimination law in Canada is about substantive equality,[98] then the cases mentioned above demonstrate that accommodation for people with chronic illnesses does not meet our expectations of the law. So long as disability is viewed as something permanent and predictable, the disability paradigm will continue to fail those people with chronic conditions. Instead, this class of disabled workers can be better accommodated with an approach that recognizes the societal need for caregivers, the necessity for flexibility and work-life balance, and the importance of benefits. These objectives have been highlighted in discrimination cases concerning gender and family status, which can collectively be thought of as caregiving case law. While not perfect, the approaches taken in these decisions can help to bridge the gaps related to chronic illness in the disability paradigm. What follows is a discussion about how this area of law provides helpful guidance concerning accommodation of chronic conditions, and why the analogy to gender, and caregiving in particular, works.

How We Accommodate Caregivers

Before getting to the law of discrimination and caregiving, it is helpful to recognize that there are some similarities in the rhetoric concerning people who are chronically ill and those who are parents. For example, women who take time off work to have and raise children – or who do not take time off but simply divert some time and energy away from their roles as professionals and towards their roles as mothers – are seen as less committed, less able, and less competent.[99] This gendered pattern is reflected in women's remuneration, advancement, and retention in private legal practice and other forms of employment.[100] The Law Society of Upper Canada reports that, for women, having children is the greatest obstacle to equality in the legal profession.[101]

It is true that men may take on parenting, and other caregiving, responsibilities, but this kind of work is still typically undertaken by women in our society and is also linked to the fact that it is women who gestate, give birth, and breastfeed. Further, there is new evidence that shows that men who seek workplace accommodation for caregiving are subject to a "flexibility" stigma.[102] Thus, gender and family status discrimination are related and bear examination.

The discussion here focuses on two landmark cases. The first is the Supreme Court's decision in *Brooks v Canada Safeway*,[103] in which discrimination on the basis of pregnancy was recognized as discrimination on the basis of gender. The second is the fairly recent Federal Court decision in *Canada (Attorney General) v Johnstone*,[104] which widened the purview of protections for caregiving under family status.

First, however, it should be pointed out that there appears to be some irony reflected in the cases discussed here. Both of these influential gender and family status discrimination cases look to the accommodation of disability as a model for comparison. This may be due to the fact that disability is a very powerful metaphor with respect to concepts of disadvantage because it undercuts arguments of a blameworthiness or choice in terms of an individual's circumstances and promotes notions of social responsibility. The *Granovsky* and *Honda v Keays* cases discussed above illustrate how these aspects of the disability paradigm seem to fall away in cases of chronic illness, often because of comparisons made to others who are either permanently disabled or not disabled at all. The gender and family status cases become that much more important because assertions of collective responsibility override ideas of individual blame. These human rights cases also recognize important social goals missing from the disability law realm that are valuable when dealing with chronic illness, like work-life balance, flexibility, the importance of caregiving, and the need to protect careers and job-related benefits.

Brooks signified a sea change in Canadian law. The Supreme Court overruled its earlier decision in *Bliss v Attorney General of Canada*,[105] in which it had found that discrimination on the basis of sex did not include discrimination because of pregnancy. At issue in *Brooks* was the employer's sickness and accident group insurance plan that specifically excluded pregnant employees for a number of weeks prior to and following the birth of a child. In reversing its position, the Court refutes the idea that pregnancy is a voluntary state and that inequality "is not created by legislation but by nature."[106] By doing this, the Court extends the realm of social responsibility and flips the rhetoric around choice, thus removing the onus from the affected individual and placing it with those who have the power to make policy.

Also significant is the Court's reasoning concerning the social importance of gendered caregiving and making room for it in the world of work. As the decision clarifies, "[c]ombining paid work with motherhood and accommodating the childbearing needs of working women are ever increasing imperatives. That those who bear children and benefit society as a whole thereby should not be economically or socially disadvantaged seems to bespeak the obvious."[107]

An application of this sentiment to cases of chronic illness could see an expansion of the societal importance of caregiving needs to include not just those who are taking care of others, but also those who are taking care of themselves. When it comes to adults with chronic illness, there is a false dichotomy between caregivers and those who receive care because an adult with a chronic illness is often his or her own caregiver. As in the case of family status accommodation, it is in society's wider interest to ensure that the time required for such care is protected; it is an investment in prevention of further harm to that person and of increased healthcare and other costs that would otherwise be levied against the society at large.[108]

Johnstone, which builds on *Brooks*, is a family status case and a decision that makes some strong statements in a relatively new and evolving area of human rights law.[109] Essentially, the case definitively expands family status to include child-caregiving obligations. The claimant in this case challenged her employer's refusal to grant her a fixed-shift schedule to manage the childcare needs of her two children. Instead, the employer responded that the only way it would concede a fixed schedule was if Johnstone gave up her full-time position for part-time work. This change in employment status would mean that Johnstone would have to give up her long-term career objectives with the employer and forsake the benefits associated with her current position. The Tribunal's finding of discrimination was upheld on judicial review and the ruling hailed as "[a] landmark federal court decision that states workplaces are obliged to accommodate reasonable childcare-related requests from their employees."[110]

Extrapolating from the *Johnstone* decision to accommodation of chronic illness, there is a clear recognition of the importance of work-life balance. This means that, as a matter of fairness, so long as the caregiving needs are of "substance" and the worker has made attempts to "reconcile" care and work obligations, the employer must be flexible and provide accommodation.[111] Flexibility in the form of offering a choice of part-time employment without benefits was deemed to be an insufficient accommodation. The decision demonstrates that work is central to a person's life and livelihood, but not at the expense of other needs. Choices concerning "fundamental societal relationships" of caregiving are not to be treated as tradeoffs or compromises in terms of work and are protected under human rights law.[112] When push comes to shove, workplaces must give way to caregiving in a manner that recognizes that an employee need not be a warrior to preserve a stake in things like benefits and career objectives.

Why the Analogy Works
As noted above, because most of the caregiving work in families is still done by women, related issues include an unavoidable link to gender. Chronic illness is also both gendered and gendering. These conditions are gendered because they have a disproportionate impact on women's bodies.[113] They are gendering because, culturally, there has been a blurring of the lines between what it means to be ill, frail, and feminine. Women are seen to be motivated not by their minds, but by their bodies; bodies that are viewed as "leaky," uncontrollable, and lesser in comparison to the male norm.[114] In Victorian literature, for example, women were portrayed as "biologically inferior" and were romanticized for their susceptibility to "disease and pain."[115] Today, the fashion industry promotes an image of the ultra-thin woman – a body-type achieved sometimes through eating disorders and at the expense of menstruation – as the picture of beauty.[116] On the other hand, men's bodies are valued for their "strength, activeness, speed, virility, stamina, and fortitude."[117] Understanding these traditional, and oppositional, perceptions of male and female helps to bring the utility of a gender discrimination analogy into focus.

At the same time, it is important to set out some caveats with respect to comparisons. Being disabled is not the same as being oppressed because of gender. Such an analogy would fail to recognize the unique experience that results from physical and mental difference.[118] It is also a problem to conflate disability and gender, as the experience of being disabled can also be degendering.[119] One cannot simply substitute the words "chronically ill" for the word "female" and vice versa. It must be understood that the experiences are different. That said, there is a kind of similarity that exists when it comes to the relationship each class has to the warrior trope.

Martha Minow's book *Making All the Difference: Inclusion, Exclusion, and American Law* is an exploration of how relationships of difference function in our society.[120] In particular, Minow examines how concepts of what is normal and what is different are created and enforced to maintain power relationships. She writes: "The attribution of difference hides the power of those who classify and of the institutional arrangements that enshrine one type of person as the norm, and then treat classifications of difference as inherent and natural while debasing those defined as different."[121]

The chronically ill lawyer and the caregiving lawyer are both perceived as deviant when held up against the warrior-litigator norm. Societal notions of what it means to be a caregiver function in opposition to what we imagine to be an ideal worker. Parents, and in particular mothers, are perceived as less competent, committed, dependable, and authoritative than other workers.[122] And hence, they are viewed as less effective for a law firm's bottom line.

When it comes to disability, Iris Marion Young applies Minow's proposition to explore how employers are able to define what it means to be a good worker.[123] Young writes:

> Among such norms of work that have an impact on people with disabilities is the norm of the "hale and hearty" worker. The "normal" worker is supposed to be energetic, have high concentration abilities, be alert to adapt to changing conditions, and be able to withstand physical, mental or interactive stress in good humor. Workers who fail to measure up to one or more of these standards are "normally" considered lazy, slackers, uncooperative or otherwise inadequate.[124]

The adherence to the idea of a normal or ideal worker functions to preserve particular power dynamics, in this case the dominant position of the healthy male. This relationship to the masculine, nondisabled norm is similar in character and effect for members of both groups.[125] Both, therefore, also benefit from refuting the warrior-worker norm and replacing this idealized image with values related to flexibility, guarding benefits and work-life balance, and the social importance of caregiving obligations, be it for oneself or a family member.

Still, the analogy between gender discrimination and chronic illness discrimination remains imperfect. Unlike the mothering model, chronic illness involves care for oneself as opposed to care for others. Mothers are supposed to engage in self-sacrifice, not self-care.[126] That said, there is also no possibility of contracting out much of one's own care when it comes to an illness – it is impossible to pay someone to have your migraine or undergo your treatment, for example – a difference that possibly makes claims for chronic illness even stronger than claims for the care of others; although, this line of argument has significant social class implications.

It is also important to issue a word of warning against the trend of women-warrior worship. Advancing arguments for women to simply adhere to a masculine warrior norm by "manning up" or "leaning in"[127] in the work-place may erode gains made in terms of recognizing that the old model does not work for everyone, especially people with chronic illnesses.[128] It is of particular concern now, as some Canadian jurisdictions have been slow to take up the cause of family status discrimination.

All told, however, the exercise of carefully analogizing the experiences of discrimination based on gender and chronic illness is helpful. It highlights that "the privileging of masculinity has worked to shape and intensify the special rights and privileges of the able bodied."[129] There are more similari-ties than differences, both in terms of the problems and the solutions.

Where Does the Analogy Lead Us?

As a society, we seem able to recognize that the warrior-worker norm poses problems for caregivers, many of whom are women. This is as true in the legal field as it is for other workers. That norm also leads to many of the same obstacles for people with chronic illnesses. Lawyers who can-not live up to high standards of competitiveness and commitment to work above all else face challenges, both in terms of day-to-day accom-modation and also with respect to their ability to remain and thrive with-in the profession.

Several trends emerge in terms of the character of discrimination workers with chronic illnesses face and the failures of the disability para-digm to mend the damage. While chronic illness forms a class of dis-ability, and is even recognized as such under the law, the way we often conceive of disability is unhelpful, even harmful, to those who fall within Susan Wendell's classification of "unhealthy" disabled. The social model of disability tends to prioritize permanent and physical disability that may be accommodated by way of permanent and physical accommoda-tion. Chronic conditions are different because they often result in unpre-dictable impairments that affect people who appear to be just as strong and healthy as everyone else.

When it comes to the law, this conceptual hierarchy of disability, which places those with chronic illnesses near the bottom, further marginalizes this group of workers by virtue of comparisons made to those who are either "dauntingly" disabled, as Justice Binnie puts it, or those who are not disabled and we believe have made a decision to work and earn less. People who are chronically ill lose their status as truly disabled and appear less deserving of accommodation, compensation, and promotion. And, as the language in the *Granovsky* decision demonstrates, concepts of commitment and effort become matters of choice.

This problem leads to an obvious and pressing question: Now what? How do we use the caregiver analogy, along with the gender and family status case law, to advance the cause for those people with chronic conditions?

For starters, the language of accommodation for chronic illness needs to cast things like the value of flexible work arrangements, self-care, and work-life balance as social rather than individual goods, just as has been done in cases like *Brooks* and *Johnstone*. We all gain from these ideals, both because we are all human and vulnerable to the impacts of illness and aging, and also because we collectively bear the costs of the harms that result from failing to accommodate the chronically ill. As part of this, we need to expand the idea of what constitutes caregiving from caring for children and family members to include caring for oneself.

Further, building on the understanding that comparing pregnant workers to nonpregnant workers is pointless, the same needs to be done with comparisons regarding chronic illness. That is, we must stop comparing workers who are periodically disabled to those who are permanently disabled or those who choose to curtail their workload. There has never been a better time to make this argument, as the Supreme Court has expressed its support for eliminating comparator groups in discrimination analysis.[130] Removing the comparison step will help ensure that employers must demonstrate undue hardship in more chronic illness cases.

The big lesson we can take and apply from *Johnstone* is that caregiving, of any kind, is not something done at the expense of careers. Protecting work-life balance is not simply about protecting jobs. Rather, protecting careers means that workers are able to maintain rights to benefits, salaries, and advancement. Because these gains have been made for caregivers using the metaphor of disability, it should be possible to transfer back some of the analytical benefit.

All of the above also requires a cultural shift. We must recognize that people have a real interest in doing well at work. At the same time, we need to question the value of the warrior norm and be willing to replace it with values like flexibility, work-life balance, and caregiving while simultaneously recognizing the importance of careers, salaries, and related benefits. If we come to view these things as broad social goods, then it will also be incumbent on us to make policy decisions that support workers who are chronically ill, along with their employers. More work needs to be done to develop the forms these supports could take, and this would properly be the subject of much investigation and many more papers.

We do not need more research to know that achieving this shift will be challenging. Because people with chronic illnesses do not come together as a visibly identifiable group and are, understandably, reluctant to self-declare, we miss out in terms of clearly grasping the extent of the problem. As well, promoting productive workplaces is important, and battling the warrior mentality may have a cost when it comes to things like profit.

All of which brings us to the last reason for making the caregiving and accommodation analogy. There is a kind of utility derived from riding the coattails of the women's movement, to use a gendered cliché. As evidenced by the *Touchstones* Report,[131] women have been able to successfully draw attention to issues of discrimination and the practice of law and pave the way for some progress, even if only incrementally. Linking the problems of discrimination on the basis of chronic illness to those of discrimination on the basis of caregiving can provide reasons to seek common, and more effective, solutions.

NOTES

I am grateful for the support and encouragement of Dr. Ravi Malhotra, who provided very helpful feedback on an earlier draft of this paper. I wish to thank Prof. Katherine M Franke, Isidor and Seville Sulzbacher Professor of Law and Director of the Center for Gender and Sexuality Law at Columbia Law School, for her supervision of this paper; Prof. Elizabeth Emens, Isidor and Seville Sulzbacher Professor of Law at Columbia Law School, for her comments and ongoing support; Prof. Susan Boyd, Professor Emerita at the University of British Columbia's Peter A Allard School of Law, for suggestions that helped inform this work and my larger dissertation project; and the Institute for Feminist Legal Studies at York University's Osgood Hall Law School. I would also like to thank the anonymous peer reviewers for their very helpful and constructive feedback. An earlier version of this paper was presented at the annual meeting of the Law and Society Association, Minneapolis, MN, 30 May 2014, and it received an honourable mention for the Roderick A Macdonald Student Essay Prize from the Canadian Law and Society Association, Calgary, AB, 28 May 2016. All errors remain my own.

1 Canadian Bar Association, Task Force on Gender Equality in the Legal Profession, *Touchstones for Change: Equality, Diversity and Accountability* (Ottawa: Canadian Bar Association, 1993) (Chair: Hon Bertha Wilson) [*Touchstones*]. For a critique of

the report with respect to disability issues, see Dianne Pothier, "A Comment on the Canadian Bar Association's Gender Equality Task Force Report" (1993) 16 Dalhousie LJ 484. Pothier notes that the task force reflected on how other equality-seeking groups might also be implicated by the legal profession's practices, but their analysis "comes across as an afterthought" and is "inadequate," particularly in terms of disability (at 490–91).

2 *Touchstones, supra* note 1 at 3.

3 *Ibid* at ch 4.

4 See, e.g., Jordan Furlong, "Why Women Leave Law Firms, and When They'll Return" (28 February 2013), *Law21* (blog), online: <http://www.law21.ca/2013/02/why-women-leave-law-firms-and-when-theyll-return/> ("The typical contemporary law firm is nobody's idea of a good business model, a satisfying workplace, or a solid bet for long-term future success. It shouldn't surprise us that women abandon this model in droves"). See also, e.g., Omar Ha-Redeye, "Introducing Men's Voice into the Parenting Debate" *Slaw* (30 June 2013), online: <http://www.slaw.ca/2013/06/30/introducing-mens-voice-into-the-parenting-debate/> ("Men are very much part of the discussion within families on balancing work and life, as families jointly struggle to figure out how they fulfill parenting duties and maintain careers of both parents").

5 I borrow this term from Beth Symes, Janet Minor, Jessica Wolfe & Sharon Walker, "Panels Full of Women: 40 Years Later, Has Anything Changed?" (Plenary panel at the annual conference of the Law Union of Ontario, Toronto, 16 March 2013). Further discussion about the warrior-litigator can be found in the section "When Lawyers Are Chronically Ill" below.

6 Tamsin McMahon, "Time to Man Up," *Maclean's* (18 March 2013) 54; Sheryl Sandberg, *Lean In* (New York: Alfred A Knopf, 2013). This bestseller by Facebook's chief operating officer, Sheryl Sandberg, outlines how she believes working women make choices that negatively impact their careers and advises them on how to achieve success.

7 I chose to use the word "disabled" here, and at points throughout the chapter, instead of person-first terminology because the passive terminology invites the reader to question our collective role in creating conditions of disablement. As Sheila McIntyre points out, by using such language, "the focus shifts from debates about appropriate comparators to analysis of relations between excluders and the excluded, stigmatizers and stigmatized, expropriator and dispossessed." Sheila McIntyre, "Answering the Siren Call of Abstract Formalism with the Subjects and Verbs of Domination" in Fay Faraday, Margaret Denike & M Kate Stephenson, eds, *Making Equality Rights Real: Securing Substantive Equality under the Charter* (Toronto: Irwin Law, 2009) 99 at 103.

8 Further discussion on what constitutes a chronic illness can be found the section "Chronic Illness as Disability" below.

9 Susan Wendell, "Unhealthy Disabled: Treating Chronic Illnesses as Disabilities" (2001) 16:4 Hypatia 17. These terms are explained further in the section "Chronic Illness as Disability" below.

10 I use the word "illness" throughout this chapter in the common or colloquial sense. Again, I largely borrow from the work of Susan Wendell, who uses the term to refer

to "suffering, imitation and/or loss of function experienced by a person and attributed by her/him (or others) to a loss of health and not to a physical or mental condition
present from birth or acquired by an injury to a specific part of the body." *Ibid* at
32, n 1.

11 For example, the 2012 *Canadian Survey on Disability* by Statistics Canada uses a
new set of questions, making it impossible to accurately compare the data with
the former Participation and Activity Limitation Survey (PALS). Online:
<http://www23.statcan.gc.ca/imdb/p2SV.pl?Function=getSurvey&SDDS=
3251&Item_Id=133011&lang=en#a4>. Interestingly, the survey did ask respondents
to report the cause of any conditions and lists "disease of illness" among the
possible responses. To date, no results reflecting this part of the survey have
been released.

12 Health Council of Canada, *Population Patterns of Chronic Health Conditions in Canada* (Toronto: Health Council of Canada, 2007) at 6–7, online: <http://theconference.
ca/pdf/healthcouncil_populationpatternsofchronichealthconditionsincanada.
pdf>. These figures account for only seven chronic conditions: arthritis, cancer,
chronic obstructive pulmonary disease, diabetes, heart disease, high blood pressure,
and mood disorders. It is therefore important to note the absence of autoimmune
disorders, most mental health issues, and so on.

13 Kimberly Elmslie, "Against the Growing Burden of Disease" (PowerPoint presentation, delivered at the Canadian Conference on Global Health, Ottawa, 22 October
2012) at 5, online: <http://www.ccgh-csih.ca/assets/Elmslie.pdf>. These numbers
reflect only four kinds of chronic diseases: cancer, cardiovascular diseases, diabetes,
and hypertension. Again, it is notable that autoimmune disorders and mental illnesses are not included.

14 Tyler Meredith & Colin Chia, *Leaving Some Behind: What Happens When Workers
Get Sick* (Montreal: Institute for Research on Public Policy, 2015) at 5, online: <http://
irpp.org/wp-content/uploads/2015/09/report-2015-09-03.pdf>, citing Public Health
Agency of Canada, *The Chief Public Health Officer's Report on the State of Public
Health in Canada, 2014: Public Health in the Future* (Ottawa: Minister of Health,
2014), online: <http://www.phac-aspc.gc.ca/cphorsphc-respcacsp/2014/assets/pdf/
2014-eng.pdf>.

15 I take no position here on the value of participating in the labour force other than to
say that it is the current norm and that, as a consequence, people who wish to work
should be able to do so. I recognize that the social model of disablement has been
criticized for its central focus on paid employment, because of resulting exclusion of
disabled people who cannot work or whose work is undervalued. See AJ Withers,
Disability Politics and Theory (Halifax: Fernwood, 2012) at 89–90. There is also an
argument that the equation of work and identity is a capitalist concept and that those
with some forms of disability must be accorded a right not to work. See Sunny Taylor, "The Right Not to Work: Power and Disability" (2004) 55:10 Monthly Rev,
online: <http://monthlyreview.org/2004/03/01/the-right-not-to-work-power-and
-disability>.

16 This chapter also does not take up the challenge of dealing with the intersection of
disability and other identity axes such as race, indigeneity, immigrant status, age,
or sexual orientation. See, e.g., Mia Mingus "Changing the Framework: Disability

Justice" (12 February 2011), *Leaving Evidence* (blog), online: <https://leavingevidence. wordpress.com/2011/02/12/changing-the-framework-disability-justice/>.

17 In 2011, the employment rate for disabled people in Canada between the ages of 25 and 64 was 49 percent, compared to 79 percent for people who did not report a disability. Martin Turcotte, *Persons with Disability and Employment* (Ottawa: Statistics Canada, 3 December 2014) at 1–2, online: <http://www.statcan.gc.ca/pub/75 -006-x/2014001/article/14115-eng.pdf>.

18 Many people with "a severe or very severe disability," to borrow the survey's language, say they experience discrimination in employment on the basis of disability. The numbers range significantly depending on age and gender; they are highest among younger, male workers, with 62 percent reporting that they believe they were denied employment in the past five years because of their disability. *Ibid* at 9.

19 Wendell, *supra* note 9 at 20–21.

20 *Ibid.*

21 *Ibid* at 20.

22 Sharon Dale Stone, "Resisting an Illness Label: Disability, Impairment, and Illness" in Pamela Moss & Katherine Teghtsoonian, eds, *Contesting Illness: Processes and Practices* (Toronto: University of Toronto Press, 2008) 201 at 202.

23 The Supreme Court has interpreted the meaning of "disability" very broadly in *Quebec (Commission des droits de la personne et des droits de la jeunesse) v Montréal (City); Quebec (Commission des droits de la personne et des droits de la jeunesse) v Boisbriand (City)*, 2000 SCC 27, [2000] 1 SCR 665 [*Quebec v Montreal*]:

> The liberal and purposive method of interpretation along with the contextual approach, which includes an analysis of the objectives of human rights legislation, the way in which the word "handicap" and other similar terms have been interpreted elsewhere in Canada, the legislative history, the intention of the legislature and the other provisions of the *Charter*, support a broad definition of the word "handicap," which does not necessitate the presence of functional limitations and which recognizes the subjective component of any discrimination based on this ground. (at para 71)

24 The practice of law plays an important role in defining equality, and there is, therefore, a unique onus placed on its practitioners to lead by example. Sheila McIntyre and Elizabeth Sheehy thoughtfully make this point in the introduction to their book *Calling for Change: Women, Law, and the Legal Profession* (Ottawa: University of Ottawa Press, 2006) at 1–2:

> [There] is an understanding of legal practice as more than a job: it is also a crucial location and a vehicle of the struggle for social justice. Equality proponents and activists within the profession approach practice as a calling, and embrace an understanding of lawyering as a public service, an enabling profession.

25 The Toronto law firm Davies Ward Phillips & Vineberg LLP earned some notoriety for its "Slavies" recruitment campaign, which attempted to capitalize on the firm's

reputation for overworking students and young lawyers. See Elie Mystal, "Truth in Advertising: Firm Jokes about Working Associates like 'Slavies,'" *Above the Law* (25 January 2012), online: <http://abovethelaw.com/2012/01/truth-in-advertising-firm-jokes-about-working-associates-like-slavies/>. See also Jeff Gray, "Davies Apologizes for 'Slavies' Ads," *Globe and Mail* (27 January 2012), online: <http://www.theglobeandmail.com/report-on-business/streetwise/davies-apologizes-for-slavies-ads/article621161/>.

26 See, e.g., Howard Scher, "Litigation: The 5 Traits of Highly Effective Trial Lawyers," *Inside Counsel* (30 August 2012), online: <http://www.insidecounsel.com/2012/08/30/litigation-the-5-traits-of-highly-effective-trial?t=litigation>. The author lists the five most important qualities for litigators as credibility, civility, confidence, curiosity, and competitive spirit. Carrie Griffin Basas, who has written about female lawyers with disabilities in the United States, describes the desirable traits of lawyers as, "bravado, strength, stamina, courage, maneuvering, scruples, strategy, intractability, endurance, and wile." Carrie Griffin Basas, "The New Boys: Women with Disabilities and the Legal Profession" (2010) 27 Berkeley J Gender L & Just 32 at 95.

27 Pothier, *supra* note 1 at 486.

28 Jerry Kang et al, "Are Ideal Litigators White? Measuring the Myth of Colorblindness" (2010) 7 J Empirical Leg Stud 886 (this study found that mock jurors exhibited both explicit and implicit biases in favour of white lawyers over Asian lawyers).

29 Lauren A Rivera, "Hiring as Cultural Matching: The Case of Elite Professional Service Firms" (2012) 77 American Sociological Rev 999 (this study found that hiring in professional firms often has more to do with cultural similarities than assessment of skills).

30 Osgoode Business Law Society, "The Firm Culture Guide" (2007), online: <http://obls.wordpress.com/the-firm-culture-guide/> (a student club at Osgoode Hall Law School, York University, surveyed a number of major Canadian law firms).

31 *Ontario Human Rights Commission and O'Malley v Simpsons-Sears Ltd*, [1985] 2 SCR 536, 23 DLR (4th) 321 [*O'Malley v Simpsons-Sears*]. This was the first duty to accommodate case decided by the Supreme Court of Canada. The accommodation sought in this case was with respect to religious belief and the scheduling of shifts. See also *British Columbia (Public Service Employee Relations Commission) v BCGSEU*, [1999] 3 SCR 3, 176 DLR (4th) 1 (setting out the substantive and procedural elements of the duty to accommodate, and that such a duty is a fundamental legal obligation).

32 *Central Alberta Dairy Pool v Alberta (Human Rights Commission)*, [1990] 2 SCR 489, 72 DLR (4th) 417. The Supreme Court set out the following as potential factors for consideration of undue hardship in employment: financial cost, impact on the collective agreement, morale of other employees, health and safety, adaptability of the workforce and facilities, and the size of the operation (at para 62).

33 James Cameron, Kim Patenaude & Shauna Troniak, "Invisible Disability and the Duty to Accommodate in the Workplace" (presentation delivered to Health Canada on behalf of Reach Canada, 3 December 2008), online: <http://www.ravenlaw.com/

James-Cameron-Speaks-Health-Canada-Seminar-International-Day-Persons
-Disabilities.html>.

34 See, e.g., the Law Society of Upper Canada, *Rules of Professional Conduct* (Law Society of Upper Canada, 2000), r 5.04(1):

> A lawyer has a special responsibility to respect the requirements of human rights laws in force in Ontario and, specifically, to honour the obligation not to discriminate on the grounds of race, ancestry, place of origin, colour, ethnic origin, citizenship, creed, sex, sexual orientation, age, record of offences (as defined in the Ontario Human Rights Code), marital status, family status, or disability with respect to professional employment of other lawyers, articled students, or any other person or in professional dealings with other licensees or any other person.

35 See, e.g., American Bar Association Commission on Mental and Physical Disability Law, *ABA Disability Statistics Report* (1 February 2010) at 4, online: <http://www.americanbar.org/content/dam/aba/migrated/disability/PublicDocuments/ABADisabilityStatisticsReport.authcheckdam.pdf>.

36 The theft analogy is interesting because it seems to expose a tendency to view those with invisible disabilities as deceitful. Law Society of British Columbia, *Lawyers with Disabilities: Identifying Barriers to Equality* (Vancouver: Law Society of British Columbia, 2001) at i, online: <http://www.lawsociety.bc.ca/docs/publications/reports/DisabilityReport2004.pdf> [LSBC].

37 The Law Society of Upper Canada, *Students and Lawyers with Disabilities: Increasing Access to the Legal Profession* (Report of the Disability Working Group) (December 2005), online: <http://rc.lsuc.on.ca/pdf/equity/studentsandlawyerswithdisabilitiesreport.pdf> [LSUC]; Fiona M Kay, Cristi Masuch & Paula Curry, *Diversity and Change: The Contemporary Legal Profession in Ontario* (September 2004), online: <http://rc.lsuc.on.ca/pdf/equity/diversityChange.pdf>. In 2011, the Ontario Bar Association surveyed lawyers and law students with disabilities but no results were published, due to a small response rate.

38 LSBC, *supra* note 36.

39 Basas, *supra* note 26.

40 See, e.g., Sharon-Dale Stone, Valorie A Crooks & Michelle Owen, "Going through the Back Door: Chronically Ill Academics' Experiences as 'Unexpected Workers'" (2013) 11 Social Theory & Health 151 (an examination of academics with multiple sclerosis). See also Joy E Beatty, "Career Barriers Experienced by People with Chronic Illness: A U.S. Study" (2012) 24 Employee Responsibilities and Rights J 91 (an American study of people with chronic illnesses in various professions).

41 Christine Miserandino, an American woman diagnosed with lupus, has developed "spoon theory" as a way to explain what it is like to live with a chronic illness. The spoon metaphor, which has been gaining in popularity, illustrates how energy is a limited resource, measured in "spoons," that is rationed and spent on daily tasks. Christine Miserandino, "The Spoon Theory," online: <http://www.butyoudontlooksick.com/wpress/articles/written-by-christine/the-spoon-theory/>.

42 Kay, Masuch & Curry, *supra* note 37 at 57:

Lawyers working in non-private practice are also more likely to have access to alternative work arrangements. Part-time work is more readily available: 57% of lawyers in non-private practice compared to 47% of lawyers working law firms, reported that part-time work was an option. Job sharing, although not widely available, is more common in non-private practice (34% compared to 16%) as is telework (56% compared to 42%). Interestingly, flexible full-time hours were equally available in both settings: 65% of lawyers employed in non-private practice and 64% of lawyers in law firms reported flexible hours for full-time work.

43 LSBC, *supra* note 36 at 2, 22, 25; LSUC, *supra* note 37 at 14.
44 Stone, Crooks & Owen, *supra* note 40.
45 *Ibid* at 156–57.
46 Basas, *supra* note 26 at 59.
47 *Ibid* at 59–60.
48 Allan McChesney, Richard Nolan & Martin Schmieg, *Advancing Professional Opportunities and Employment Accommodation for Lawyers and Other Law Graduates Who Have Disabilities* (Ottawa: Reach Canada, 2001) at 110, online: <http://www.reach.ca/_uploads/_media/advancing_opportunities.pdf>. Kay, Masuch & Curry, *supra* note 37 at 99.
49 See Eli Wald, "Glass Ceilings and Dead Ends: Professional Ideologies, Gender Stereotypes, and the Future of Women Lawyers at Large Law Firms" (2010) 78 Fordham Law Review 2245. This article examines past trends in law firm culture designed to promote "objective standards of excellence" and "competitive meritocracy." The author also notes that firms are becoming more "hypercompetitive" and that this is having disproportionate impact on women's equality within these work environments.
50 LSUC, *supra* note 37 at 14.
51 See, for example, Kay, Masuch & Curry, *supra* note 37 at 95: "I left the full-time practice of law at a big firm because they were unable/unwilling to accommodate my special needs due to my health issues. I have an illness that is unpredictable and therefore requires me to have flexible hours. This was not possible in a Bay Street firm."
52 LSBC, *supra* note 36 at 19.
53 *Ibid* at 2.
54 Beatty, *supra* note 40.
55 *Ibid* at 101.
56 *Ibid* at 103.
57 *Ibid* at 104.
58 *Ibid* at 107. Interestingly, a recent labour arbitration ruling in Ontario found that collective agreement language that characterized absences separated by three-weeks time as separate periods of illness for the purposes of limiting short-term sick-pay benefits unfairly impacted employees with chronic illnesses under the province's *Human Rights Code*. See "Arbitrator Finds Hospital Sick Leave Policy Discriminatory" (13 April 2015), online: <http://ravenlaw.com/2015/04/13/arbitrator-finds-hospital-sick-leave-policy-discriminatory/>.

59 As cited in Donald H Stone, "The Disabled Lawyers Have Arrived: Have They Been Welcomed with Open Arms into the Profession? An Empirical Study of the Disabled Lawyer" (2009) 27 Law & Inequality 93 at 95, n 14.

60 Kevin D MacNeil, *The Duty to Accommodate in Employment* (Toronto, ON: Thomson Reuters, 2012), ch 26 at 2, 4–5 (loose-leaf; consulted 2 August 2013). Some collective agreements are worded so as to allow vacation accrual during paid sick leave. See, e.g., *Public Service Alliance of Canada v Sydney Airport Authority*, 2015 NSSC 38 (CanLII).

61 The history of the Law Society of British Columbia's fitness question is outlined in *Gichuru v The Law Society of British Columbia*, 2009 BCHRT 360 at paras 66–88, [2009] BCHRTD No 360.

62 *Ibid* at para 61.

63 *Ibid*. For the decisions concerning remedy, see *Gichuru v The Law Society of British Columbia*, 2011 BCHRT 185, [2011] BCHRTD No 185, aff'd *Gichuru v The Law Society of British Columbia*, 2013 BCSC 1325, [2013] BCJ No 1629 (with the exception of the miscalculation of employment insurance benefits).

64 Michael Lynk, "Accommodating Disabilities in the Canadian Workplace" (1999) 7 CLELJ 183 at 189.

65 Vicki Schultz, "Life's Work," (2000) 100 Columbia L Rev 1881, at 1886–92.

66 *Canadian Human Rights Act*, RSC, 1985, c H-6, s 2.

67 Philosopher Gregory Kavka argued that, while the right is not absolute, people with disabilities should have a legal right to paid employment, arising from moral considerations of one's "right to participate as an active member in the productive processes of one's society." Further, he said that this right places obligations on both government and private employers and that it is insufficient to make determinations about a disabled person's employability based on an economic cost-benefit analysis alone. Gregory S Kavka, "Disability and the Right to Work" in Leslie Pickering Francis & Anita Silvers, eds, *Americans with Disabilities: Exploring Implications of the Law for Individuals and Institutions* (New York: Routledge, 2000) 174 at 174–75. For a discussion on disability and "the right not to work," see Taylor, *supra* note 15.

68 Wendell, *supra* note 9 at 21.

69 *Council of Canadians with Disabilities v VIA Rail Canada Inc*, 2007 SCC 15, [2007] 1 SCR 650.

70 *Eldridge v British Columbia (Attorney General)*, [1997] 3 SCR 624, 151 DLR (4th) 577.

71 It is worth noting that, while the accommodations in these cases may appear straightforward, the achievement of such victories has in no way been simple or easy for disability advocates. After all, the provincial and federal governments were so invested in denying the accommodation that both claims clawed their way up the rungs of litigation to the Supreme Court of Canada. The decade-long ascension of the *VIA Rail* case was so arduous that it nearly bankrupted the Council of Canadians with Disabilities. David Baker & Sarah Godwin, "All Aboard: The Supreme Court of Canada Confirms that Canadians with Disabilities Have Substantive Equality Rights" (2008) 71 Sask L Rev 39 at 40.

72 Michael Oliver, *Understanding Disability: From Theory to Practice* (New York: St. Martin's Press, 1996) at 32.

73 Jill C Humphrey, "Researching Disability Politics, or, Some Problems with the Social Model in Practice" (2000) 15 Disability & Society 63 at 63. See also, Wendell, *supra* note 9 at 31:

> [Focus on the medical model] can lead us to ignore the social conditions that are causing or increasing disability among people who have impairments. Moreover, given the history of eugenics, there is reason to be skeptical about whether prevention and cure are intended primarily to prevent suffering or to eliminate "abnormalities" and "abnormal" people.

74 The Supreme Court endorsed the social model, albeit not to the exclusion of the medical model, in *Quebec v Montreal, supra* note 23. Citing Bickenbach, the Court states, "By placing the emphasis on human dignity, respect, and the right to equality rather than a simple biomedical condition, this approach recognizes that the attitudes of society and its members often contribute to the idea or perception of a 'handicap.' In fact, a person may have no limitations in everyday activities other than those created by prejudice and stereotypes" (at para 77).

75 Jerome E Bickenbach, *Physical Disability and Social Policy* (Toronto: University of Toronto Press, 1993) at 13.

76 *Ibid* at 138 [emphasis in original].

77 For an account of the relationship between the social model and the disability rights movement in Canada, see Withers, *supra* note 15 at 81–97.

78 Carol Thomas, *Female Forms: Experiencing and Understanding Disability* (Buckingham, UK: Open University Press, 1999) at 75.

79 *Ibid* at 43.

80 Fiona Sampson, *The Judicial Treatment of Gendered Disability Discrimination* (PhD Thesis, Osgoode Hall Law School, York University, 2005) at 20 [unpublished].

81 Humphrey, *supra* note 73 at 67.

82 *Ibid* at 69.

83 Wendell, *supra* note 9 at 28–29.

84 Susan Wendell, *The Rejected Body: Feminist Philosophical Reflections on Disability* (New York: Routledge, 1996) at 27 (emphasis in original).

85 *Granovsky v Canada (Minister of Employment and Immigration)*, 2000 SCC 28, [2000] 1 SCR 703 [*Granovsky*].

86 Sampson, *supra* note 80 at 275. On the other hand, while Ravi Malhotra characterizes *Granovsky* as a disappointing decision that retreats from notions of substantive equality, he also goes on to note that the Supreme Court exhibited a sophisticated understanding of the social model of disablement. Ravi Malhotra, "Has the *Charter* Made a Difference for People with Disabilities? Reflections and Strategies for the 21st Century" (2012) 58:2 SCLR 273 at 286–87.

87 Sampson, *supra* note 80 at 261.

88 *Canada Pension Plan Act*, RSC, 1985, c C-8, s 44(2)(b).

89 *Canadian Charter of Rights and Freedoms*, s 15(1), Part 1 of the *Constitution Act, 1982*, being schedule B to the *Canada Act 1982* (UK), 1982, c 11.

90 It is worth noting here, however, that the Court does reject arguments that Granovsky is not disabled. Malhotra, *supra* note 86 at 287.

91 Sampson, *supra* note 80 at 277.

92 The "supercrip" characterization is the flipside of projections of pity and is considered equally harmful by critical disability scholars and members of the disability rights movement. The supercrip is a disabled person who defies his or her disability, goes on to excel in the face of adversity, and is then regarded as amazing or inspirational by others. The result is that the responsibility for disablement is placed on the individuals affected as opposed to those who perpetuate inequality. For more see Joseph P Shapiro, *No Pity: People with Disabilities Forging a New Civil Rights Movement* (New York: Random House, 1993) ch 2, "Tiny Tims, Supercrips, and the End of Pity." See also Anna Hamilton, "The Transcontinental Disability Choir: Disability Archetypes: Supercrip" (18 December 2009), *Bitch Media* (blog), online: <http://bitchmagazine.org/post/the-transcontinental-disability-choir-disability-archetypes-supercrip>.

93 *Granovsky, supra* note 85 at para 28.

94 *Honda Canada Inc v Keays*, 2008 SCC 39, [2008] 2 SCR 362.

95 MacNeil, *supra* note 60, ch 26 at 5–6.

96 *Re Versa Services Ltd. and Milk & Bread Drivers, Dairy Employees, Caterers & Allied Emplyees Union, Local 647* (1994), 39 LAC (4th) 196 at 201, aff'd (unreported, 7 February 1995, Ont Div Ct) (requiring employees on long-term disability to reimburse employer for the cost of benefits is not discriminatory). See also *Re Soldiers Memorial Hospital and ONA (Robinson)* (1996), 58 LAC (4th) 72, rev'd [1997] OJ No 2744 (Ont Div Ct), rev'd 42 OR (3rd) 692 (CA), leave to appeal to SCC refused 169 DLR (4th) vii (adjusting seniority date for employees on unpaid leave due to disability is discriminatory, but limiting service accrual and benefit contributions is not).

97 I'd like to thank Susan Boyd, Professor Emerita at the University of British Columbia's Peter A Allard School of Law, for pointing out that the comparison used in these cases illustrates the often problematic invocation of formal equality principles in antidiscrimination case law.

98 *Andrews v Law Society of British Columbia*, [1989] 1 SCR 143, 56 DLR (4th) 1; *O'Malley v Simpsons-Sears, supra* note 31.

99 Shelly J Correll, Stephen Benard & Ian Paik, "Getting a Job: Is There a Motherhood Penalty?" (2007) 112 Amer J Sociology 1297 at 1298.

100 Joan C Williams, "Want Gender Equality? Die Childless at Thirty" (2006) 27 Women's Rts L Rep 3. These harms are described, not in terms of a glass ceiling, but rather as a "maternal wall." It is not enough to compare men and women without also factoring in how women who are mothers fare.

101 See Law Society of Upper Canada, *Executive Summary: Retention of Women in Private Practice Working Group* (Toronto: Law Society of Upper Canada, 2008), online: <http://www.lsuc.on.ca/media/convmay08_retention_of_women_executive_summary.pdf>.

102 The "flexibility" stigma is twofold for men, who are regarded as poor workers and effeminized. Joan C Williams, Mary Blair-Loy & Jennifer L Berdahl, "Cultural

Schemas, Social Class, and the Flexibility Stigma" (2013) 69 J Social Issues 209 at 220. See also Tara Siegel Bernard, "The Unspoken Stigma of Workplace Flexibility" *New York Times* (14 June 2013), online: <http://www.nytimes.com/2013/06/15/your-money/the-unspoken-stigma-of-workplace-flexibility.html?pagewanted=all&_r=0>. Also Laurie A Rudman & Kris Mescher, "Penalizing Men Who Request a Family Leave: Is Flexibility Stigma a Femininity Stigma?" (2013) 69 J Social Issues 322 at 336: "[I]t appears that when men 'act like women' they are charged with violating proscriptions against weakness and prescriptions for agency – gender rules that play a key role in employment discrimination."

103 *Brooks v Canada Safeway*, [1989] 1 SCR 1219, 59 DLR (4th) 321 [*Brooks*].

104 *Canada (Attorney General) v Johnstone*, 2013 FC 113, 357 DLR (4th) 706 [*Johnstone*]. The Federal Court of Appeal affirmed the lower court's decision in early 2014, clarifying that protection of family status under the *Canadian Human Rights Act* covers a parent's legal obligations for care but does not extend to "voluntary family activities," which are regarded as "personal choices." 2014 FCA 110 at paras 70–74, 372 DLR (4th) 730.

105 *Bliss v Attorney General of Canada*, [1979] 1 SCR 183.

106 *Brooks, supra* note 103 at paras 1237, 1242.

107 *Ibid* at para 1243.

108 Notably, the divide between the concepts of self-care and care for others appears to be bridged in the *Employment Insurance Act*, SC 1996, c 23, which provides coverage for leave from employment due to pregnancy or parenting, sickness, and the care of family members, among other reasons. Even more specifically, the two forms of care are dealt with in the United States by the *Family Medical Leave Act*, 29 USC § 2601 (1993), which allows eligible employees to take unpaid, protected leave for certain family and medical reasons.

109 Ontario Human Rights Commission, "Family Status and Human Rights in Canada," online: <http://www.ohrc.on.ca/en/human-rights-and-family-ontario/family-status-and-human-rights-canada> (noting that family status, as a ground for protection from discrimination, was incorporated into human rights legislation in the late 1970s and early 1980s and is not found in all jurisdictions). As well, the threshold that must be met to demonstrate discrimination on the basis of family status remains higher in British Columbia following the decision in *Health Sciences Assoc of BC v Campbell River and North Island Transition Society*, 2004 BCCA 260, 240 DLR (4th) 479.

110 "Employers Told They Must Accommodate Staff's Child-Care Requests" *CBC News* (5 February 2013), online: <http://www.cbc.ca/news/canada/story/2013/02/05/court-ruling-employers-family-life.html>. One of the arguments made, and rejected, in the case was that family status simply protected against discrimination but did not entail accommodation. *Johnstone, supra* note 104 at para 102.

111 *Johnstone, supra* note 104 at paras 120, 128.

112 *Johnstone v Canada Border Services*, 2010 CHRT 20 at para 231, [2010] CHRD No 20, aff'd *Johnstone, supra* note 104 at para 61.

113 Wendell, *supra* note 9 at 19.

114 I have been very influenced by the work of my friend Julie Devaney, who writes and teaches, often through performance, about her experiences with chronic illness. Julie Devaney, *My Leaky Body: Tales from the Gurney* (Fredericton, NB: Goose Lane Editions, 2012) at 286–87, citing Margrit Shildrick, *Leaky Bodies and Boundaries: Feminism, Postmodernism and (Bio)ethics* (London,: Routledge, 1997). Sara Bergstesser's work also notes that women's bodies, which are different from men in their capacity for reproduction, are seen as inferior because they are "leaky, permeable, and disgusting." Sara M Bergstresser, "Embodied Threats to Bounded Selfhood: Reflections on the Female Body, 'Self-Mutilation,' and Autoimmunity" (paper presented to the Future of Disabilities Studies Project with the Center for the Study of Social Difference at Columbia University, New York, 1 March 2013) [unpublished, on file with author].

115 For an examination of such depictions of women in American literature, see Diane Price Herndl, *Invalid Women: Figuring Feminine Illness in American Fiction and Culture, 1840–1940* (Chapel Hill: University of North Carolina Press, 1993) at 34.

116 In her essay "Illness as Metaphor," Susan Sontag explores the romantic notions associated with tuberculosis and even goes so far as to propose that the "cult of thinness" that is associated with women's fashion is a vestige of such ideals. Susan Sontag, *Illness as Metaphor; and, AIDS and Its Metaphors* (New York: Picador, 2001) at 29.

117 Robert F Murphy, *The Body Silent* (New York: Henry Holt and Co., 1987) at 95. Carrie Griffin Basas also looks at disability, more generally, as feminizing. Basas, *supra* note 26 at 47: "If people with disabilities are devalued and subjugated in the workplace, women with disabilities bear both the "inferiority" of the "weaker sex" and the largest label of weakness imaginable – disability."

118 See Tobin Siebers, "Disability and the Pain of Minority Identity" (2012) [unpublished, on file with author].

119 See, e.g., Russell P Shuttleworth, "Disabled Masculinity: Expanding the Masculine Repertoire" in Bonnie G Smith & Beth Hutchison, eds, *Gendering Disability* (Piscataway, NJ: Rutgers University Press, 2004) 166 (an exploration of how physical disability impacts men who are unable to adhere to socially expected performances of masculinity).

120 Martha Minow, *Making All the Difference: Inclusion, Exclusion, and American Law* (Ithaca, NY: Cornell University Press, 1990).

121 *Ibid* at 111.

122 Correll, Benard & Paik, *supra* note 99 at 1298.

123 Iris Marion Young, "Disability and the Definition of Work" in Leslie Pickering Francis & Anita Silvers, eds, *Americans with Disabilities: Exploring Implications of the Law for Individuals and Institutions* (New York: Routledge, 2000) 169 at 171.

124 *Ibid* at 172.

125 Bonnie G Smith, "Introduction" in Bonnie G Smith & Beth Hutchison, eds, *Gendering Disability* (Piscataway, NJ: Rutgers University Press, 2004) 1 at 1–6.

126 Again, I would like to thank Susan Boyd, who offered this observation and phrasing.

127 See *supra* note 6 and accompanying text.

128 Rachel Cohen-Rottenberg, "Why This Disabled Woman No Longer Identifies as a Feminist" (30 July 2013), *Disability and Representation* (blog), online: <http://www.disabilityandrepresentation.com/2013/07/30/why-this-disabled-woman/> (brands of feminism that aim to replicate the warrior mentality, or privilege notions of strength, independence, and accomplishment, as Cohen-Rottenberg puts it, can be alienating to people with disabilities); see also Wendell, *supra* note 9.

129 Smith, *supra* note 125 at 6.

130 *Withler v Canada (Attorney General)*, 2011 SCC 12 at para 63, [2011] 1 SCR 396.

131 *Touchstones, supra* note 1.

Towards Full Inclusion
Addressing the Issue of Income Inequality for People with Disabilities in Canada

MEGAN A. RUSCIANO

Help is useful only when it leads to empowerment.
  – James I. Charlton, *Nothing about Us without Us*[1]

It may come as a surprise to some that today in Canada there are still laws on the books that allow people with disabilities to be paid a subminimum wage.[2] But far from being a vestige of a past era of sheltered workshops and segregated employment, wage disparity and inequality remain a reality for people with disabilities. Indeed, the lived experiences of many people with disabilities reflect failed promises of full social inclusion and gainful employment. When people with disabilities do enter the workplace, the work they perform is not equally valued, they are unable to hold jobs for long periods of time due to a lack of accommodations, and they must curb the income they receive in order not to jeopardize their access to provincial benefits. Thus, a narrative of degradation, powerlessness, and oppression continues today.

This chapter examines the concept of income inequality faced by people with disabilities through an investigation of a recent case presented before the Ontario Human Rights Tribunal: *Garrie v Janus Joan Inc.*[3] Using the social model of disability, this chapter approaches disability as "a socially-created category derived from labour relations" in our capitalist society.[4] Yet, an initial caveat is needed. While there are commonalities in the experiences people with disabilities face in this system, there clearly are different experiences of disability that render a "master narrative" difficult.[5] This chapter uses the example of the narrative of Terri-Lynn Garrie, a woman with a developmental disability, to investigate the reality of income inequality faced by people with disabilities. However, given that "disability" is a wide and variegated class, Ms. Garrie's narrative is only one version of this story.

Following a brief background on the issue of income inequality and wage discrimination as faced by people with disabilities, this chapter summarizes the case of Terri-Lynn Garrie, a forty-three-year-old woman from St. Catharines, Ontario, who was paid subminimum wage at her employment for over a decade.[6] It then investigates whether there are any legal mechanisms available to people with disabilities to combat the unequal wages, subordination, and devaluation of labour they experience in the workplace. In doing so, this chapter analyzes and deconstructs the ability of the *Accessibility for Ontarians with Disabilities Act* (*AODA*), the *Employment Equity Act*, relevant Supreme Court of Canada jurisprudence, the United Nations *Convention on the Rights of Persons with Disabilities* (*CRPD*), and the Ontario Human Rights Tribunal to address the issue of income inequality. By doing so, this chapter limits its focus to the broad and formal legal avenues available to people with disabilities in Canada. It argues that although all of these legal tools are flawed, the Ontario Human Rights Tribunal can provide a space to begin a constructive discussion about income inequality faced by people with disabilities. It finds that, at minimum, this Tribunal is a forum that is receptive to furthering the *CRPD*'s promise of self-fulfillment and human flourishing for people with disabilities.

Background

The Role of the Impaired Body in the Workplace

The employment history of people with disabilities reveals a narrative of "liminality" in the workplace.[7] Sheltered workshops offered a space wherein people with disabilities, positioned on the cusp of social inclusion, were given "easy to learn" and repetitive tasks in return for subminimum wages.[8] Thus, although they were included as part of the workforce when needed, people with disabilities were excluded from gainful employment. Today, the sheltered workshop model has yielded to one of supported employment; however, the effects of this transition are still felt.[9] While roughly 50 percent of people with disabilities are employed, a glance at the wages they receive reveals vast discrepancies in contrast to the wages of people without disabilities.[10] Today in Canada, almost half a million people with disabilities who are at a working age are living below the poverty line.[11] In many ways, people with disabilities remain liminal figures in the workplace. Although they may be proffered opportunities to work, people with disabilities continue to be excluded from opportunities to obtain living wages.

This reality stems from a political and economic structure that reinforces the oppression of the impaired body in the workplace. Put simply, the labour of a person with disabilities is degraded in the capitalist market, as he or she is seen as a "non-productive member" of the economic system.[12] The capitalist market values people's bodies for their production, and so people whose bodies do not conform to "the standard worker's body" are excluded from paid work.[13] Here, just as "capitalism forces workers into the wage relationship, it equally forcefully coerces disabled workers out of it."[14] People with disabilities become part of Marx's "reserve army of labour" and thus are "a resource to be tapped" only "in times of expansion."[15] Because a person's value is tied to his or her productive capacity and income, a person with a disability is reduced to being a member of the surplus population.

At the same time, disability benefit programs enable the "capital class" to "avoid hiring or retaining non-standard workers" and shift the cost of supporting people with disabilities "onto poverty-based government programs."[16] Many people struggle to survive on the notably inadequate support provided by disability benefits.[17] This arrangement merely perpetuates the impoverishment of people with disabilities.

In this system, disability, as Marta Russell and Ravi Malhotra point out, is a product of "the exploitative economic structure of capitalist society."[18] Keeping an eye on this broader political and economic structure allows us to remain cognizant of how the labour of people with disabilities continues to be degraded "systematically" through relationships "of domination and resistance" inherent in capitalist economies.[19]

In light of this system of exploitation, some disability rights advocates have argued that that there should be a shift away from defining value and worth in terms of traditional notions of labour and productivity altogether. For example, Russell and Malhotra ask, "Is work the defining quality of our worth?"[20] Indeed, the degradation of "non-productive" work in the economic system arguably degrades other valuable activities, including hobbies, volunteerism, and political activism, which can enable a path to human flourishing. Reflecting on Sunny Taylor's critique in her article "The Right Not to Work," we must be vigilant about how we conceive of meaningful work so as not to devalue the self-fulfilling contributions people with and without disabilities make outside of the conventional labour market.[21] The reality remains that "full citizenship" in our society currently rests on securing meaningful employment; however, what is defined as "meaningful" is subjective and must be deconstructed to include activities that are otherwise labelled as "non-productive."[22] While, in a capitalist society, worth is tied to productivity, it is important to critique the notion that meaningful employment is tied to work that yields the highest wages.

However, regardless of the definition of meaningful employment, the employment realities for people with disabilities continue to yield a cycle of poverty, exclusion, and dependence on social assistance programs. Many people with disabilities rely on precarious employment to survive.[23] Such employment reflects the reality that people with disabilities have a tendency to be "concentrated in poorly paid positions" and are less likely to be promoted over people without disabilities.[24] Precarious employment is characterized by "non-standard work arrangements," including part-time work and temporary positions that lead to fewer benefits, less job security, and a lower probability of being protected by existing labour laws.[25] In such employment, a person with a disability may not be able to control the conditions and pace of his or her work or obtain a living wage.[26] These barriers to full and meaningful inclusion are reinforced by the fact that roughly 17.6 percent of people who are not participating in the workforce commonly do not look for work because of a fear of losing their disability benefits.[27] Public assistance programs often do not allow for additional earned income and thereby fail to "assist people to become more engaged in society."[28] Instead, these programs reinforce cycles of poverty. The degradation of the labour of people with disabilities leads to the creation of social structures that reinforce their exclusion from a promise of gainful employment.

Nevertheless, while the current state of labour reveals a narrative of unemployment and underemployment for people with disabilities, the issue of income inequality has gained more traction as a policy issue. Recently, the Council for Canadians with Disabilities released a report, "Disabling Poverty and Enabling Citizenship," that seeks to "draw attention to policy and program factors that stand the greatest likelihood of helping people with disabilities move out of poverty into income adequacy – of disabling poverty and enabling citizenship."[29] This chapter explores and evaluates some of the current legal tools available that can address the issue of income inequality for people with disabilities, as is brought to life through the experience of Terri-Lynn Garrie.

The Limits of Legal Tools

Although this chapter now turns to evaluate legal mechanisms available to combat income inequality, it does so cognizant that legal tools are limited as viable mechanisms for change. On a fundamental level, as Julio Cortazar remarked, "nothing can be denounced if the denouncing is done within the system that belongs to the thing denounced."[30] The legal tools examined in this chapter have been developed within a political and economic system that has largely excluded people with disabilities. Therefore, we cannot expect that turning to these same legal tools to address the issue of income inequality will proffer the most meaningful solutions.

Indeed, the legal system is not always a forum that actively advances and protects the rights of people with disabilities. The words of Marc Galanter resonate – that the "architecture of the legal system," which creates distinctions between the "repeat players" and the "one-shotters," also "limits the possibilities of using the system as a means of redistributive ... change."[31] Here, access to justice remains a major barrier that prevents people with disabilities from being able to both claim and protect their legal rights. Moreover, legal institutions have remained places where, in order to gain access to benefits, rights, and protections, people with disabilities have to label themselves as "incompetent" or unable to complete work. Thus, although this chapter analyzes legal mechanisms available in Canada to address the issue of income inequality, it proceeds aware of the reality that legal mechanisms may not offer the most satisfying or liberating solutions.

Yet, in spite of these limitations, legal tools have offered an incremental step to societal change. For example, the *Americans with Disabilities Act* (ADA) was seen by some disability rights activists as the "culmination" of the civil rights movement because it changed dialogues around accommodation and accessibility.[32] While many scholars today argue that the ADA has not gone far enough in addressing disability discrimination, especially in the employment context,[33] this very debate reveals that, at minimum, the ADA was a first step in bringing key issues of exploitation and marginalization to the fore. Indeed, it is the duty of advocates within the legal system to utilize legal mechanisms to initiate progressive dialogues about the failures of the current system and the means available to address systemic issues of discrimination.

Terri-Lynn Garrie's Case

Terri-Lynn Garrie's narrative presents a lens through which the realities of income inequality for people with disabilities are brought into clear view.

What follows is a recitation of the findings of the Ontario Human Rights Tribunal regarding Ms. Garrie's case.

The Initial Application

In November 2009, Ms. Garrie filed an application under Ontario's *Human Rights Code* alleging that she had experienced discrimination in the area of employment and on the ground of her disability.[34] Terri-Lynn Garrie had worked at Janus Joan Inc. for a decade starting in the late 1990s and continuing until 2009.[35] The company employed people with and without disabilities, and all performed the same duties producing wine bottles.[36] Nevertheless, all of the individuals with developmental disabilities were paid using a "training honorarium" of $1.00 per hour, which, after a number of years, was increased to $1.25 per hour.[37] Employees without developmental disabilities were paid minimum wage or higher.[38]

Ms. Garrie reported being happy at her job. Her parents testified that they were aware of the pay differential and uncomfortable with it but did not complain because Ms. Garrie "enjoyed her work."[39] Because of her reduced pay, Ms. Garrie did not experience a reduction in her provincial benefits from the Ontario Disability Support Program (ODSP).[40] In 2009, however, Ms. Garrie was fired due to an allegation that she was unhappy with her job. Within a month, the company also terminated all the other employees with developmental disabilities.[41] Ms. Garrie testified that her termination made her "upset, sad, mad, and depressed."[42] Janus Joan Inc. failed to file any response to Ms. Garrie's claim.[43]

The Human Rights Tribunal, however, found that the statutory deadline for Ms. Garrie's application had passed. It noted that the act of paying Ms. Garrie $1.25 per hour was just "one" act of "alleged discrimination" in a contract formed in the late 1990s.[44] Although this act had continuing effects on her until her employment ended, the Tribunal found that it did not have the jurisdiction to make a ruling on the claim.[45] The Tribunal did find that Ms. Garrie's termination constituted discrimination because it was done on the basis of her disability. Nevertheless, the outcome of this case was unsatisfactory for Ms. Garrie, as it did not address the reality that for over a decade she had been paid subminimum wages.

Reconsideration

Yet, in a rare occurrence, the Tribunal reconsidered its own decision later that year and found that the wage differential was an ongoing contravention and not just a single occurrence in Ms. Garrie's employment contract.[46] The reconsideration panel, however, did not reach a decision on the merits and sent the case back to the original adjudicator for review.[47]

When the Human Rights Tribunal finally did conduct a review of the decision, Janus Joan Inc. and its manager, Stacey Szuch, provided a response. Ms. Szuch stated that she had formed the company to provide support, services, and training for people with developmental disabilities.[48] She stated that she did not provide "supported employment" but merely "volunteer trainee placements" for people with disabilities, who were given "a bi-weekly allowance/honorarium, which it was agreed would be reported by their family or support worker" to the ODSP.[49] Ms. Szuch alleged that, if the company had discriminated against Ms. Garrie, so had the social service agencies that were aware of the pay differential, the applicant's support worker, who was also aware of this differential, and the applicant's mother who, as Ms. Szuch stated, was a supervisor at the organization and was complicit in the alleged discrimination.[50] Ms. Garrie's mother acknowledged that she worked at Janus Joan Inc. and that she knew of the pay differential but claimed that she was not a supervisor.

The Tribunal heard testimony from both Ms. Garrie and her mother at this hearing, which Ms. Szuch did not attend. Interestingly, at this juncture the adjudicator questioned whether a litigation guardian needed to be appointed for Ms. Garrie. The adjudicator had doubts about Ms. Garrie's capacity to bring the claim. Only after Ms. Garrie's counsel testified that she was capable of providing instructions was the adjudicator persuaded that Ms. Garrie was competent to bring the claim.

The Tribunal found that the act of paying Ms. Garrie subminimum wages was discriminatory.[51] It found that Ms. Garrie was paid less solely because of her disability. Moreover, the Tribunal held that, although Ms. Garrie was paid just enough to continue receiving her ODSP benefits, her subminimum wages inflicted an arbitrary disadvantage on her on the basis of her disability. The Tribunal drew from the words of Gerald Robertson, a disability rights scholar from the University of Alberta, who emphasized that minimum wage legislation "tells us something about how we perceive self-worth and human worth"[52] and held that paying Ms. Garrie a subminimum wage constituted discrimination and was an affront to her dignity. The Tribunal awarded her damages based on wages she should have received at the minimum-wage level. In addition, the Tribunal issued an order that Janus Joan Inc. cease this payment practice and expressed concerns that others, including Ms. Garrie's support worker, were complicit in this practice. The Tribunal sent a copy of the decision to the Human

Rights Commission to investigate how widespread this practice was in the province.[53]

Analysis: Legal Tools Available to Combat Income Inequality

This section evaluates how the legal system responded to Terri-Lynn Garrie's experience of discrimination. It looks at the effectiveness of legislation, Supreme Court jurisprudence, the *CRPD*, and the findings of the Human Rights Tribunal itself in combatting the issue of income inequality in this case. This section concludes that all of the legal tools presented have considerable flaws, yet, at minimum, the Ontario Human Rights Tribunal proffers a space wherein claimants and advocates can begin to have a dialogue about some of the broader and systemic issues of income inequality and degradation of the labour of people with disabilities.

Legislation: Concerns about Ambiguity and Underinclusivity

No single piece of legislation combats the problem of income inequality faced by people with disabilities. Instead, the legislative approach is piecemeal, with various laws providing different protections for people with disabilities. Two of the laws that provide protections are the *Accessibility for Ontarians with Disabilities Act* [*AODA*][54] and the *Employment Equity Act*.[55] Yet, while these laws can, in theory, protect against income inequality, in practice, claimants such as Terri-Lynn Garrie have not benefited from such protections.

The Accessibility for Ontarians with Disabilities Act

Consider the hallmark disability legislation in Ontario: the *AODA*. While the *AODA* does not specifically deal with income equality, its purpose is "developing, implementing and enforcing standards in order to achieve accessibility for Ontarians with disabilities with respect to goods, services, facilities, employment, accommodation and buildings."[56] Section 30 of the *AODA*'s implementation regulations considers a need to make accommodations when looking to performance standards and employee productivity, which is important in determining whether an employee might be eligible for a higher paying job.[57] Moreover, Section 29 of the regulations requires employers to establish "return to work" processes for employees who are absent from work because of their disability.[58] These provisions ensure continuity and stability, which are imperative to combat precarious employment. They also support the notion that people with disabilities can expect consistency and progression in their employment.

Undoubtedly, the *AODA* is an indispensable tool for disability rights advocates in Ontario.

Nevertheless, the *AODA* fails to extend some of its protections to volunteers. While the *AODA* should be interpreted broadly to apply to all individuals with disabilities engaged in work, whether paid or unpaid, certain provisions of its regulations exclude volunteers.[59] This exclusion occurs within in a broader context wherein many people with disabilities "engage in unpaid work ... often as a pathway to paid employment."[60] Indeed, many individuals engage in "volunteer" work opportunities as a means to acquire skills that are beneficial in the labour market.[61] Yet, this "volunteer" population is excluded from the Employment Standards protections of the *AODA*. Thus, while the purpose of the *AODA* is to promote accessibility in the workplace for people with disabilities, which, in turn, can combat income inequality, this goal is inhibited by a failure to extend certain protections to volunteers.

Consider this exclusion in light of Terri-Lynn Garrie's narrative. Janus Joan Inc. attempted to frame Ms. Garrie's employment as a "volunteer-like position," wherein she was receiving only a "training honorarium."[62] Under the *AODA*, as a volunteer, she would not receive some of the protections of the Employment Standards section. Indeed, the way in which the employer-employee relationship is defined has serious repercussions for the protections one is afforded under the *AODA*. More broadly, debates around this definition are often the very source of the income inequality faced by individuals with disabilities. For example, through the exceptions for rehabilitative work and trainees, the provisions of the *Ontario Employment Standards Act* can be interpreted as characterizing people with disabilities as workers who do not require minimum wage or, indeed, any reimbursement.[63] A similar limitation in the *AODA* restricts its scope. It was perhaps in recognition of this restriction that Janus Joan Inc. attempted to define the employment relationship with Ms. Garrie in such a way that she would be characterized as a "volunteer." While features of the *AODA*, such as its return to work and performance management components, are useful tools for all people with disabilities who are seeking income equality and stability in their jobs, the *AODA*'s narrow applicability limits its effectiveness.[64]

The Employment Equity Act

In this discussion, we also need to consider relevant that federal legislation – here, the *Employment Equity Act* – requires that measures be taken to counter the discrimination faced by marginalized groups, including persons with disabilities.[65] The Act applies only to "federally regulated private-sector employers, Crown corporations and other federal organizations."[66] The impetus for the Act came from the *Report of the Royal Commission on Equality in Employment* (the Abella Report) in 1984, which found that discrimination was an "arbitrary barrier" to employment for people with disabilities and that Canada should strive to ensure that "access is genuinely available in a way that permits everyone who so wishes the opportunity to fully develop his or her potential."[67] The Act's provisions require that employers identify and eliminate "barriers" and institute "positive policies and practices."[68] Here, the Act's spirit of inclusion and emphasis on removal of structural barriers to employment make it a tool to combat the income inequality faced by people with disabilities.

Yet, in the context of Terri-Lynn Garrie's narrative, this Act lacks utility. While its purpose is to "achieve equality in the workplace so that no person shall be denied employment opportunities or benefits for reasons unrelated to ability," its scope is limited to federally regulated employers and employees.[69] Thus, individuals who work for private companies, as Ms. Garrie did, cannot take advantage of these protections. Undoubtedly, Ms. Garrie would have benefited from being able to claim that she was denied "benefits" – namely, equal pay – for reasons unrelated to her ability. Similarly, the Act's requirement that an employer review its policies and practices to locate employment barriers could have been used to investigate Janus Joan Inc's use of trainee honorariums as a barrier to equality. However, given the limited application of the Act, its protections, which may be useful in addressing some aspects of income inequality, do not extend to many claimants, including Ms. Garrie.

When we view the *AODA* and the *Employment Equity Act* through the lens of the *Garrie* case, it becomes apparent that certain individuals with disabilities continue to experience disparities in employment regardless of both such legislative protections. While both laws are tools that, in some ways, can address income inequality and access to employment, the *Garrie* case reveals their limited applicability.

Supreme Court Jurisprudence: Tensions between the Social Model of Disability and Socio-Economic Rights

The Supreme Court of Canada's jurisprudence also provides a legal basis to combat income inequality. Nevertheless, while the Supreme Court continues to recognize the importance of the social model of disability, it has drastically limited recognition of socio-economic rights. Here, the issue of income inequality for persons with disabilities finds itself uniquely situated within a tension in this jurisprudence.

The Supreme Court of Canada and Disability Rights

In several cases, the Supreme Court of Canada has recognized the social model of disability and demanded that the government take steps to remedy discrimination against people with disabilities. For example, in the 1997 case of *Eldridge v British Columbia (Attorney General)* [*Eldridge*],[70] the claimants, who had hearing impairments, argued that denying sign language interpretation in hospitals was a violation of the *Charter*.[71] The Court agreed, holding that this denial violated Section 15(1) of the *Charter*, since people with disabilities could not have equal access to and the benefit of healthcare without being able to communicate with hospital staff.[72] The Court noted that people with disabilities are "subject to invidious stereotyping" and face "persistent social and economic disadvantage," including being "concentrated at the lower end of the pay scale."[73] Given this context, the Court held that the government needed to take "affirmative steps" towards inclusion, since the government had conferred a benefit (in this case, healthcare) but had done so in a way that assumed that everyone could hear, which discriminated against people with hearing disabilities.[74] The Court's holding highlights a need to redress the legacy of the social exclusion of people with disabilities and society's persistence in establishing barriers to inclusion.

Also consider the 2000 Supreme Court case of *Quebec (Commission des droits de la personne et des droits de la jeunesse) v Montréal (City)* [*Mercier*].[75] This case involved people with disabilities who were refused employment because of their health conditions, even though these conditions did not result in functional impairments.[76] As a basis for finding a *Charter* violation, Ena Chadha summarizes the Court understanding that "paternalistic ideas about the quality of lives of persons with disabilities and their ability to contribute economically remain deeply rooted in society's consciousness."[77] Stereotypes represented people with disabilities as "helpless," which led to a "legacy of the economic model of disablement."[78] The Court held that these stereotypes about what people with disabilities were not able to do in the workplace grounded their discrimination claims. Thus, the Court found that this exclusion was unconstitutional.

Finally, consider the 2003 case of *Nova Scotia (Workers' Compensation Board) v Martin* [*Martin*].[79] Here, long-term workers' compensation benefits were eliminated for the entire category of workers who suffered from chronic pain.[80] The Supreme Court held that, in certain circumstances,

Charter protections can "protect against economic disadvantage" when there was a "blanket preclusion from long-term benefits."[81] The Court noted that economic deprivation might be "symptomatic of widely held negative attitudes towards the claimants and thus reinforce the assault on their dignity."[82] These words go some distance towards recognizing the historical socio-economic disadvantage experienced by individuals with disabilities and highlight the Court's commitment to redressing discrimination faced by people with disabilities.

In all, the Supreme Court of Canada has been willing to find that barriers to meaningful inclusion and equality require that the government take steps to remedy the discrimination faced by people with disabilities.

The Supreme Court of Canada and Socio-Economic Rights

Nevertheless, when read in light of the Supreme Court's jurisprudence on socio-economic rights, any protection of income equality for persons with disabilities becomes moot. In the 2000 case of *Granovsky v Canada (Minister of Employment and Immigration)* [*Granovsky*],[83] the Court found that the "deprivation of a financial benefit was not compelling enough to constitute discrimination under the *Charter*," in part because the claimant suffered from only a temporary disability and thus was comparatively "more fortunate" than other people with disabilities.[84]

However, one of the Supreme Court's defining decisions involving socio-economic rights occurred in the 2002 case of *Gosselin v Quebec (Attorney General)* [*Gosselin*].[85] In *Gosselin*, the Court found that the deficiency of the welfare benefits for certain claimants did not create "a positive state obligation to guarantee an adequate standard of living."[86] The challenge in *Gosselin* involved evaluating the disproportionately lower social assistance benefits that were paid specifically to individuals under thirty years old who were not enrolled in workfare programs or in school. The Court refused to recognize the claimant's grossly inadequate level of social assistance as a *Charter* violation.[87] The majority noted that the question was not "whether Section 7 has ever been or will ever be recognized as creating positive rights," but found that, in this specific circumstance, Section 7 did not create a state obligation to ensure adequate living standards.[88] Justice Arbour dissented, finding that the *Charter* created a positive obligation on the part of government to provide "those in need with an amount of social assistance adequate to cover basic necessities."[89] Nevertheless, *Gosselin* delineates how the Court is unwilling to impose a positive obligation on government to ensure that individuals receive an adequate standard of living.

This brief overview of relevant Supreme Court cases highlights that, even if the Court has been willing to embrace the language of social inclusion for people with disabilities, it has not been as willing to recognize a positive obligation on the part of the government to remedy disproportionality in terms of socio-economic rights. The Court's hesitancy to impose an obligation on government to address disproportionality makes arguments that seek to remedy income inequality more difficult.

Terri-Lynn Garrie's Case Exposes a Tension within the Supreme Court of Canada Jurisprudence

The issue that the *Garrie* case exposes – the problem of discriminatory income inequality as experienced by people with disabilities – is not one that has been clearly dealt with by the Supreme Court of Canada. Considering this issue in light of the Court's decisions exposes the tension between two strands of Supreme Court jurisprudence: one that seeks to remedy systemic discrimination experienced by people with disabilities, and another that fails to remedy income inequality more broadly. On the one hand, the Court has advanced the rights of people with disabilities by embracing the social model of disability and addressing social stereotyping and barriers to inclusion. In *Eldridge*, the Court found that the government had a positive obligation to ensure that its practices, including the provision of healthcare, did not discriminate against and reinforce stereotypes about people with disabilities. Here, the Court noted that stereotypes, including stereotypes about people with disabilities' contributions to the economy, cause people with disabilities to continue to face economic hardship, lower pay, and broader barriers to social inclusion.[90]

Ms. Garrie's narrative provides an illustration of this finding, as stereotypes about her ability to contribute to the economy resulted in her subminimum wage of $1.25 per hour. Although a person with a disability may be able to fulfil the same employment requirements as a person without a disability, income inequality may still persist, because of underlying assumptions that the work of people with disabilities is of lesser value. Because of these stereotypes, people with disabilities, including Ms. Garrie, continue to encounter barriers, including refusals to provide raises and other benefits. The *Garrie* case reveals that, akin to the claimants in *Eldridge*, who were unable to access basic medical services available to others because of barriers and stereotypes, people with disabilities in an employment context are largely unable to access a living wage, or even at times a minimum wage, because of barriers and stereotypes about the value of their labour.

Indeed, in *Mercier*, the Court found that stereotypes about people with disabilities led to discrimination in and exclusion from employment.[91] Historically, these stereotypes justified the existence of sheltered workshops, which were seen as therapeutic forms of labour and means of inclusion.[92] The opportunity for people with disabilities merely to work and to be included in the workplace was seen as beneficial.[93] However, this vision of inclusion was rooted in a stereotype about the ability of people with disabilities to meaningfully contribute in employment settings. In sheltered workshops, people with disabilities were segregated and paid subminimum wages, which reflected the assumption that their work was of lesser value and was a form of therapy. In *Mercier*, the Court held that there was a need to eliminate exclusion that was based on "preconceived ideas concerning personal characteristics, which ... do not affect a person's ability to do a job."[94] Following the line of reasoning in *Mercier*, in *Garrie* there is a need to eliminate exclusion from minimum wages based on preconceived ideas of Terri-Lynn Garrie's level of functioning, which does not affect her ability to do her job. Stereotypes have no place in determining the value of people with disabilities' labour.[95]

The Court in both *Eldridge* and *Mercier* drew on the presence of stereotypes about the capabilities of people with disabilities and the barriers they face to bolster its holdings that people with disabilities had faced a form of discrimination that required the government to take affirmative steps to remedy.[96] In *Garrie*, too, it was clear that Ms. Garrie's employer had used stereotypes about her capabilities to justify Ms. Garrie's economic exclusion. When the *Garrie* case is read with *Eldridge* and *Mercier*, it appears to point towards a need for the government to take more proactive steps towards the social inclusion of people with disabilities.

However, while the Supreme Court is willing to recognize and remedy the total exclusion of persons with disabilities, it is less willing to provide redress in situations of disproportionality. For the Court, even the gross levels of disproportionality presented in *Gosselin* were not grounds for a *Charter* violation.[97] The Court found that there was no obligation to ensure adequate living standards for those claimants. Moreover, in *Martin*, the practice of eliminating long-term workers' compensation benefits for certain workers was found to be unconstitutional only because it entailed a "blanket exclusion."[98] Likewise, in *Granovsky*, the Court did not find that the deprivation of a financial benefit constituted a *Charter* violation because Mr. Granovsky's disability was perceived as only "temporary" and he was better off than others with permanent disabilities.[99] Following this line of thinking, one could argue, in reference to *Garrie*, that it is sufficient that people with disabilities are receiving a wage. In other words, the issue of income inequality arguably does not mandate positive state obligation, as long as people with disabilities are not totally excluded from the labour market.

Nevertheless, the Supreme Court's jurisprudence does not foreclose the idea that the Court could recognize that the government has a positive obligation to protect the socio-economic rights of people with disabilities. Indeed, the Court in *Gosselin* did not exclude the possibility that the *Charter* could be used to create a positive state obligation to ensure socio-economic rights. Moreover, the history of the *Charter* reveals that the wording in Section 15 of "equality before and under the law" was chosen over an "anti-discrimination" wording and therefore was intended to create a "positive obligation of government towards disadvantaged groups."[100] Advocacy groups have stressed the importance of a liberal interpretation of the right to equality in order to "require governments ... to remedy systemic inequality and to maintain and improve social programs on which the enjoyment of equality and other *Charter* rights depends."[101] Indeed, it is possible to interpret *Charter* obligations broadly to include respect for socio-economic rights. As Martha Jackman and Bruce Porter delineate, at minimum claimants have "benefited from the ability to frame socio-economic rights claims as fundamental issues of constitutional inclusion."[102] Thus, while the Supreme Court has been hesitant to recognize that the deprivation of socio-economic rights requires a state obligation to remedy inequality, it has not excluded this possibility.

In all, however, the application of the Supreme Court's jurisprudence to *Garrie* reveals that, while there are some legal arguments available to combat stereotypes about the capabilities of people with disabilities and to promote social inclusion, legal arguments are currently limited when it comes to recognizing socio-economic benefits. Although the Court may be willing to embrace socio-economic rights in the future, *Garrie* reveals a tension within the jurisprudence – between a need to respond to stereotypes and barriers that people with disabilities face and an emphasis on denying socio-economic rights when confronted with gross inequality instead of total exclusion.

The *Convention on the Rights of Persons with Disabilities*

Canadian Use of the CRPD

The 2007 United Nations *Convention on the Rights of Persons with Disabilities (CRPD)*[103] has become an important tool for disability rights advocates.

The *CRPD* recognizes social barriers that prevent people with disabilities from fully recognizing their civil, political, economic, and social rights, and it obliges state parties to remove these barriers. It is heralded as promulgating a dignity approach to human rights, which "compels societies to acknowledge that persons with disabilities are valuable because of their inherent human worth."[104] It can be an imperative legal mechanism, which can combat stereotypes and the broader systemic discrimination people with disabilities face.

Canada ratified the *CRPD* in 2010, and in late 2016, it began consultation to ratify the Optional Protocol, which opens the door to allow individuals to file disability rights complaints with the United Nations. Nevertheless, Canada has not put corresponding implementation legislation in place as of this writing. Although international treaties may not be domestically binding without implementing legislation, they still have interpretive value in domestic courts and human rights tribunals.[105] Regardless of whether one finds that all portions of the *CRPD* require implementation, it is important to note that Canadian courts and human rights tribunals use the *CRPD* to bolster arguments aiming to protect the rights of persons with disabilities in Canada.

Consider just a few uses of the *CRPD* in Canadian jurisprudence to date. In *Cole v Cole*, the Ontario Superior Court of Justice considered the *CRPD* when it addressed arguments that a person with a disability should not be presumed incompetent.[106] The Ontario Human Rights Tribunal employed the *CRPD* in *Kacan v Ontario Public Service Employees Union* to address the issue of whether a litigation guardian needed to be appointed[107] and in *Hinze v Great Blue Heron Casino* to address employment discrimination based on the applicant's disability.[108] These cases represent only a small sample of times in which the *CRPD* has been cited in Canadian jurisprudence. Indeed, despite a lack of implementing legislation, the *CRPD* has been employed as a mechanism to promote the rights of persons with disabilities in courts and tribunals in Canada.

Relevant Articles of the CRPD

Turning to the *CRPD* itself, three articles are relevant to this chapter's analysis: Article 27, Article 26, and Article 19. Article 27 concerns the right to work in a way that leads to the possibility of gaining "a living" and leading "a life of dignity."[109] It states that people with disabilities have a right to work "on an equal basis with others."[110] It goes on to note that people with disabilities have a right to "equal remuneration for work of equal value."[111] Article

26 requires states to take measures to ensure that people with disabilities can have their full "vocational ability" recognized and experience full "participation in all aspects of life."[112] During drafting, these articles together problematized the existence of sheltered workshops, which provide continuous rehabilitation "without fully guaranteeing conditions applying under the labour law."[113] When interpreting these articles together, we must remain cognizant of the drafters' intent – that people with disabilities have a right to be fully included in the workforce, not merely included for rehabilitative purposes. The environment within sheltered workshops, which excludes people with disabilities, was not found by the drafters to be in compliance with the Convention's principles.[114] Thus, both Articles 27 and 26 can be used to address the systemic issues of discrimination surrounding the income inequality faced by people with disabilities.

Finally, Article 19 requires states to recognize "the equal right of all persons with disabilities to live in the community, with choices equal to others," and "facilitate full enjoyment by persons with disabilities of this right."[115] This Article recognizes that people with disabilities have equal rights to a fulfilling life in the community. When seen in conjunction with Articles 26 and 27, Article 19 reinforces the right of people with disabilities not only to employment but to meaningful and gainful employment.

All of these articles underscore the right of people with disabilities to have their labour valued equally, to have their full vocational ability recognized, and to lead fulfilling lives within the community. Clearly, should Canadian courts and tribunals choose to utilize it, the *CRPD* can be a viable tool for addressing the systemic issue of income inequality.

The CRPD and the Garrie Case

When Articles 27, 26, and 19 of the *CRPD* are applied to *Garrie*, they highlight the profound and pervasive discrimination Ms. Garrie faced. For example, Article 27 invokes not merely a right to be able to work, but rather a right to "gain a living" and lead a "life of dignity" on an "equal basis with others."[116] As Terri-Lynn Garrie was paid significantly below minimum wage for her work, even though it was nearly identical to that being done by people without disabilities, her experience clearly was not one of "gain[ing] a living" on an "equal basis with others."[117] Her labour was degraded because she has a disability. The application of Article 27 to this case would require addressing the systemic discrimination and stereotypes Ms. Garrie faced.

Furthermore, under Article 26, Ms. Garrie has the right to recognize her "full vocational ability," meaning she has a right to pursue and attain a vocation consistent with her skills and aspirations. Coupled with her right to earn a living, this right implies an opportunity to advance in her career, not to be considered a "trainee" for over ten years. Ms. Garrie should have had the chance to be challenged in her employment rather than to simply complete the same repetitive tasks she had shown she was able to complete. If the *CRPD* is said to "compel societies" to recognize the inherent worth of individuals with disabilities, then an approach to employment that devalues the work of individuals or does not provide them with opportunities because of their disabilities cannot be tolerated.[118] In fact, this is the precise exclusion from equal opportunity that the *CRPD* seeks to remedy by creating a legal mechanism that protects and promotes the human rights of people with disabilities.

Terri-Lynn Garrie's experience also goes to the heart of the debate that occurred during the *CRPD*'s drafting on the merits of sheltered workshops and the intersection between Articles 26 and 27. In that debate, what emerged was an understanding that it was not sufficient that such workshops simply provide employment for individuals with disabilities.[119] Rather, what was required was the meaningful and full inclusion of individuals with disabilities in the workplace.[120] The payment of a "training honorarium" for ten years does not reflect a movement towards inclusion. Instead, it represents segregation from the rest of the workforce and exclusion from earning a minimum wage. The full inclusion of people with disabilities into the community is not achieved when they are paid at a lower rate because of their disabilities.

Finally, Ms. Garrie's treatment also contravenes Article 19 of the *CRPD*, which recognizes that people with disabilities have a right to full inclusion and participation in the community and to the full enjoyment of this right.[121] Full enjoyment of the right to live in the community evokes the right to flourish as an individual – not merely to be present in the community, but to be a fully participating member of society. Article 19 reflects the notion that "connecting people back into their community and in living arrangements and settings that reflect their own wishes and preferences is vital to personhood and human flourishing."[122] An absence of a living wage provides little opportunity for this full enjoyment and self-fulfillment. Instead, it creates a cycle of powerlessness and poverty. The *CRPD* pushes beyond ensuring that people with disabilities are included in the community; it seeks to recognize their full enjoyment of rights in the community. In this context, the gross income inequality facing individuals with disabilities is unacceptable.

Although the *CRPD* is a useful legal tool to address the issue of income inequality faced by persons with disabilities in Canada, its weight in Canadian law is tempered by the reality that Canada has yet to pass implementing legislation ensuring its enforcement. Yet, even in the absence of such legislation, the use of the *CRPD* within Canadian courts and tribunals shows that it can still be used to address the fundamental income inequalities faced by individuals with disabilities.

The Ontario Human Rights Tribunal

The Requirements to Bring an Individual Discrimination Claim
The last legal tool that this chapter analyzes is the Ontario Human Rights Tribunal itself. To begin, it is important to consider the purpose of this Tribunal, which is "not aimed at determining fault or punishing conduct. It is remedial. Its aim is to identify and eliminate discrimination."[123] In light of this purpose, the Tribunal can both order monetary damages and also create remedies that take active steps to ensure that discrimination does not occur in the future.

For an individual discrimination claim, the Human Rights Tribunal's test requires that the applicant prove on a balance of probabilities and supported by "clear, convincing, and cogent evidence" that a *Human Rights Code* violation occurred.[124] In order for a Code violation to be found, there must be a link between the discrimination, a ground (disability in Ms. Garrie's case), and an area (employment in Ms. Garrie's case).[125] The test for individual claims involves applicants proving that: (1) they had a disability, (2) they received adverse treatment, and (3) this treatment was on account of the disability.[126]

The Tribunal's Handling of the Garrie Case
In *Garrie*, the Tribunal found a clear violation of the Ontario *Human Rights Code*. Before that finding, however, the case faced two initial hurdles. The first related to whether Ms. Garrie's claim was timely. This was eventually remedied by the Tribunal's decision on reconsideration, which found that a contravention of the Code occurred every time Ms. Garrie was paid a sub-minimum wage. This finding is useful for future income inequality claims.

The second hurdle constituted what could be a more profound problem: namely the ability of people with disabilities to bring claims themselves. By raising concerns that Ms. Garrie might have needed a litigation guardian, the adjudicator unnecessarily questioned her capacity to bring the claim herself. The adjudicator stated that, in light of Ms. Garrie's testimony, he was unsure whether she was capable and that "if the applicant's counsel had not represented that she has been able to obtain instructions directly from the applicant, I likely would have made additional enquiries with respect to the scope of the applicant's capacity to manage her financial matters."[127] It was only because Ms. Garrie's counsel stated that she had received instructions from Ms. Garrie that the adjudicator allowed the claim to continue without a litigation guardian. Nevertheless, previous decisions of the Human Rights Tribunal as well as Article 12 of the *CRPD* recognize that Ms. Garrie would be capable of bringing this claim herself.[128] While the adjudicator's decision ultimately affirmed Ms. Garrie's capacity, there was no need for the adjudicator to question her capacity. Raising concerns about an individual's capacity to bring a claim could inhibit others from bringing income inequality claims or, if they are forced to appoint a litigation guardian, could prevent claims from preceding in a way that preserves the dignity of claimants or conforms to human rights principles.

Yet, once these initial issues were overcome, the Tribunal was able to assess Ms. Garrie's claim that she faced discrimination by receiving unequal pay. Turning to the Human Rights Tribunal's test for individual claims, the first category was satisfied because it was determined that Ms. Garrie has a developmental disability under the Code.[129] The second step of proving adverse treatment was also straightforward: Ms. Garrie had received a "training honorarium" of approximately $1.25 per hour for over ten years despite the reality that individuals without developmental disabilities were paid minimum wage levels or higher for the same work.

Importantly, when finding that Ms. Garrie had experienced adverse treatment, the adjudicator was able to address some of the systemic issues of discrimination that emerge from the fact that her pay was capped so that her ODSP benefits would not be affected. The adjudicator found that this reasoning was not a viable argument to justify such discrimination. The finding that a party cannot claim that lower wages are not discriminatory simply because they enable people with disabilities to work and to continue to receive their full benefits is crucial for future litigants. Here, the fact that Ms. Garrie's work was degraded was sufficient to constitute discrimination. The Tribunal went on to underscore how the minimum wage is entwined with a basic notion of protecting self-worth. While not mentioned in the ruling, these arguments accord with Articles 19, 26, and 27 of the *CRPD* and their recognition of Ms. Garrie's right to a living wage and to a life of self-fulfillment, not merely one where she could retain her social welfare benefits. Finally, these arguments are presented in a way that changes the narrative about people with disabilities in courts and tribunals from one of incompetency and incapability to one of self-fulfilment, dignity, capability, and potential. In addition to the recognition that Ms. Garrie experienced adverse treatment, these findings and arguments are important to further the discussion about income inequality and the systemic discrimination faced by people with disabilities.

Regarding the third prong of the test, which requires that the adverse treatment be connected to the disability, the Tribunal found that this prong was also satisfied. There was a causal link between Ms. Garrie's pay and her disability, as all other employees who were not people with disabilities were paid minimum wage or higher. Ms. Garrie was paid a "training honourarium" because of her disability, even though she performed the same tasks as other workers. A glance at the principles embedded within the *CRPD* or even within the Supreme Court jurisprudence of *Eldridge* and *Mercier* reveals that Ms. Garrie was paid a lower wage because of stereotypes that her work was not of equal value due to her disability. Thus, the third prong of this test was met.

Based on this reasoning, the Tribunal found that Ms. Garrie's rights were violated, awarded her damages for lost wages at the minimum wage rate, and demanded that Janus Joan Inc. cease its discriminatory payment practice. The Tribunal also sent the decision to the Human Rights Commission so it could investigate the pervasiveness of paying people with disabilities subminimum wages and the knowledge that support workers may have about this practice. Because Janus Joan Inc. is insolvent, it is unlikely that Ms. Garrie will receive money as a result of this decision. Nevertheless, these remedies do make efforts to address the income inequality Ms. Garrie faced and take small steps to ensure other people with disabilities do not encounter this discrimination in the future.

While the Human Rights Tribunal has provided some recourse to address the issue of income inequality faced by people with disabilities, it is not a forum without faults. In particular, the fact that the Tribunal questioned Ms. Garrie's capacity reveals the barriers people with disabilities face in accessing justice. We also see an absence of Ms. Garrie's narrative presented in her own words. Indeed, there is little documentation about whether Ms. Garrie felt empowered by the proceedings. There are few quotes from her about the proceeding, and in one news article, she stated that she was happy that the experience was over and that she hoped this would not happen to any other people with disabilities in the future.[130] Finally, it is not apparent that these proceedings recognize Ms. Garrie's crosscutting identities. Ms. Garrie may have experienced discrimination as a result of being a woman with a disability, which the Tribunal was not able to consider. We should remain cognizant at this juncture that, while the Tribunal's decisions may go some length towards addressing systemic issues that people with disabilities face, these decisions are limited by how advocates are able to frame the arguments and, more broadly, who is able to access this forum.

Despite the limitations of the Human Rights Tribunal as a forum to combat income inequality, the Tribunal provides a space wherein we can begin to have dialogues about the systemic issues of income inequality that people with disabilities face. Indeed, because the Tribunal has recognized the principles of the *CRPD* in past cases, this forum can allow for more individualized discussions about the vocational and employment aspirations of people with disabilities in a way that can expose broader stereotypes and systemic barriers. With the recent closure of Ontario's sheltered workshops,[131] and as other claimants – including Kris McCormick, a man with a developmental disability who was also paid subminimum wage – bring claims in the Tribunal,[132] advocates will have the opportunity to pursue more innovative arguments about the income inequality faced by people with disabilities.

Counterargument: The Transition from Sheltered Workshops to Supported Employment

In this section, I consider a counterargument, that perhaps the experience of a person with a disability receiving a lower wage is not adverse treatment that highlights discrimination. This argument posits that the emphasis on social inclusion reveals a need to hire more individuals with disabilities, which comes at a cost of being unable to pay individuals with disabilities higher wages.[133] In this context, the wage that is supplied is not as important as the benefit of being included in the workplace and being able to establish social connections. In her case, Ms. Garrie did note that she was content at her job, which raises the question of whether her treatment can be characterized as "adverse." It is also arguable that her lower wages ensured that she did not lose access to her ODSP benefits, while still affording her gainful employment.

Nevertheless, it is important to note that these arguments rest on a presumption that the work of people with disabilities is of a lower value than that of people without disabilities. These arguments perpetuate common stereotypes about people with disabilities, which lead to their continued segregation. People with disabilities must be included in the workplace, and this must imply *full* inclusion, with living wages and meaningful vocational opportunities. The *CRPD* represents a shift in this thinking by promoting not only inclusion but also human flourishing. An argument that contends that the status quo is adequate does not take into account such commitments in the *CRPD* and its broader vision of a fully inclusive society.

This chapter has demonstrated that, while many tools exist to address the income inequality of people with disabilities, they are not without inadequacies. Legislation may not apply to a considerable number of people with disabilities, and the Supreme Court is generally unwilling to recognize positive obligations on the part of the state to provide remedies in cases of disproportionality in socio-economic contexts. That said, human rights tribunals are forums that can adopt the tenets of Supreme Court's jurisprudence on the need to address stereotypes surrounding people with disabilities and couple them with the core principles of the *CRPD* in order to address issues of income inequality for people with disabilities.

Indeed, of all the tools surveyed in the context of Terri-Lynn Garrie's claim, the Ontario Human Rights Tribunal is the most promising legal mechanism available to address issues of income inequality facing people with disabilities. It has the authority to consider the use of the *CRPD* in its analysis and to expose the systemic issues of discrimination that continue to reinforce the poverty faced by people with disabilities. While the Tribunal is not without shortcomings, this chapter has shown how the Tribunal can provide an initial forum in which advocates and claimants can have meaningful dialogues about the income inequality faced by people with disabilities. The *Garrie* case provides an example of the start of such a dialogue. In all, however, while there are various legal tools in Canada that seek to enable people with disabilities achieve equal wages, to be truly effective, these mechanisms must ultimately empower the people they seek to help.

NOTES

1 James I Charlton, *Nothing about Us without Us: Disability Oppression and Empowerment* (Berkeley: University of California Press, 1998) at 5.
2 See, e.g., *Employment Standards Code*, RSA 2000 c E-9 s 67.
3 *Garrie v Janus Joan Inc*, 2014 HRTO 272 [*Garrie III*].
4 Marta Russell & Ravi Malhotra, "Capitalism and Disability" (2002) 38 Social Register 211 at 212, online: <http://socialistregister.com/index.php/srv/article/view/5784#.VRoL2WYhzOo>.
5 Race, gender, and sexual identification also add additional layers to this narrative that are not considered in this chapter.

6 *Garrie v Janus Joan Inc,* 2012 HRTO 1955 (CanLII) [*Garrie* II].
7 Dustin Galer, *"Hire the Handicapped!" Disability Rights, Economic Integration and Working Lives in Toronto, Ontario, 1962–2005* (PhD Thesis, University of Toronto, 2014) [unpublished], online: <https://tspace.library.utoronto.ca/bitstream/1807/65661/11/Galer_Dustin_201406_PhD_thesis.pdf>.
8 Canadian Association for Community Living, "Achieving Social and Economic Inclusion: From Segregation to 'Employment First'" (June 2011) at 6, online: <http://www.cacl.ca/publications-resources/achieving-social-and-economic-inclusion-segregation-employment-first> [CACL].
9 *Ibid* at 7–11.
10 Chantal Collin, Isabelle Lafontaine-Émond & Melissa Pang, "Persons with Disabilities in the Canadian Labour Market: An Overlooked Talent Pool" (March 2013) at 3, online: <www.parl.gc.ca/Content/LOP/ResearchPublications/2013-17-e.pdf>. See also Cameron Crawford, "Disabling Poverty and Enabling Citizenship: Understanding the Poverty and Exclusion of Canadian with Disabilities" (December 2014), online: <http://www.ccdonline.ca/en/socialpolicy/poverty-citizenship/demographic-profile/understanding-poverty-exclusion#sec-labour>.
11 Crawford, *supra* note 10.
12 Robert D Wilton, "Working at the Margins: Disabled People and the Growth of Precarious Employment" in Dianne Pothier & Richard Devlin, eds, *Critical Disability Theory: Essays in Philosophy, Politics, Policy, and Law* (Vancouver: UBC Press, 2006) 129; Charlton, *supra* note 1 at 24.
13 Russell & Malhotra, *supra* note 4 at 213.
14 *Ibid.*
15 Charlton, *supra* note 1 at 24.
16 Russell & Malhotra, *supra* note 4 at 214–15.
17 *Ibid* at 215. See, generally, Mark C Weber, "Disability Rights Welfare Law" (2011) 32:6 Cardozo L Rev 101.
18 Russell & Malhotra, *supra* note 4 at 214–15.
19 Wilton, *supra* note 12 at 130.
20 Russell & Malhotra, *supra* note 4 at 223.
21 Sunny Taylor, "The Right Not to Work: Power and Disability" (2004) 55:10 Monthly Rev 30.
22 Wilton, *supra* note 12 at 129.
23 *Ibid.*
24 *Ibid.*
25 *Ibid* at 131.
26 *Ibid.*
27 Deborah Stienstra, *About Canada: Disability Rights* (Black Point, NS: Fernwood, 2012) at 53.
28 Andrew Power & Janet E Lord, *Active Citizenship and Disability: Implementing the Personalisation of Support* (Cambridge: Cambridge University Press, 2014) at 6–7.
29 Crawford, *supra* note 10.
30 Charlton, *supra* note 1 at 22.
31 Marc Galanter, "Why the 'Haves' Come out Ahead: Speculations on the Limits of Legal Change" (1974) 9:1 Law & Soc'y Rev 95 at 95.

32 Weber, *supra* note 17 at 103.
33 See, generally, Marta Russell, "What Disability Rights Cannot Do: Employment and Political Economy" (2002) 17:2 Disability & Society 117. See also Weber, *supra* note 17.
34 *Garrie v Janus Joan Inc*, 2012 HRTO 68 (CanLII) at paras 1–2 [*Garrie* I]; *Human Rights Code*, RSO 1990, c 19.
35 *Garrie* I, *supra* note 34 at paras 8–12.
36 *Ibid* at para 8.
37 *Ibid* at para 9.
38 *Ibid*.
39 *Ibid* at para 11.
40 *Ibid* at para 10.
41 *Ibid* at para 12.
42 *Ibid* at para 15.
43 *Ibid* at para 4.
44 *Ibid.* at para 23.
45 *Ibid*.
46 *Garrie* II, *supra* note 6 at para 46.
47 *Ibid* at para 49.
48 *Garrie* III, *supra* note 3 at para 19.
49 *Ibid*.
50 *Ibid*.
51 *Ibid* at paras 70–74.
52 *Ibid*.
53 *Ibid* at paras 84–112.
54 *Accessibility for Ontarians with Disabilities Act*, SO 2005 c 11 [*AODA*].
55 *Employment Equity Act*, SC 1995, c 44.
56 *AODA*, *supra* note 54 at s 1.
57 O Reg 191/11, s 30.
58 *Ibid* at s 29.
59 *Ibid* at s 20 ("The standards set out in this Part apply to obligated organization that are employers and ... do not apply in respect of volunteers and other non-paid individuals"). But see generally, Lisa Stam, "Can You Discriminate against a Volunteer?" (10 October 2012), *Employment and Human Rights Law in Canada* (blog), online: <http://www.canadaemploymenthumanrightslaw.com/2012/10/articles/discrimination/can-you-discriminate-against-a-volunteer/>.
60 Canadian Mental Health Association Ontario, "Response to the Draft Proposed Integrated Accessibility Regulation under the Accessibility for Ontarians with Disabilities Act, 2005" (2011) at 4, online: <http://ontario.cmha.ca/public_policy/response-to-the-draft-proposed-integrated-accessibility-regulation-under-the-accessibility-for-ontarians-with-disabilities-act-2005-final-public-review-period/#.UrEyb3CH218> [CMHAO, "Response"].
61 CACL, *supra* note 8 at 13–14.
62 Garrie III, *supra* note 3 at para 19.
63 *Ontario Employment Standards Act*, RSO 2000 c 41 at ss 2, 5.
64 *AODA*, *supra* note 54.

65 In Ontario, prior to the enactment of the federal *Employment Equity Act*, the provincial *Employment Equity Act* was in place but was repealed in *Ferral v Ontario (Attorney General)* (1998), 42 OR (3d) 97 when the Court found that it was constitutional to provide this protection and then remove it because the government was under no obligation to enact it. See also Mary Cornish, "A Living Wage as a Human Right" (October 2012), at 8, online: <http://www.policyalternatives.ca/sites/default/files/uploads/publications/Ontario%20Office/2012/10/Living%20Wage%20as%20a%20Human%20Right.pdf>.

66 Employment and Social Development Canada, "Employment equity in federally regulated workplaces" (2016), online: <https://www.canada.ca/en/employment-social-development/programs/employment-equity.html>.

67 Judge Rosalie S. Abella, *Report of the Commission on Equality in Employment* (Ottawa: Minister of Supply and Services Canada, 1984), at 2.

68 *Employment Equity Act, supra* note 55 at s 5.

69 *Ibid* at ss 3–4.

70 *Eldridge v British Columbia (Attorney General)*, [1997] 3 SCR 624 [*Eldridge*].

71 *Ibid* at para 1.

72 *Ibid* at para 80.

73 *Ibid* at para 56.

74 Pauline Rosenbaum & Ena Chadha, "Reconstructing Disability: Integrating Disability Theory into Section 15" (2006) 33 (2d) SCLR 343 at 357. See also *Eldridge, supra* note 70 at para 57.

75 *Quebec (Commission des droits de la personne et des droits de la jeunesse) v Montréal (City)*, 2000 SCC 27, [2000] 1 SCR 665 [*Mercier*].

76 *Ibid* at paras 2–4.

77 Ena Chadha, "The Social Phenomenon of Handicapping" in Elizabeth Sheehy, ed, *Adding Feminism to Law: The Contributions of Justice Claire L'Heureux-Dubé* (Toronto: Irwin Law, 2004) at 219. See also *Mercier, supra* note 75 at 39.

78 *Ibid*.

79 *Nova Scotia (Workers' Compensation Board) v Martin*, 2003 SCC 54, [2003] 2 SCR 504 [*Martin*].

80 *Ibid* at para 1.

81 Ravi Malhotra & Morgan Rowe, "Justice Gonthier and Disability Rights: The Case of *Nova Scotia (Workers' Compensation Board) v. Martin*" (2012) 56 SCLR 515.

82 *Martin, supra* note 79 at para 101.

83 *Granovsky v Canada (Minister of Employment and Immigration)*, [2000] 1 SCR 703 [*Granovsky*].

84 Ena Chadha & Laura Schatz, "Human Dignity and Economic Integrity for Persons with Disabilities: A Commentary on the Supreme Court's Decisions in *Granovsky* and *Martin*" (2004) 19 J L & Soc Pol'y 107. *Granovsky, supra* note 83 at para 79.

85 *Gosselin v Quebec (Attorney General)*, 2002 SCC 84 [*Gosselin*].

86 *Ibid* at para 82.

87 *Ibid*.

88 *Ibid*. See also Martha Jackman & Bruce Porter, "Socio-Economic Rights under the Canadian Charter" in M Langford, ed, *Socio-economic Rights Jurisprudence: Emerging*

Trends in Comparative International Law (Cambridge: Cambridge University Press, 2009) at 28.

89 *Ibid.*
90 *Eldridge, supra* note 70, at para 80.
91 *Mercier, supra* note 75 at paras 36–39.
92 Geoffrey Reaume, "No Profits, Just a Pittance: Work, Compensation, and People Defined as Mentally Disabled in Ontario, 1964–1990" in Steven Noll & James W Trent Jr, eds, *Mental Retardation in America: A Historical Reader* (New York: New York University Press, 2004) 474.
93 *Ibid.*
94 *Mercier, supra* note 75 at para 36.
95 Chadha & Schatz, *supra* note 84 at 97.
96 *Eldridge, supra* note 70 at para 57; *Mercier, supra* note 75 at para 36.
97 *Gosselin, supra* note 85 at para 83.
98 Malhotra & Rowe, *supra* note 81 at 515.
99 *Granovsky, supra* note 83 at para 79.
100 Jackman & Porter, *supra* note 88 at 28.
101 *Ibid* at 28–29.
102 *Ibid* at 27–29.
103 *Convention on the Rights of Persons with Disabilities,* GA Res. 61/106 (2007) [*CRPD*].
104 Michael Ashley Stein, "Disability Human Rights" (2007) 95 Cal L Rev 106.
105 Ravi Malhotra & Robin Hansen, "The United Nations Convention on the Rights of Persons with Disabilities and Its Implications for the Equality Rights of Canadian with Disabilities: The Case of Education" (2011) 29:1 Windsor YB Access Just 73 at 83–84. See also *Suresh v Canada (Minister of Citizenship and Immigration)* 2002 SCC 2, [2002] 1 SCR 3.
106 *Cole v Cole,* 2011 ONSC 4090 (CanLII) at para 6.
107 *Kacan v Ontario Public Service Employees Union,* 2010 HRTO 1717 (CanLII) [*Kacan*].
108 *Hinze v Great Blue Heron Casino,* 2011 HRTO 93 (CanLII).
109 Sabrina Ferraina, "Analysis of the Legal Meaning of Article 27 of the UN CRPD: Key Challenges for Adapted Work Settings" (2012) at 7, online: <http://digitalcommons.ilr.cornell.edu/gladnetcollect/560/>.
110 *CRPD, supra* note 103 at art 27.
111 *Ibid.*
112 *Ibid* at art 26.
113 Ferraina, *supra* note 109 at 18.
114 *Ibid.*
115 *CRPD,* supra note 103 at art 26.
116 *Ibid* at art 27; Ferraina, *supra* note 109 at 7.
117 *CRPD, supra* note 103 at art 27.
118 Stein, *supra* note 104 at 106.
119 Ferraina, *supra* note 109 at 18.
120 *Ibid.*
121 *CRPD, supra* note 103 at art 19.

122 Office of the United Nations High Commissioner for Human Rights, "Getting a Life: Living Independently and Being Included in the Community" (2012) at 11, online: <www.europe.ohchr.org/documents/Publications/getting_a_life.pdf>.

123 *Robichaud v Canada*, [1987] 2 SCR 84 at para 13.

124 *FH v McDougall*, 2008 SCC 53, [2008] 3 SCR 41 at para 46.

125 *Chuchala v Szmidt*, 2010 HRTO 2545 (CanLII).

126 *Local 789 v Domtar*, 2009 BCCA 52 (CanlII) at para 36.

127 *Garrie* III, *supra* note 3 at para 30.

128 *CRPD*, *supra* note 103 at art 12; *Kacan*, *supra* note 107.

129 *Garrie* II, *supra* note 6 at para 46.

130 Laurie Monsebraaten, "Disabled Woman Win Discriminatory Pay Case at Ontario Human Rights Tribunal," *Toronto Star* (7 March 2014), online: <http://www.thestar. com/news/gta/2014/03/07/disabled_woman_wins_discriminatory_pay_case_at_ ontario_human_rights_tribunal.html>.

131 Moira Welsh, "Ontario's Sheltered Workshops to Close Forever," *Toronto Star* (29 November 2015), online: <http://www.thestar.com/news/canada/2015/11/29/ontarios -sheltered-workshops-to-close-forever.html>.

132 Kathy Dobson, "Sarnia Man Says Workshop's Meager Pay Violates His Human Rights," *Sarnia Journal* (15 July 2015), online: <http://thesarniajournal.ca/sarnia-man -says-workshops-meager-pay-violates-his-human-rights/>.

133 Reaume, *supra* note 92 at 475.

Compensating Work-Related Disability
The Theory, Politics, and History of the Commodification-Decommodification Dialectic

ERIC TUCKER

In 2015, the last year for which we have complete Canadian data, workers' compensation boards recognized that 852 Canadian workers died from work-related injuries and diseases and 232,629 workers experienced disabling injuries requiring them to take time off work. About 13 percent of those injured will have permanent disabilities of varying severity.[1] These figures significantly underestimate the true burden of work-related disability for at least three reasons. First, the percentage of the paid Canadian workforce covered by workers' compensation has been shrinking. In 2008, it was estimated to stand at about 80 percent, although coverage bounced back to about 85 percent in 2015.[2] Second, there is widespread evidence of claims suppression and underreporting of lost-time injuries. A 2014 review estimated that workers do not claim 20 percent of their injuries and illnesses and that employers do not report 7–8 percent of injuries, misreport 3–9 percent of lost-time injuries as non-lost-time injuries, and actively suppress some inestimable number of eligible claims.[3] Finally, for a claim to be recorded it must be accepted by the compensation board, and there is evidence that compensation boards are rejecting claims more frequently. For example, in Ontario, the percentage of denied claims increased from 4 percent in 2001 to 8 percent in 2010.[4]

But even if the current official toll of death, disease, and injury significantly underestimates its true incidence, the situation today is likely as good as it has been since the rise of industrial capitalism, which has taken a terrible toll on workers' bodies.[5] It is not surprising, therefore, that regulating hazardous working conditions and compensating workers who suffered disabling work-related injuries were among the earliest working-class demands and among the first to be addressed by protective labour laws. Yet despite widespread recognition that it is unacceptable for workers to be killed and injured because of dangerous work and that compensation must be paid to those who are, conflict over health and safety and workers' compensation laws regularly recurs. The goal of this chapter is to explore the theory and politics of recurring regulatory dilemmas in labour law and to examine a few key moments in the history of workers' compensation, which illustrate why these conflicts are endemic and so intractable.

The Theory and Politics of Regulatory Dilemmas in Labour Law

In capitalism, workers commodify their time and capacity to work by selling it on labour markets to employers. In theory, the terms and conditions of employment contracts are the product of negotiation and are mutually acceptable. From the perspective of capital, labour is an ordinary commodity, bought and sold in labour markets just as other commodities are bought and sold in other commodity markets. But labour power is not an ordinary commodity, as unlike, say, steel beams it cannot be separated from its seller, who retains agency over its use even after its sale. Moreover, labour power is not produced for the market in response to market demand but is socially reproduced outside the market. When the commodification of labour threatens the well-being of workers, materially or psychologically, or undermines the conditions of social reproduction, resistance is likely to ensue. The conflict between the drive to commodify workers' capacity to work and resistance to its dysfunctional and harmful consequences produces an enduring if uneven commodification-decommodification dialectic, which is a central insight of the work of both Marx and Polanyi.[6]

For Marx, problems arise principally after the transaction is complete. As he famously put it, workers, having freely sold their labour power (their "hide") in the labour market, follow the capitalist into the hidden abode of production, where they can expect nothing but a hiding.[7] Workers discover that the commodification of their labour power results in their legal subordination to their employers, who are driven to maximize their output in order to extract surplus value and maximize profits. For Marx, the retention of surplus value (the difference between the value of what is produced and what the worker is paid) by the employer constitutes exploitation. At certain points in time, workers view this exploitation of their labour power, and the laws that enable or tolerate it, as normatively unfair, and they resist it at the point of production and/or through political action, producing a commodification-decommodification dialectic driven by the politics of class conflict.[8]

A variation of the Marxist account contemplates some situations in which class collaboration may emerge within this dialectic. Erik Olin Wright identifies situations in which worker organization reaches a sufficient level of strength that prevents employers from dominating the class-conflict game, imposes intolerably high costs of conflict, or actually assists employers in overcoming their own collective action problems that, if resolved, would leave employers better off as a class. Under these circumstances, a politics of class cooperation may develop in regard to particular issues. Such cooperation does not change the underlying structural conditions of the commodification-decommodification dialectic, but it does allow for a different kind of politics to emerge in response to it, a politics of class cooperation.[9]

From a Polanyian perspective, the fictive nature of labour as a commodity also arises from the fact that labour is not produced for the market. But for Polanyi, the dysfunctional consequences of labour's commodification do not emerge principally in the hidden abode of production but rather in the threat commodification poses to social reproduction, as norms of reciprocity and redistribution are replaced by the pursuit of self-interest without regard to others. In a similar vein, Nancy Fraser has recently discussed what she characterizes as the background conditions that make capitalism possible. These include social reproduction, the earth's ecology, and political power.[10] From a Polanyian/Fraser perspective, the unbridled commodification of labour and its subordination to market forces creates existential threats to society and, in Polanyi's famous formulation, produces a counter- or double-movement that, if successful, results in the partial decommodification of labour by re-embedding the market in the social. Although Polanyi does not have a clear theory of how this will occur, his theoretical framework suggests that a broader coalition of social forces, potentially including some employers, will emerge to produce this countermovement. Fraser writes of "boundary struggles" to defend human or social reproduction from economic production that are not only driven by functionalist imperatives but are also informed by norms and social practices indigenous to non-economic spheres. As a result, class is not the only level at which struggle over the commodification-decommodification dialectic occurs; rather, multiple sets of actors enter the fray under the banner of diverse norms.

Although there are important differences in Polanyi and Fraser's perspectives, their analyses lead to a common conclusion that the dialectic may be driven by a broader-based politics that draws on norms of social solidarity. For simplicity's sake, we will call this the politics of social protection.

Workers' compensation is an excellent case for exploring the politics of the commodification-decommodification dialectic and how that politics has unfolded over time. From the beginning of industrial capitalism, work injuries have proven to be particularly problematic, as they illustrate in the most dramatic way possible the inability to separate labour power from the worker who sold it; when a worker is injured or killed at work, it is not just the worker's labour power that is damaged or destroyed but the human being. Moreover, in a social formation in which unwaged dependants rely on the income of a waged worker, those dependants also suffer the consequences of work-related disabilities and deaths, both economically (the loss of access to the wage and the increased cost of care) and personally. These devastating losses explain why struggles to prevent work injuries and to compensate injured workers began with the rise of industrial capitalism, which set the dialectic in motion and has kept it in play.

Because the commodification-decommodification dialectic is a structural feature of capitalist relations of production, it is endemic as long as those relations exist. However, conflict is not constant, and its development and the forms it takes are contingent on a wide range of historically specific factors, which we will look at more closely when we turn from theory to history. However, it will be helpful first to distinguish between two ideal types of conflict. The first challenges the commodity status of labour and is typically based on normative claims grounded outside the market. "Our health is not for sale" is a slogan that captures this ethos. The second accepts the commodity status of labour and draws on norms rooted within the market. Claims from within labour market norms might take the form of a demand for higher wages or a higher wage replacement rate for injured workers. Of course, these are ideal types, and in the messy reality of workers' compensation struggles the lines between the two kinds of claims are often blurred. For example, from one perspective a claim for full compensation for a partially disabled worker to continue until the worker is able to find employment might be viewed as a purely economic demand, which employers resist because of its cost. However, the demand may also be fuelled by a deep sense of injustice about being treated as a disposable commodity, and employer resistance may be driven by a concern that full compensation would partially decommodify labour by enabling injured workers to remain out of the labour market. Despite these complications, the distinction is analytically useful for understanding and interpreting the history and politics of workers' compensation struggles.

History of the Commodification-Decommodification Dialectic in Workers' Compensation

A full history of this dialectic in workers' compensation is beyond the scope of this chapter and so instead it focuses on a few key moments and issues: the creation of a contract-based compensation regime and the shift to the tort regime and then the no-fault regime, followed by an overview of the recurring conflict over the compensation of workers with permanent disabilities within the no-fault regime.

It was not until the nineteenth century that workers and their families first began suing their employers for work-related disabilities and fatalities. While the earliest case concerned a boy employed in a mercantile setting, soon thereafter the litigation was dominated by adult male workers employed in industries at the core of the first Industrial Revolution, including railways and factories. Because there was no legal precedent for these claims, common law judges were left to develop the guiding principles and in so doing opted for a contract regime rooted in market liberalism. In a string of cases, beginning with *Priestly v Fowler* in 1837 and crisscrossing the Atlantic, judges fashioned the legal presumption that workers voluntarily assumed the risk of injury from hazards that were known or ought to have been known to be present in the workplace, including the risk of injury from the negligence of fellow servants.[11] The reason for adopting this presumption was market economics. Workers would "naturally" demand higher wages to incur risks and so it was legally presumed that in their contracts of employment they agreed to incur the risk of injuries from hazards known to be present in the workplace in exchange for the wages they were paid. Therefore, they were not entitled to further compensation if those risks materialized in disabling injuries. The same result was reached even if the court acknowledged that the old master and servant law implied a duty of care on the part of employers. In a liberal market economy, the implied terms of employment contracts washed away older duties arising from status relations.[12]

The creation of this regime can be understood through the lens of the politics of class conflict, although it was a pretty one-sided affair, skewed heavily towards employers, occurring at a time when workers generally had little organizational or political power. Although the judges responsible for selecting the model might not have seen themselves as acting in class terms, they were not naive about what they were doing. They were ideologically committed to the individualistic or laissez-faire outlook that predominated among men of their class at the time. They embraced the view that labour should be treated as a commodity, no different in principle than any other.[13] Canadian common law judges slavishly followed English precedent, giving it full effect while revealing little of their own thoughts on the law.[14]

The contract model served employers' interests well; it made the cost of hazardous working conditions low and fairly certain by effectively relieving employers of any legal obligation to compensate injured workers. Workers were ill served by the model, which deprived them of access to post-injury compensation. Moreover, because most workers lacked the bargaining power to command significant risk premiums, employers had little incentive to reduce hazards. However, the certainties that the model produced helped to concentrate and make visible the respective and contradictory interests of workers and employers and also attracted the attention of some reformers who became concerned about its impact on child and female labour in factories and its adverse effects on social reproduction. Such concerns created space for the politics of class conflict and social protection.

The widespread perception among reformers and workers that it was unfair to expose workers to hazardous conditions and to not compensate them when injuries materialized led them to demand reforms soon after the contract model was entrenched. Both class and social protection politics drove occupational health and safety (OHS) reform. For workers, the rosy image of the labour market as a realm of freedom was, in this regard, a lie; they experienced hazardous work as an imposition rather than as a choice. Social reformers, on the other hand, were much more concerned that the unrestrained pursuit of profit was creating physical and moral dangers that were interfering with the reproduction of the next generation. Darcy Bergin, a Conservative member of Parliament, spoke to these concerns in support of protective factory legislation he introduced in 1885: "The future of the children is in our hands ... their health, their life, their faith and their morals are at stake ... that they may not become holocausts on the altar of mammon – these are among the objects of this Bill."[15]

England enacted protective labour law before Canada did, and that often set a precedent followed in this country. In the area of work-injury compensation, workers in England successfully lobbied for legislation in 1880 that provided workers with a statutory claim for compensation from their employers if they could establish that their injuries were the result of employer negligence, making tort rather than contract the underlying basis for compensation. However, if the worker pursued a statutory claim, recovery was limited to a maximum of three years' wages, even in the case of a fatality.[16] Developments in Ontario took a slightly different route, but reached the same result. In 1881, the Ontario legislature enacted the *Railway Accidents Act* (RAA). The preamble signalled dissatisfaction with the results of the contractual model: "Whereas frequent accidents to railway servants and others are occasioned by the neglect of railway companies to provide reasonable measures of protection against their occurrence." The Act then went on to set standards for railway construction and maintenance and allowed workers injured as a result of violations to sue as if they were not employees. The effect was that workers could make tort-like claims for these injuries because the contractual presumption of voluntary assumption of risk was removed.[17] Five years later, under pressure from a revived trade union movement led by the Knights of Labor and facing more workers at the polls as a result of amended election laws, the Ontario government followed England's lead and enacted the *Workman's Compensation for Injuries Act* (WCIA), bringing in the negligence model of liability for work injuries.[18]

The creation of a tort-based regime of compensation was a departure from market voluntarism insofar as it gave workers a nonwaivable right to sue for injuries resulting from employer negligence, but it did little to decommodify labour power. Damages were measured by the injured worker's lost income, capped by a three-year limit, if the worker chose to sue under the statute, but without a minimum entitlement independent of income level.[19] In short, the change affected how labour power was priced and compensated but hardly touched its commodity status.

While the creation of the WCIA/tort regime can be understood chiefly as the product of class conflict, the shift from tort to no-fault workers' compensation is better explained by a politics of class cooperation, with class conflict playing a secondary role. The starting point of the story is the failure of the tort regime to stabilize the regulatory dilemmas of market liberalism. Although the tort model allowed some workers to obtain some compensation some of the time, numerous problems remained. For the majority of injured workers, who did not have access to private benefit plans,[20] their first recourse was to seek compensation directly from their employer. While some employers may have paid compensation voluntarily, benevolence was in limited supply and workers would have to sue and prove negligence in order to recover damages. Where employers purchased employer liability insurance, as a number of large employers did, any claims would have been referred to the insurer, who had a direct pecuniary interest in minimizing payouts. Here workers often faced delay or received settlement offers significantly below their legal entitlement, which might be accepted because of economic duress. If no settlement were reached, the employee might sue, but this was risky because the downside could be crushing; if the suit failed, not only would the worker be left without compensation, but he or she would be liable to pay the legal costs of the employer as well as his or her own. Even if the worker were successful in the initial action, the employer/insurer might appeal, resulting in further delay and more legal costs. As a result, many workers were left dependent on scarce family resources or on the community at large through charity or municipal welfare where it was available. Thus, compensation for work-related disability remained highly uncertain even after the WCIA.

The tort model also had considerable drawbacks for employers. While the outcome of litigation was less certain than it had been under the contract model, Ontario judges seemed almost relieved not to administer the contract regime, and they implemented the WCIA in the spirit in which it was enacted.[21] The effect was to increase employers' liability for work injuries, making their cost a greater concern. Some employers purchased employer liability insurance, but it is doubtful that insurance markets were sufficiently developed to provide coverage for small employers and, in any event, the practices of insurance companies in resisting claims created ill-will between injured workers and employers. This concern increased in the first decade of the twentieth century as a result of deepening class divisions and the growing popularity of socialist and radical ideology. In addition, employers were unhappy about the perceived inefficiency of private insurance because the proportion of premiums paid in benefits to injured workers was low relative to the high commissions paid to brokers and the large costs of defending claims.[22]

As a result, employers had a collective interest in an alternative to the tort model, one that compensated injured workers regardless of fault, provided that it would neither significantly increase their costs nor put them at a competitive disadvantage. A public insurance scheme based on mandatory participation and collective employer liability, at least within industry groups, could go a long way towards meeting these concerns by taking compensation costs out of competition and allowing them to be passed on to the consumer. This was certainly the view of William Meredith, who headed the commission appointed by the Ontario government to study the problem and whose report proposed something along these lines. Employers would be "simply tax gatherers" from the public, who would pay the cost of workers' compensation through higher prices.[23] This made the no-fault alternative to tort tolerable.

However, a public insurance scheme did not resolve employer concerns completely. First, an insurance scheme with standardized premiums created its own collective action problems, in particular the possibility of free-riding employers seeking to gain a competitive advantage by underinvesting in safety, as they would not have to bear the full cost of their accidents. The problem of policing free riders was partly addressed by health and safety legislation that required employers to meet public standards, but enforcement was generally lax. So other steps were taken. Some provision was made for premiums to be adjusted through merit rating, although these powers were little used initially because of their inconsistency with the principle of collective liability.[24] The other legislative measure provided for the creation of German-style industry safety associations funded by workers' compensation premiums. These associations were given the authority to promulgate and enforce rules, as well as to educate their members, thereby lowering information costs about risk reduction and providing a mechanism to police employers whose hazardous practices threatened to increase everyone's premiums.[25]

But the politics of class compromise do not tell the whole story. Employer acceptance of no-fault workers' compensation insurance can also be traced to a more general change in thinking about the causes of workplace injuries. While nineteenth-century market liberalism embraced notions of individual responsibility, increasingly in the twentieth century statistical thinking about accidents began to predominate. Work injuries were seen as a predictable result of engaging in productive activity. As I.M. Rubinow noted in his early treatise on social insurance, "'an industrial accident is not an accident at all.' Rather, it is a definite and constant characteristic of modern industry, subject to definite rules and laws."[26] As such, the search for individual fault seemed misguided as a basis on which to award compensation to workers who predictably suffered disabling injuries.

The retreat from individual fault paralleled and complemented an ideological shift away from laissez-faire principles and practices. One of the most striking examples of this change comes from an unsigned article published in 1910 in the *Labour Gazette*, a monthly publication of the federal Department of Labour, on the topic of workmen's compensation:

The basic fact from which legislation of the class specifically designated as "Labour Legislation" proceeds is that labour, though bought and sold, is not a "commodity" in the ordinary sense of the term, inasmuch as its purchase and sale always involve in the most intimate way the welfare of a human being ... The securing of the comprehensive body of legislation of this class ... marks the overthrow of the economic doctrine of *laissez faire* ... the effect of which was to minimize or abolish the distinction between labour and other commodities and to leave the condition of the labourer to be determined almost wholly by competition and the law of supply and demand.[27]

Karl Polanyi could not have said it better. Clearly, one of the most dysfunctional consequences of unchecked commodification was the adverse effect of work injuries and disability on the family wage system.

But to what extent did workers' compensation decommodify labour? Here we need to return to the distinction between conflict over the price of work-related disability and conflict over labour's commodity status. Employers were deeply concerned about both issues. In regard to price, even though the no-fault regime took compensation costs out of competition, employers still had a collective interest in holding down the system's costs. Employers understood that even if, in principle, the public would pay, consumer demand for most products was elastic and at some point higher prices would noticeably reduce consumption levels. Moreover, even in the early twentieth century Ontario producers in some sectors were competing with out-of-province and international producers, who were not covered by the provincial scheme and whose compensation costs could be lower. Thus, compensation costs were not fully taken out of competition. It was also crucial to employers that the boundaries of the system be maintained so that only costs associated with work injuries would be compensated, otherwise employers and consumers would be "unfairly" burdened with the cost of benefits that should be paid out of general revenues if they were to be provided at all.[28]

Measures to address these concerns included a wage-replacement rate of 55 percent, capping insurable earnings at $2,000, and imposing a seven-day waiting period before benefits were payable. Employers also pushed for employees to pay part of the premium, but Meredith held firm, arguing that workers already contributed by the restrictions placed on the amount of their compensation.

Employers were equally concerned about anything in the system that might weaken labour's commodity status or the work incentive. Therefore, injured workers should be given neither the permission nor the means to stay out of the labour market longer than was absolutely neces-sary for them to recover. Thus, benefit levels were not just a cost issue but also went to employers' interest in maintaining workers' labour mar-ket dependency.[29]

Disagreements over price and commodification sometimes played them-selves out in debates about whether workers' compensation was "social legislation." For example, workers argued for minimum compensation lev-els regardless of income in order to keep workers and their families out of poverty, something that previous regimes had failed to do.[30] Meredith was sympathetic to this concern: "I suppose everybody recognizes, at least I cer-tainly do, that this Bill is more than a mere compensation to workmen Bill. It is social legislation and it is intended to provide for the workman and save the community from bearing the burden of his impairment."[31] However, apart from funeral expenses in the case of fatal accidents, Meredith was adamantly opposed to minimum entitlements, even for dependent spouses and children.[32]

Common interests coalesced around the basic principle of a public, compulsory, no-fault workers' compensation (WC) system. The benefit to workers was the certainty of a modest entitlement to compensation, even though they lost the right to sue employers for potentially greater sums where employer negligence caused the injury. For employers, the WC sys-tem promised to remove a source of worker discontent, standardize the cost of workplace injuries within industries at modest levels, and make insur-ance more efficient by increasing the percentage of premiums that went to injured workers.

But the system also built in conflicts that could only be managed, not resolved. One endemic conflict was over the level of compensation. Work-ers had an interest in increasing benefit levels to improve their standard of living after a disabling injury, while employers had an interest in lim-iting them to contain costs. The scheme set out a replacement rate and capped insurable earnings, but there was nothing sacred about these de-terminations. Inflation would inevitably eat away at the earnings cap, so that over time workers would demand that the cap be increased just to retain the value of the coverage. Employer resistance to more generous benefits went beyond their economic cost and reflected a concern that higher compensation levels would weaken workers' incentive to return to the labour market.

Another structural conflict revolved around how workers with per-manent disabilities would be compensated. The scheme was based on the principle that workers were to be partially compensated for their lost earning capacity. But how was that loss to be calculated? From the employers' perspective, permanently disabled workers should be compensated only for the percentage of lost earning capacity directly caused by the injury. This portion could be permanently retired and excused from the labour market. The remaining capacity, however, had to remain commodified and active in the labour market. Therefore, any additional problems the worker experienced in selling his or her residual labour power was non-compensable, as it could be affected by factors such as the unemployment rate, a problem outside the scheme. Workers regarded the distinction between the retired and the active portion of labour power as entirely artificial, as it overlooked the reality that the worker was still a whole human being and that the damaged portion of his or her capacity could not be neatly severed without affecting residual earning power. Regardless of the prevailing labour market conditions, workers with disabilities attributed their difficulty in finding employment to the work injury and demanded full compensation for their wage loss until they found work that, with their compensation, returned them to their pre-injury income.

We can see that workers with permanent impairments grasped intuitively that disability was socially constructed by political economic relations – that, under capitalism, a worker with an impairment was disadvantaged when seeking to find employment, as a result of employers' expectations that workers with impairments would be less productive than able-bodied workers, that they would be more prone to re-injury, or that they would require some accommodation to be able to perform their jobs. Workers with impairments knew from experience that, even at marginally lower wage rates, they faced discrimination in the capitalist labour market because employers anticipated that less surplus value could be extracted from them.[33]

The no-fault compensation system coalesced workers' and employers' distinct collective interests but the strength of those collective interests, as well as the capacity to act collectively, varied over time.[34] Space does not permit a more comprehensive historical examination of how these contradictions played out in the Ontario WC regime; however, a focus on the compensation of workers with permanent disabilities provides a good lens through which to view the recurring dilemmas within the regime.

The original 1914 *Workmen's Compensation Act* mandated a wage-loss system for compensating workers with permanent disabilities. According to that model, a Workmen's Compensation Board (WCB; the name was changed to the Workers' Compensation Board in 1981 and to the Work-place Safety and Insurance Board [WSIB] in 1998) determined a compensation benefit solely by calculating the wage loss caused by the injury, not taking into account any "social" factors that might make the worker less employable and result in additional wage losses. This approach was consistent with insurance and commodification principles, but it was difficult to administer: it required not only isolating the portion of the loss due exclusively to the injury, which was difficult, but also ongoing monitoring of workers' future earnings to determine whether the wage loss was continuing. In 1917 the statute was amended to permit the board to adopt a rating system based on a "meat chart" that established the percentage of wage loss associated with the loss of a body part or a capacity. This too was a way of commodifying the loss suffered by the worker, but it was administratively simpler and provided rough justice in that it ignored the fact the same loss of capacity did not affect the wage earnings of all workers equally as the "meat chart" provided.[35]

Standardized calculations of wage loss did not satisfactorily resolve the issue for labour, which continued to demand full compensation for the *actual* wages lost. Labour movement pressure during the Great Depression in the 1930s led a number of provincial governments to appoint commissions to investigate WC and make recommendations.[36] In Ontario, the commission was headed by Justice W.E. Middleton, who made his perspective clear: "The whole scheme of the Act and the principle underlying it is in the nature of insurance." Thus any proposal inconsistent with insurance principles was rejected. This sealed the fate of labour's demand that workers with permanent partial disabilities be fully compensated, despite Middleton's recognition that workers with permanent disabilities were disadvantaged in the labour market: "[T]oo frequently this condition is accentuated by general industrial conditions and it seems inequitable to place any burden of unemployment insurance upon the industries concerned under the guise of workmen's compensation."[37]

Middleton's report did not satisfy the labour movement, but it was not until the Second World War when labour militancy reached unprecedented levels that it gained the political clout necessary to get the government to enact legislation partially responsive to its concerns. In 1942, the Ontario government amended the Act to empower the compensation board to award additional benefits to permanently injured workers if the board believed that would be more equitable than the rating system.[38] However, the board was not required to award additional benefits, and so the labour

movement continued to press the issue in the postwar era, albeit with
limited success. The Roach Commission, appointed in 1950, reiterated the
position of the Middleton Commission, as did the McGillvray Commission
report seventeen years later. Both reports took the position that high unemployment among disabled workers was a problem for the welfare system to
address, not for WC.[39]

In the late 1960s, the rise of a militant injured workers' movement, centred among Italian immigrants in Toronto, altered the political context of
the commodification-decommodification dialectic, giving workers' compensation issues unprecedented political traction.[40] Initially, the board expanded rehabilitation services in an effort to address the serious problems
workers with disabilities experienced re-entering the labour market, but
this strategy met with limited success. In the face of this reality, it became
increasingly difficult to uphold the distinction between compensating only
for the functional loss and not for the real labour market impact of the
impairment. Under growing pressure, in 1974 the Ontario government
amended the Act to give the board the power to award benefit supplements
to injured workers who returned to work for less than their pre-injury
earnings. As well, those who did not return to work could continue to receive full benefits unless they failed to cooperate in a medical or vocational
rehabilitation program or did not accept suitable work that was available.[41]
The legislation was amended one year later to permit the board to provide
supplemental benefits to workers with permanent partial disabilities when
the impairment of earning capacity was significantly greater than normal,
provided the worker participated in a program of medical or vocational
rehabilitation or accepted or was willing to take an available job that the
board deemed suitable.[42]

In the years that followed, injured workers fought with the board to be
awarded these new supplemental benefits and met with some success. Improved benefits for injured workers, however, increased the costs of compensation and raised employer premiums, which attracted the attention of
employers, who mobilized and pressed their concerns before the board and
the government. In response to these pressures, the compensation board
commissioned a report from private consultants, which found that more
generous benefits were reducing the incentive to return to work. The WCB
followed up with its own paper, which valorized employers' concerns that
rising compensation costs were making Ontario industry uncompetitive.
The politics of decommodification and price were clearly engaged. As a
solution, the WCB paper proposed a dual award system that would more

accurately compensate permanently injured workers for their "real" wage loss. Robert Elgie, the minister of labour, then commissioned Harvard law professor and former chair of the British Columbia Labour Relations Board Paul Weiler to undertake a system review.[43]

Weiler stepped into an "unhappily polarized" environment marked by "incipient class struggle" over workers' compensation.[44] In his 1980 report, he made a number of recommendations that workers supported, but the recommendation that attracted the most attention and antipathy from injured workers was the dual award system, which would see permanently injured workers receive a lump-sum payment that acknowledged their non-economic losses and an ongoing payment tied to actual wage loss. This approach would replace the rating system, which had only recently been amended to enable more disabled workers to get supplemental benefits. Workers feared that a return to the wage-loss system, abandoned by the board in 1917, would lead to benefits being reduced if the WCB deemed that a worker could earn an income from a suitable job, even if a suitable job was not available. Employers were more favourably inclined towards the proposal, but they were worried that the board might not take into account labour market conditions in calculating actual wage loss, especially in the context of a recession.

The twisted politics that followed cannot be fully recounted here but, in a nutshell, while the Ontario government did not immediately implement the wage-loss plan, it did make other changes, including higher wage replacement levels, more vocational rehabilitation, and an independent appeal tribunal. Employers became even more alarmed that the workers' compensation system was being incrementally transformed into a social welfare program that enabled injured workers to remain outside the labour market and gave them access to generous social services, driving up the cost of the system.[45] They were supported by a 1987 KPMG report, which found that real claim costs had indeed increased and singled out supplemental benefits as the most significant contributor to the rising cost per claim.[46] In June 1988, the government introduced Bill 162, which would implement the dual award system recommended by Weiler but which also would provide injured workers with a limited right to be reinstated to their old jobs. In announcing the Bill, the minister emphasized that its goal was to tie compensation more closely to economic losses and help injured workers return to the workforce.[47] Both workers and employers were wary of how it would be implemented, but eventually the employers were won over and the Bill was enacted in 1989.[48]

There is relatively little research on the impact of the Bill 162 reforms on compensation costs, but there is some evidence that it failed to produce the cost savings employers wanted, largely because its implementation occurred under a New Democratic Party (NDP) government, which was elected in 1990.[49] As a result, the WCB was reluctant to reduce economic loss benefits by deeming workers able to earn a wage even though they were not employed.[50] The defeat of the NDP government in 1995 and its replacement by an ideologically right-leaning Conservative Party opened the door for change, especially given the strong employer demand for the costs of the system to be reined in.[51] The government enacted legislation in 1997 that prioritized returning injured workers to work, either with the employer where the injury occurred or through a labour market re-entry (LMR) plan.[52]

There were numerous problems with this approach, including an annual review of loss of earnings (LOE) benefits for six years after the injury, but one consequence was that, after workers completed the LMR program, they were deemed capable of earning a wage, and their loss of earnings compensation was reduced accordingly, even if no suitable job was available. Many disabled workers suffered benefit cuts as result, as LMR programs were often of poor quality, and only about half of all workers who completed these programs found employment.[53]

In 2004, a Liberal government took office. Legislative reform of workers' compensation was not high on its list of priorities, but in 2007 it removed the word "deem" from the Act and reinserted the requirement that a suitable job had to be "available" before workers could have their LOE benefits reduced.[54] Yet, despite this change, injured workers continue to have their LOE benefits cut.[55]

The WSIB (renamed from WCB) subsequently launched a Benefits Policy Review Consultation, chaired by Jim Thomas. In his 2013 report, he refers back to his earlier involvement in workers' compensation issues in the 1980s and 1990s:

> I recall it was impossible to find enough common ground within the stakeholder community to move forward with benefits policy reforms. It would appear that little has changed since then. Stakeholder opposition, stemming from the fact that what is a "win" for injured workers is an additional cost for employers, and vice versa, has thwarted attempts at reforming benefit policies.

He goes on to bemoan this state of affairs and express the belief that "a principle-based approach to benefits policy might be a key to unlock the paralysis that has occurred over decades of failed attempts at policy reform."[56]

Thomas's report did result in a policy change by the board, but one that was deeply controversial. Effective November 1, 2014, the board's policy on pre-existing conditions changed to give adjudicators greater scope to reduce benefits for permanently injured workers who had a pre-existing condition, even if that condition had not been adversely affecting their ability to work prior to the accident. Not surprisingly, injured worker advocates have denounced the policy change as a betrayal of a foundational principle of workers' compensation law: that all workers are entitled to the full benefit of the law without discrimination based on their physical condition.[57]

This brief history of workers' compensation in Ontario demonstrates the strength of the commodification-decommodification dialectic as a driving force in producing the recurring regulatory dilemmas that are endemic to this area of law. Workers' interests in challenging their commodity status or demanding a greater share of socially produced wealth, in this case by insisting on being fully compensated for their work injuries, runs into capital's interest in maintaining labour market discipline and maximizing profit by extracting surplus value. The politics of the commodification-decommodification dialectic vary, as does the intensity of conflict. There have been moments when workers successfully mobilized, sometimes attracting the support of reformers concerned about the dysfunctional consequences of gloves-off capitalism on social reproduction, but the current turn of governments towards austerity politics has penetrated the workers' compensation system, shifting the focus to cost containment at the expense of benefits for injured workers generally, and especially those with permanent work-related disabilities.

NOTES

1 Association of Workers' Compensation Boards of Canada, *Detailed Key Statistical Measures Report – 2015*, online: <http://awcbc.org/?page_id=9759>.

2 *Ibid* and Jaclyn Gilks & Ron Logan, "Occupational Illnesses and Diseases in Canada, 1996–2008" (Ottawa: Research and Analysis, Occupational Health and Safety Division, Labour Program, Department of Human Resources and Skill Development Canada, 2010). In Ontario, only 65.8 percent of the workforce was covered in 2015. Workplace Safety and Insurance Board, *By the Numbers: 2015 WSIB Statistical Report*, online: <http://www.wsibstatistics.ca/en/s1workplaces/>.

3 Institute for Work and Health, *Suppression of Workplace Injury and Illness Claims: Summary of Evidence in Canada* (Issue Briefing, October 2014).

4 Ontario, Workplace Safety and Insurance Board, *Statistical Supplement to the 2010 Annual Report* (Toronto: Workplace Safety and Insurance Board, 2011), Table 3. The WSIB stopped publishing these data in more recent reports.

5 There is no good quantitative study of work injuries in industrializing Canada. For the United States, see Mark Aldrich, *Safety First* (Baltimore, MD: Johns Hopkins University Press, 1997); for England, see PWJ Bartrip & SB Burman, *The Wounded Soldiers of Industry, 1833–1897* (Oxford: Clarendon Press, 1983).

6 Beverly J. Silver, *Forces of Labor* (Cambridge: Cambridge University Press, 2003) at 16–20.

7 Karl Marx, *Capital*, vol. 1 (New York City: International Press, [1867] 1967), c 6.

8 Kevin Purse, "The Evolution of Workers' Compensation Policy in Australia," (2004) 14 Health Sociology Rev 8, makes the argument that policy development is driven by the conflicting interests of business and organized labour.

9 Erik Olin Wright, "Working-Class Power, Capitalist-Class Interests, and Class Compromise," (2000) 105:4 Am J Sociology 957.

10 Karl Polanyi, *The Great Transformation* (Boston: Beacon Press, 1957); Nancy Fraser, "Behind Marx's Hidden Abode" (2013) 86 New Left Rev 55.

11 *Priestly v Fowler* (1837), 3 M&W 1; *Farwell v The Boston and Worcester Rail Road Company* 45 Mass. (4 Met.) 49 (1842); *Bartonshill Coal Co v Reid* (1858), 3 Macq. 266.

12 In theory, an employee could still sue his or her employer if the injury were caused by a hazardous condition, personally created by the employer, not in the contemplation of the parties, and not partly caused by the worker's own negligence, an almost impossible task. See *Deverill v Grand Trunk Railway* (1866), 25 UCR 517 (UCQB).

13 For example, see Michael Ashley Stein, "Victorian Tort Liability for Workplace Injuries" [2008] Illinois L Rev 933 at 964–75; Leonard W Levy, *The Law of the Commonwealth and Chief Justice Shaw* (Cambridge, MA: Harvard University Press, 1957) at 319.

14 Eric Tucker, "The Law of Employers' Liability in Ontario, 1861–1900: The Search for a Theory" (1984) 22 Osgoode Hall LJ 213; RCB Risk, "The Law and the Economy in Mid-Nineteenth Century Ontario: A Perspective" (1984) 27 UTLJ 403; Bruce Ziff, "Warm Reception in a Cold Climate: English Property Law and the Suppression of the Canadian Legal Identity" in John McLaren, AR Buck & Nancy E Wright, eds, *Despotic Dominion: Property Rights in British Settler Societies* (Vancouver: UBC Press, 2005) 103.

15 *House of Commons Debates*, 5th Parl, 3rd Sess, Vol 2 (1 April 1885) at 881 (Hon Darby Bergin).

16 Bartrip and Burman, *supra* note 5 at 126–57; *Employer's Liability Act, 1880*, 43 & 44 Vic, c 42.

17 *Railway Accidents Act*, SO 1881, c 22.

18 *Workman's Compensation for Injuries Act*, SO 1886, c 28. Gregory S Kealey, *Toronto Workers Respond to Industrial Capitalism* (Toronto: University of Toronto Press, 1980).

19 The act did not preclude workers from suing under the common law, but if they did then they were back in the contract model.

20 We know relatively little about the operation of these plans in mid- to late nineteenth-century Ontario, but existing evidence suggests their coverage was limited and benefits were generally low. See Dustin Galer, "A Friend in Need or a Business Indeed? Disabled Bodies and Fraternalism in Victorian Ontario" (2010) 66:1 Labour/ Le Travail 9. As well, a few employers (mostly railroads) provided mandatory insurance plans, funded largely by employee contribution, which required employees to waive any other claims against the company. The 1886 law provided limited space for employer insurance plans to displace statutory tort actions, provided they paid benefits at least as generous as those under the act.

21 Tucker, *supra* note 14; RCB Risk, "'This Nuisance of Litigation': The Origins of Workers' Compensation in Ontario" in David H Flaherty, ed, *Essays in the History of Canadian Law,* vol 2 (Toronto: Osgoode Society, University of Toronto Press, 1983) 418.

22 Michael Piva, "The Workmen's Compensation Movement in Ontario" (1975) 67 Ontario History 39 at 46–47; Risk, *supra* note 21 at 458–63. Also see FW Wegenast, *Workmen's Compensation for Injuries* (Toronto: Canadian Manufacturers Association, 1911) for comments on the inefficiencies of the insurance system. Robert Maton aptly described this system as one of variable benefits to workers and variable costs to employers. See Robert Maton, *The Emergence of Neo-Liberalism in Ontario's Workers' Compensation System* (PhD Thesis, University of Toronto, 1991) at 43–49 [unpublished].

23 Quoted in Risk, *supra* note 21 at 461.

24 Donald W Rogers, *Making Capitalism Safe* (Champaign: University of Illinois Press, 2009) at 140–41, cites a Canadian compensation official who warned his American colleagues about the danger severe merit rating posed to collective liability.

25 Javier Silvestre, "Improving Workplace Safety in the Ontario Manufacturing Industry, 1914–1939" (2010) 84 Business History Rev 527.

26 IM Rubinow, *Social Insurance* (New York: Henry Holt, 1913) at 49.

27 "Legislation with Respect to Workmen's Compensation in Canada," *Labour Gazette* (November 1910) 546 at 546. A similar view is expressed in another unsigned article, "Compensation for Injuries to Canadian Workingmen" (1918) 54 Can LJ 281 at 281–82:

> The tendency to look upon the laboring man as a mere chattel in industry is rapidly passing away; there is a general admission to-day not only that labour is a vital necessity in all industrial endeavour, but also that it must be conserved, protected and inspired to its best use. It is agreed that society is held together by the laws of social solidarity; the interests of all its classes are bound together in the general welfare of the community's life; ... it is impossible for society or one class of society to rise while one social group is held down by unjust and unnecessary limitations. It is further agreed that labour has made a vast and indispensable contribution to our industrial development; the products of industry are all composite structures and the labouring

man can look upon them and justly claim that not merely his muscle, but also his brain, his skill and his sagacity have entered into their creation. It is only to be expected, therefore, that the working man, when accidently injured or killed, should receive a large and increasing share of attention.

28 Grant Duncan, "Workers' Compensation and the Governance of Pain" (2003) 32 Economy and Society 449, makes a similar point from a Foucauldian perspective.
29 See Robert Storey, "From Invisibility to Equality? Women Workers and the Gendering of Workers' Compensation in Ontario, 1900–1925" (2009) 64 Labour/Le Travail 75 at 83–84, for a discussion of early concerns to avoid decommodification in the workers' compensation system.
30 *Ibid.* For the United States, see John Fabian Witt, *The Accidental Republic: Crippled Workingmen, Destitute Widows, and the Remaking of American Law* (Cambridge, MA: Harvard University Press, 2006) at 129–34.
31 Sir William Ralph Meredith, *Final Report on Laws Relating to the Liability of Employers to Make Compensation to Their Employees for Injuries Received in the Course of Their Employment which Are in Force in Other Countries* (Toronto: L.K. Cameron, 1913) Minutes of Evidence, vol 2, 577–78.
32 *Workmen's Compensation Act,* SO 1914, c 25, s 33(5). Meredith's support for insurance principles also led him to reject a proposal from employers that pensions for workers with permanent disabilities be limited in amount or duration. See, Meredith, *supra* note 31 at 464–71.
33 Marta Russell & Ravi Malhotra, "Capitalism and Disability" (2002) 38 Socialist Register 211.
34 Nob Doran, "Maintaining the Simulation Model in the Era of the 'Social': The 'Inquiry' System of Canadian Workers' Compensation, 1914–1984" (1994) 31:4 Can Rev of Sociology & Anthropology 446, makes a similar point from a more Foucauldian perspective about the way in which the workers' compensation scheme involved the creation of a grammar of compensation that provided the dominant framework within which organized labour and workers operated, but that from time to time was contested by workers whose common sense experiences conflicted with the bureaucratic discourse within which they had to fit themselves. Jeffrey Hilgert, "Building a Human Rights Framework for Workers' Compensation in the United States: Opening the Debate on First Principles" (2010) 55 Am J Industrial Medicine 512, does not see the workers' compensation regime as containing a commodification-decommodification dialectic, but rather views it as another way of instantiating market liberalism and trumping social rights.
35 SO 1917, c 34. Maton, *supra* note 22 at 73–80 has an excellent discussion of this issue.
36 *Labour Gazette* (February 1931) 122 (ON); (March 1931) 267 (NB); (April 1931) 389 (AB). Nova Scotia, *Report of Workmen's Compensation Commission* (Halifax: King's Printer, 1937).
37 Ontario, *Report of the Commissioner in the Matter of the Workmen's Compensation Act* (Legislative Assembly, Sessional Paper 37, 1932) at 6, 7, 14.
38 SO 1942, c 41.

39 Ontario, *Report on the Workmen's Compensation Act* (Toronto: King's Printer, 1950); Ontario, *Report of the Royal Commission in the Matter of the Workmen's Compensation Act* (Toronto: Commission in the Matter of the Workmen's Compensation Act, 1967) at 36–51.

40 Robert Storey, "'Their Only Power Was Moral': The Injured Workers' Movement in Toronto, 1970–1985" (2008) 41 Histoire sociale/Social History 99; Robert Storey, "Social Assistance or a Worker's Right: Workmen's Compensation and the Struggle of Injured Workers in Ontario, 1970–1985" (2006) 78 Studies in Political Economy 67; Injured Workmen's Consultants, "Brief to the Resources and Development Committee of the Legislative Assembly of Ontario" (27 June 1972).

41 SO 1974, c 70.

42 SO 1975, c 47, s 6.

43 Maton, *supra* note 22; Storey, "Social Assistance," *supra* note 40; and Nick McCombie, "Justice for Injured Workers: A Community Responds to Government 'Reform'" (1984) 7 Can Community LJ 137.

44 Paul Weiler, *Reshaping Workers' Compensation for Ontario* (Toronto: Ministry of Labour, November 1980) at 17.

45 See, for example, J Edward Nixon, "Financial Status of Workers' Compensation, Current Trends and Bill 162" in Harold P Rolph, ed, *Workers' Compensation: New Costs, New Challenges, New Opportunities* (Toronto: Canadian Institute, 1988) A-1.

46 KPMG Peat Marwick, *Workers' Compensation Board Cost Study, Main Report* (Toronto: KPMG Peat Marwick, September 1987).

47 Ontario, Ministry of Labour, *Workers' Compensation Reform 1988* (Toronto: Ontario Ministry of Labour, 1988) at 7–8.

48 SO 1989, c 47.

49 E.g., Richard Allingham & Douglas Hyatt, "Measuring the Impact of Vocational Rehabilitation on the Probability of Post-Injury Return to Work" in Terry Thomason & Paul Chaykowski, eds, *Research in Canadian Workers' Compensation* (Kingston, ON: IRC Press, 1995) 158, focuses on return to work outcomes, not costs.

50 Tellingly, the NDP did not repeal the wage-loss system but rather appointed a former NDP member of the Legislative Assembly and injured worker activist, Odoardo Di Santo, as chair of the WCB. It subsequently created a bipartite governance structure but also modified the indexing formula in a manner that would reduce future benefit increases. SO 1994, c 24.

51 For a critique of the crisis claims, see David K Wilken, "Manufacturing Crisis in Workers' Compensation" (1998) 13 J L & Social Policy 124.

52 SO 1997, c 16.

53 Garth Dee, "Dealing with the Aftermath of the *Workplace Safety and Insurance Act, 1997*" (1990) 14 J L & Social Policy 169; Joan M Eakin, Ellen MacEachen & Judy Clarke, "'Playing It Smart' with Return to Work: Small Workplace Experience under Ontario's Policy of Self-Reliance and Early Return" (2003) 1:2 Policy and Practice in Health and Safety 19; Bonnie Kirsh & Pat McKee, "The Needs and Experiences of Injured Workers: A Participatory Research Study" (2003) 21 *Work* 221; Ellen MacEachen et al, "The 'Toxic Dose' of System Problems: Why Some Injured Workers Don't Return to Work as Expected" (2010) 20 J Occupational Rehabilitation 349;

KPMG, *WSIB Labour Market Re-entry (LMR) Program Value for Money Audit Report* (KPMG, 3 December 2009), online: <http://www.wsib.on.ca/WSIBPortal/faces/WSIBDetailPage?cGUID=WSIB014204&rDef=WSIB_RD_ARTICLE> at 19.

54 SO 2007, c 7, Sch 41, s 1(1).

55 Injured Workers' Consultants, "Deeming Adds Insult to Injury" (2007), online: <http://injuredworkersonline.org/documents/law-and-policy-submissions/Subm_IWC_20071107_Bill187_Deeming.pdf>.

56 Jim Thomas, *WSIB Benefits and Policy Review Consultation Process: Report to the President and CEO of the WSIB* (May 2013) at 3.

57 *WSIB Ontario Operational Policy*, 15-02-03 (03 November 2014); Sara Mojtehed-zadeh, "Injured Workers Routinely Cut Off WSIB by Improper Rulings," *Toronto Star* (21 July 2016), online <www.thestar.com>.

Editors and Contributors

Editors

Ravi Malhotra has been published widely in peer-reviewed law journals, including the *Alberta Law Review*, the *Ottawa Law Review*, the *Windsor Yearbook of Access to Justice*, and the *Manitoba Law Journal*. In addition, he has contributed chapters to several books, including one on John Rawls in Dianne Pothier and Richard Devlin's anthology, *Critical Disability Theory: Essays in Philosophy, Policy, Politics and Law* (2006). He is also the author (with Morgan Rowe) of *Exploring Disability Identity and Disability Rights through Narratives: Finding a Voice of Their Own* (2013) and the editor of *Disability Politics in a Global Economy: Essays in Honour of Marta Russell* (2016). He is a graduate of Harvard Law School, a disability law scholar, and a full professor at the Faculty of Law, Common Law Section at the University of Ottawa.

Benjamin Isitt has published two monographs, *From Victoria to Vladivostok: Canada's Siberian Expedition, 1917–19* (2010) and *Militant Minority: British Columbia Workers and the Rise of a New Left, 1948–1972* (2011). His research on labour and the left in British Columbia has also appeared in leading peer-reviewed journals, including the *Canadian Historical Review*, the *Canadian Journal of Political Science*, *BC Studies*, *Labour/Le Travail*, and *International Labor and Working-Class History*. Isitt's research has been recognized with several SSHRC grants and by the Labor and Working-Class History Association, an international professional association, which awarded him its Best Graduate Research Award.

Contributors

Odelia R. Bay is a doctoral student at Osgoode Hall Law School, York University, and holds a SSHRC Canada Graduate Scholarship to Honour Nelson Mandela. She has taught at the University of Victoria's Faculty of Law in the areas of labour law, statutory interpretation, and antidiscrimination theory. She articled in union-side labour law with Cavalluzzo Shilton McIntyre Cornish LLP in Toronto before completing her LLM at Columbia Law School, where she studied comparative antidiscrimination law and was a graduate student fellow with the Future of Disability Studies project. She is also a graduate of the University of Ottawa, Faculty of Law, Common Law Section. Prior to studying law, she worked as a broadcast journalist.

Jay Dolmage is an associate professor of English at the University of Waterloo. His work brings together rhetoric, writing, disability studies, and critical pedagogy. His book *Disability Rhetoric* was published in 2014. He is the founding editor of the *Canadian Journal of Disability Studies*. His award-winning essays have appeared in *Rhetoric Review, Cultural Critique, Enculturation,* and many other journals and edited collections. His two current book projects are *Disabled upon Arrival*, which focuses on the connected rhetorical constructions of disability and race through eugenic, anti-immigration discourse, and *Academic Ableism*, a project investigating the ways in which North American institutions of higher education are implicated in eugenic and neo-eugenic practices of disablement.

Anne Finger is a writer of fiction as well as creative nonfiction and has long been an activist in social movements, including the disability rights and reproductive rights movements. Her short story collection *Call Me Ahab* (2009) won the Prairie Schooner Award. She has had published four other books: *Elegy for a Disease: A Personal and Cultural History of Polio* (2006); a collection of short stories, *Basic Skills* (1988); *Past Due: A Story of Disability, Pregnancy and Birth* (1990), and a novel, *Bone Truth* (1994). Her work has also been published in the United States, Germany, and the United Kingdom. Her short fiction has appeared in *Southern Review, Kenyon Review, Discourse,* and *Ploughshares*, among other journals. She has taught creative writing at at Wayne State University and at the University of Texas at Austin, as well as teaching workshops in the community – as writer-in-residence at the Woman's Building in Los Angeles, at the San Francisco Independent Living Resource Center – and in schools. She has also been awarded residencies at Yaddo, Djerassi, Centrum, and Hedgebrook. She lives in Oakland, California.

Dustin Galer received his PhD in history from the University of Toronto. His book, *Working toward Equity: Disability Rights Activism and Employment in Late Twentieth Century Canada* (2017) explores the relationship between disability and work and documents the history of the disability rights movement in Canada. Galer completed a postdoctoral fellowship in the School of Health Policy and Management at York University, focusing on the relationship between disability rights and antipoverty activism. He currently serves as a collaborator at the Centre for Research on Work Disability Policy. Galer founded MyHistorian (www.myhistorian.ca), a personal history services company, where he works to preserve the oral histories of individuals and organizations.

Mark Leier is the author of *Bakunin: The Creative Passion*, and five books on British Columbia labour history, including a revised edition of *Rebel Life*, published in 2013. He worked at several jobs, including busker, bridge tender, and labourer, before going to university, and is currently a professor of history at Simon Fraser University.

Bryan D. Palmer is the author/editor of more than twenty books and currently serves as an editor of *Labour/Le Travail*. He writes, as well, for a number of magazines and journals, including *Jacobin, Canadian Dimension*, and the *Socialist Register*. His most recent books are *Revolutionary Teamsters: The Minneapolis Truckers' Strikes of 1934* (2013); *Marxism and Historical Practice*, volume 1: *Interpretive Essays on Class Formation and Class Struggle* and volume 2: *–Interventions and Appreciations* (2015); and he coauthored *Toronto's Poor: A Rebellious History* (2016).

Geoffrey Reaume is an associate professor in the Critical Disability Studies program at York University, where he has taught since 2004. His publications include *Remembrance of Patients Past: Patient Life at the Toronto Hospital for the Insane, 1870–1940* (2000) and *Lyndhurst: Canada's First Rehabilitation Centre for People with Spinal Cord Injuries, 1945–1998* (2007). Reaume introduced and has taught mad people's history at the University of Toronto, Ryerson University, and York University, where he also teaches a course on disability history.

Jen Rinaldi is an assistant professor in the Legal Studies program at the University of Ontario Institute of Technology. Her graduate scholarship explored how disability diagnostic technologies affect reproductive decision making. Her work engages with narrative and arts-based methodologies to re-imagine eating disorder recovery in relation to the queer community. She also works with Recounting Huronia, an arts-based collective that stories traumatic histories of institutionalization.

Megan A. Rusciano received JD degrees from the University of Ottawa Faculty of Law and American University Washington College of Law and has been admitted to the Maryland bar. She has published on topics ranging from the forcible medication of people with psychosocial disabilities to equal access to information and communications technology by people with disabilities. She interned at The Arc of the United States, the United States Department of Justice, and West End Legal Services of Ottawa. Currently she works as a client advocate for people with disabilities at the Arc of Northern Virginia. Through ongoing volunteer work with the Nidus Personal Planning and Resource Centre in British Columbia, she promotes the use of supported decision making as an alternative to guardianship in both the United States and Canada.

Eric Tucker is a professor at Osgoode Hall Law School, York University. He has published extensively on the history and current state of labour and employment law and occupational health and safety regulation. He is the author of *Administering Danger in the Workplace* (1990) and coauthor of *Labour before the Law* (2001) and *Self-Employed Workers Organize* (2005). He is also the editor of *Working Disasters: The Politics of Recognition and Response* (2006) and coeditor of *Work on Trial: Canadian Labour Law Struggles* (2010) and *Constitutional Labour Rights in Canada: Farm Workers and the Fraser Case* (2012), among other volumes.

Mark Walters is a PhD candidate in communication and science studies at the University of California, San Diego. His research investigates the connections between sensory embodiment, technology, and the development of underwater listening devices during and after the First World War. He has also presented work on theories of disability and complex embodiment and twentieth-century avant-garde musical aesthetics.

Index